An Agrarian Republic

CIVIL WAR AMERICA

Gary W. Gallagher, Peter S. Carmichael, Caroline E. Janney, and
Aaron Sheehan-Dean, editors

This landmark series interprets broadly the history and culture of the Civil War era through the long nineteenth century and beyond. Drawing on diverse approaches and methods, the series publishes historical works that explore all aspects of the war, biographies of leading commanders, and tactical and campaign studies, along with select editions of primary sources. Together, these books shed new light on an era that remains central to our understanding of American and world history.

An Agrarian Republic

Farming, Antislavery Politics, and Nature Parks

in the Civil War Era

ADAM WESLEY DEAN

The University of North Carolina Press   Chapel Hill

The paper in this book meets the guidelines for permanence and durability
of the Committee on Production Guidelines for Book Longevity of the Council
on Library Resources. The University of North Carolina Press has been a
member of the Green Press Initiative since 2003.

Cover illustration: Winslow Homer, *The Veteran in a New Field* (1865).
Metropolitan Museum of Art, www.metmuseum.org.

Complete cataloging information can be obtained online at the
Library of Congress catalog website.
ISBN 978-1-4696-1991-0 (pbk: alk. paper)
ISBN 978-1-4696-1992-7 (ebook)

THIS BOOK WAS DIGITALLY PRINTED.

For Joan and Gary

Contents

Acknowledgments

I dedicated this book to Joan Waugh and Gary W. Gallagher, my two main academic mentors throughout my undergraduate career at the University of California, Los Angeles, and my graduate studies at the University of Virginia. Joan encouraged a nineteen-year-old student from Utah to start thinking and writing historically. She convinced me that it was indeed possible to have a career as an academic historian. I still remember her care in reading and editing my senior thesis, meeting with me on weekends in Westwood Village to discuss changes. Joan also drove me to the Huntington Library to meet scholars in residence—an opportunity rarely afforded undergraduates. I think her influence shines through in every word I write.

Gary took a chance on a young scholar straight out of college with big ideas and a bit of intellectual overconfidence. Slowly, I developed a truer type of wisdom: just how much I had yet to discover about nineteenth-century U.S. history and the American Civil War. It is this wisdom that I seek to convey to each and every one of my own students at Lynchburg College. Gary provided wit, careful advice, criticism, and needed encouragement over my five years at the University of Virginia. Every student who takes one of Gary's classes, joins him on one of his famous battlefield tours, or has the privilege of working under his supervision as a Ph.D. student is truly blessed.

Even earlier, when I was an awkward teenager in Salt Lake City, Utah, high school teachers Carl Sturges, Bill Baxter, and Carolyn Hickman kindled my interest in history and challenged me to become a better writer. Thanks to their guidance, I entered college as a dedicated history major.

I would also like to thank the Jefferson Scholars Foundation at the University of Virginia. Julie Caruccio, Jimmy Wright, Doug Trout, and all the staff, past and present, at the foundation encourage a blend of scholarship, teaching, and leadership that make for a unique graduate school experience. Without the support of the foundation and donors like John L. Nau III, I could not have attended one of the best history programs in the country. Finally, I would like to especially thank Brian Balogh, Edward Ayers, and Michael Holt as meaningful professors in UVA's history department.

Friends and family are also indispensable. This book would not be possible without the advice and support of Adam Robert Trusner. Adam and I spent countless nights at the University of Virginia "range" sipping bourbon and talking about the ideas that would eventually flow into the pages of this book. Anyone who has met Adam knows his unique blend of incredible intelligence, generosity, and wide-ranging historical insight. My golden retriever, Greeley, spent many days curled up at my feet while I wrote this manuscript and encouraged much needed walk breaks. Jesse, Nathan, and Linda Dean all offered support during this project. In the summer of 2014, I had the honor and pleasure of marrying Dr. Kara Eaton. Kara is a brilliant musician and educator. She helped me put the finishing touches on this book and continually reminds me of the importance of patience.

Finally, I need to thank the University of North Carolina Press and the Lynchburg College History Department. Mark Simpson-Vos introduced himself after I participated in a panel at an American Society of Environmental History meeting. Mark is now the editorial director of UNC Press. The organization is lucky to have him. I also appreciate the now-retired David Perry's advice on the publication process and talks about fly-fishing. Lisa Brady, Aaron Sheehan-Dean, and an unnamed reviewer also deserve tremendous thanks for making this book more effective. Despite their careful attention, all facts and interpretations presented in this book are solely my responsibility.

I had the honor of joining the Lynchburg College history department as a tenure-track professor in 2012. Drs. Scott Amos, Nichole Sanders, Lindsay Michie, Brian Crim, Dorothy Potter, Clifton Potter, Michael Santos, and James Owens have created a wonderful working environment that encourages the exchange of ideas. I would also like to thank Dean Kimberly McCabe, Dean Sally Selden, and Vice President Julius Sigler for supporting faculty research and writing. Lynchburg College is truly a special place.

INTRODUCTION

In the spring of 2013, I made my first trip to Charleston, South Carolina. Despite years of living in the South, first as a history graduate student and then as a professor specializing in the Civil War era, I had never visited Charleston and perhaps its most famous landmark: Fort Sumter. Upon arrival at the fort on a rainy and humid day, the friendly National Park Service ranger gave a presentation. The first five minutes of the talk focused on the causes of the Civil War. Why, the ranger sought to explain, did South Carolinians fire on Fort Sumter on that fateful day in April 1861? First touching on the controversy over slavery in the West, the ranger concluded with a statement that many Americans have long believed. "The North had an industrial economy in conflict with the agricultural people of the South," he asserted. Despite admonitions by several scholars since the 1950s, who point out that most northerners were farmers as well, such views continue to percolate among the historically interested public. Part of the reason is that though historians know that most northerners lived in rural communities in 1860, they continue to present the industrial revolution as the leitmotif for nineteenth-century America.

There is nothing inherently wrong with such a story. The United States *did* become the world's preeminent industrial power. By 1900, the former Confederacy lagged far behind New England in manufacturing. Even in 1861, the eleven Confederate states had about as many manufacturing workers as the North had manufacturing facilities. The origins of these differences can also be seen in hindsight. In the late eighteenth and early nineteenth centuries, an economy of small farms and artisans gave way to a system in which farmers and producers created goods for a distant marketplace. The transportation networks critical to industrial capitalism started to dot the North prior to the Civil War. Yet, the standard narrative presented about the 1800s can prevent historians—both public and academic—from gaining a deeper understanding of how northerners lived their lives and interpreted political events in light of their occupation as farmers. Until 1920, most Americans continued to live in rural areas. Farmers produced both for themselves and urban markets. Historians should not argue that manufacturing facilities and big cities represented the North when the majority of northerners were still involved in farming and lived in rural communities.[1]

Indeed, while the North had more industrial capacity than the Confederacy at the start of the war, most of its people were still small farmers. Over 14.5 million lived in rural areas with populations smaller than 2,500, while just 5 million lived in cities such as New York, Boston, and Chicago. The labor force in the North consisted of 10,533,000 people, of which 60 percent did farmwork. Small family farms predominated among the over 1,300,000 landholdings in the free states. The average farm size was 113 acres in rural New York and Pennsylvania, 125 in today's upper Midwest, and 169 in the areas beyond the Mississippi River. While increasing land prices in the late 1850s hurt the goal of farm ownership for many northerners, most still sought small plots of land. Lands in the West seemed to provide the best opportunity, making the question of slavery's presence in the region particularly salient.[2]

While both northerners and southerners were mostly farmers, they had different land-use practices. In the 1850s, in contrast to their southern neighbors, many northerners adopted the ideal of farming a small plot of land for multiple generations—a principle called "agricultural improvement" by contemporaries. This ideal reflected physical differences in the soil between the North and the South. As Lisa Brady points out in a recent environmental history of the Civil War, in areas "loyal to the Union, nutrient-rich alfisols laid the foundation for the practice of continuous cultivation. . . . Ultisols, which have limited nutrients, are the most common soil types across much of the region that became the Confederacy, making shifting cultivation the more profitable and prevalent form of agriculture." Using soil for multiple generations seemed practical and wise in the North, while in the South, the soil encouraged farmers to abandon their fields after five to six years. Thus, while the majority of farmers in the South were likewise engaged in subsistence production, their farms appeared much different to their northern brethren.[3]

The central contention of this book is that the political ideology of the Republican Party, the antislavery organization that proved so wildly popular in the North during the 1850s, was fundamentally agrarian. Republican thinking on a wide range of issues depended upon an environmental understanding of social development. Similar to Thomas Jefferson, whose party served as their namesake, Republicans believed that wise land management was inseparable from the ideal society. Tilling the soil for multiple generations on small farms produced progress—or, to use a popular nineteenth-century term, "civilization." Small farmers were a critical component of another idea that historians have long recognized as crucial to understanding the North during the Civil War: the "Union." Republicans believed that a West settled by small farmers would strengthen the all-important American Union—a term denoting not just the nation-state but democracy itself. The converse was also true. Unlike Jefferson, the Virginia slave owner, Republicans believed that slave-based monocultures destroyed the soil. The wasteful practices on plantations encouraged constant western movement in search of new land. The reason, Republicans surmised, that the "slave power" sought to expand the institution in the wake of the Mexican-American War was that white southerners were running out of land to farm at home. Slave owners, in Republican thinking, also owned too much land. Big farms, or "land monopolies," to use a term from the time, produced aristocrats incompatible with democratic government.[4]

Understanding the Republicans as men and women with backgrounds in small farming who linked appropriate land use to political stability and cultural progress unveils new links and commonalities between seemingly disparate historical events. At first glance, the events explored by this book appear disconnected. Chapter 2 examines the rise of antislavery sentiment in the North after the Mexican-American War. Chapter 3 investigates federal policy during the Civil War and the attitudes of common Union soldiers toward southern farming practices. The fourth chapter covers the establishment of Yosemite State Park and Yellowstone National Park. Chapter 5 explains how the Republican ideal of small landholders conserving the soil applied to both the South and West during Reconstruction. A critic might well ask what national parks have to do with Reconstruction policy or the rise of free-soil sentiment in the North. The answer is that all episodes reflect an underlying Republican belief that tilling the soil for multiple generations on small farms produced a strong nation. Using slave labor, by contrast, promoted waste, barbarism, and disunion. By necessity, this book focuses on the links between antislavery politics, Civil War policy, national parks, and Reconstruction. Specialists in each of these topics might be disappointed, but the benefit is a greater understanding of the connections among them.

Dealing with "ideology" as a historian is a likewise perilous undertaking. What does the term actually connote? Whose ideas are being discussed?

The ideas of average people? Elites? Politicians? Men? Women? White people? Members of a racial or ethnic minority? The problems extend to evidence. Can one person belonging to any of these groups be said to speak for that group or for an entire organization such as the Republican Party? What about a region such as the "North?" Despite these troubling questions, "ideology" is a concept worth studying. In *Free Soil, Free Labor, Free Men*, his famous study of the Republican Party, Eric Foner provides a good defense for histories of ideas. Ideology, in Foner's view, is a "system of beliefs, values, fears, reflexes, and commitments . . . of a social group, be it a class, a party, or a section." These beliefs, fears, values, and commitments spurred action. Two other deans of nineteenth-century American history—Sean Wilentz and James McPherson—have noted the unusual level of ideological fervor of the period. Wilentz notes that during the 1860 election, "Republicanism had become a virtual political religion in much of the North," spurring huge amounts of voters to the polls. McPherson argues that the majority of northerners who fought the Civil War cited ideology as the main reason for enlistment.[5]

"Environment" is also a tricky word. When leading class discussions on the term, I find that most of my students think of the environment as the natural world. Students often cite plants, trees, mountains, and animals, sometimes with and sometimes without human control, as constituting the environment. Yet, the environment also includes varying degrees of human-constructed landscapes—from cities without a green space in sight to public parks and gardens to the small farms that most northerners worked on in 1860. Scholars often refer to these landscapes as the "built environment." People in the nineteenth-century understood their environment—both built and natural—predominantly through work. For northerners, small and tidy farms that had good soil signified the ideal landscape. Slave plantations appeared wasteful and the exhausted soil became proof of the inferiority of slave-based monocultures to free-labor northern farms. The analysis extended to the built environment. Traveling south, many northerners reported on the alleged inferiority of southern towns due to slavery. The relationship northerners had with the environment helped produce the ideology they brought to the political, social, and military conflicts of the Civil War era.[6]

Chapter 1 describes how Americans in the late 1700s to the mid-1800s connected land use with what people at the time called "republicanism." Republicanism held that in order to have a small central government, citizens needed to be virtuous and orderly. The land ordinances of 1784 and 1785, as well as the Northwest Ordinance of 1787, promoted schools and communal living to encourage public virtue. While the Jeffersonian agrarian ideal and the initial critiques of slavery expansion during the Missouri Crisis influenced the Free-Soil and Republican Parties of the 1850s, there were few links between promotion of smallholder settlement and antislavery thought. Though the Northwest Ordinance contained a prohibition of slavery, many supporters of the law only opposed slavery's restriction from the Old Northwest, where they deemed it to be environmentally inappropriate. Some of the law's supporters had no problem with the institution expanding to the modern-day states of Louisiana, Mississippi, and Alabama—the so-called Old Southwest.[7]

The first chapter also investigates how, during the second-party system pitting Whigs against Democrats, ideas about proper land use became intertwined with larger questions of national development. Democrats believed in opening western settlement so that more land could become available to small farmers. Whigs wanted a vibrant internal market in the United States, advocating high tariffs to protect U.S. manufacturers and government funding to transportation projects. Desiring to build up existing U.S. towns rather than engage in further expansion, Whigs believed in restricting western settlement and recommended that farmers use land for multiple generations. Slavery was tangential to these concerns, with a few Whigs hoping that scientific agriculture and economic progress would eliminate the white South's need for the institution. For example, popular farming expert John Lorain commented in 1825 that better soil cultivation would allow "Virginians . . . with safety to themselves, their family and property, [to] set their negroes free." Only after seeing the aggressive efforts slave owners undertook in the 1840s to expand the institution did some northern Whigs and Democrats come to view slavery itself as the primary threat to small farmers and the land they worked on.[8]

Chapter 2 covers the rise of the Free-Soil and Republican Parties in the 1850s. While historians have given much scholarly attention to the ideology of the Republicans, citing their promotion of "free labor" and hostility toward the "slave power," this chapter uncovers the agrarian nature of the Republican appeal. Such an understanding is critical given how popular the Republicans were with farmers. William Gienapp, the preeminent historian of the party in the 1850s, points out that Abraham Lincoln's 1860 presidential majority "rested very heavily on his commanding majority among farmers. . . . [H]is margin was much less pronounced among workers and other groups." The party believed that civilization and loyalty in the West could only be secured by societies of small farmers practicing scientific land management. Yeomen farmers, Republicans argued, formed the strongest attachments to the Union. The land-use practices of slaveholders served as a foil to the northern ideal. Slave plantations exhausted the soil and caused nature to wither and decay. The slave South's low literacy rates, barbaric habits, dirty buildings, and lack of economic opportunity reflected its poor treatment of farmland. The immense landholdings produced an aristocracy threatening to the Union. Politicians warned that if permitted in the West, large slave plantations would exhaust the soil, ruining land better utilized by small farmers.[9]

This chapter should not be construed to imply that free states and slave states were destined for conflict in the 1850s. There was no inevitable "clash of civilizations." White Americans had devised political compromises to deal with the slavery question while writing the Constitution and again in 1820 and 1850. Even in 1860, most Americans did not foresee a war despite the fierce presidential contest. They wrote excitedly about the gold rush in Colorado, awaited news of the completion of the first telegraph line linking California with the Eastern Seaboard, and fretted about a possible Mormon uprising in Utah. Nor is the discussion of land-use politics intended to replace slavery at the heart of sectional crisis; the Civil War was about slavery and everything it represented. Rather, I want to show how ideas about land use both influenced and were influenced by the larger debate over slavery.[10]

Chapter 3 deals directly with the Civil War, exploring the secession crisis in California, wartime federal policy, and the beliefs of Union soldiers. Each of these episodes, seemingly disconnected, show how Republican opposition to slavery was based, in part, on a vision of proper land use. Republican criticism of slavery's land-use practices influenced Union support in California during 1861. According to contemporaries, California was in the process of transitioning from a rough-and-tumble frontier to a more settled agricultural society. Union loyalists argued that the state's agricultural potential could be compromised if California sided with the South and slavery. Northern soldiers made similar arguments about the slave plantations they encountered while on military service. Farmers made up nearly half of those who served in the Union army. The size, scale, and soil-management practices of slave plantations frightened these men. Soldiers argued that the concentrated wealth represented by plantations encouraged disloyal sentiments. Influenced by antislavery writings highlighting the damaging effects of plantation agriculture on the soil, these men also commented that slavery was wasteful, destructive, and unsustainable. Some believed that slavery made the otherwise beautiful natural landscape of the South ugly and decrepit.[11]

In Congress, Republicans made similar claims that slavery destroyed the land. Only free people could build ideal farming communities. When southern Democrats left for secession, Republicans saw a golden opportunity to promote small farms and agricultural permanence in the West. Ignorant of environmental realities in the region making small farms difficult to maintain, they insisted that the West could become "civilized" and loyal if settled by yeomen. Congress passed the Homestead Act, the Pacific Railroad Act, and the Land Grant College Act. It also created the U.S. Department of Agriculture (USDA). The Homestead Act promised a free farm for any family willing to work hard and move west. Farmers could learn the most advanced techniques in agricultural colleges and through USDA publications, practicing new techniques on their homesteads. With education, a small farmer could plant multiple years of crops without exhausting the soil, enabling his or her family to become members of a growing community. A transcontinental railroad would supposedly connect white westerners with the rest of the United States, enabling them to sell their crops on the international market. One of the most surprising discoveries of my research for this chapter concerns Radical opposition to slavery prior to the Emancipation Proclamation. Viewing small farmers as a natural barrier to the extension of slavery, many Republicans pushed for these four laws as a means to keep slavery from moving westward. They feared that the conflict would end with slavery largely intact.[12]

Chapter 4 investigates the creation of Yosemite State Park in 1864 and Yellowstone National Park in 1872. The story of these parks has often been told in the realm of environmental history, with scholars presenting their early history as a parable about the virtues of preservation overcoming human tendencies toward use and exploitation. Yet, both parks had their origins as pieces of legislation crafted by the Republican Party and debated within that party. Park backers believed that experiencing natural beauty would "civilize" the average person and improve his or her intellectual abilities. Supporters also argued that America should follow its republican principles by making scenes of natural beauty accessible to everyone, not just the wealthy. Finally, they claimed that the government's ability to establish parks in the midst of a bloody civil war showed the strength of the Union.[13]

The early opposition to the parks, championed by Radical Republican George W. Julian of Indiana, argued that the land should instead be reserved for yeoman farmers. No longer was the debate over land use and the corresponding social structure a fight between slavery and free labor. It was also about contrasting notions of aesthetics, natural beauty, and property rights. For die-hard supporters of small landowners, farmers enhanced areas of stunning beauty by turning them into pastoral paradises. Julian explained, "I think it might have been far wiser to carve it [Yosemite] up into small homesteads, occupied by happy families, decorated by orchards, gardens, and meadows, with a neat little post-town in their midst, and churches and school-house crowning all." The Indianan favored what scholar Leo Marx calls the "middle landscape," a pastoral environment where nature and settlement met. Early environmental controversies were not about preservation versus destruction. Instead, they were connected to the main political currents of the time.[14]

At the end of the Civil War, Republicans believed that improving the soil through hard work and scientific knowledge was the key to a strong nation. Being the most loyal segment of society, small landholders practicing agricultural permanence could help restore the Union. Thus, the fifth and final chapter explains how Republicans applied their ideas connecting land use with social structure to both the South and the West during Reconstruction. Republicans called for an end to the treaty system characterizing Indian and United States relations. They argued that forcing Indians to become small farmers would open up more land for whites and help "civilize" recalcitrant tribes. Likewise, some Republicans believed that the big plantations of the South needed to be divided and redistributed to former slaves and white unionists so that a yeomen class could form in the South. The Southern Homestead Act of 1866 used 1862 legislation pertaining to the American West as a model to grant small plots of public land to Unionist whites and freedmen in the former Confederacy. Additionally, Republicans insisted that education for freedmen and Indians would "civilize" both groups and encourage better land-use practices. Both the government and self-proclaimed philanthropic organizations established schools in the South and West.

Similar to the scholarly accounts of the early history of Yosemite and Yellowstone, there has been little interest in connecting the events of southern Reconstruction with one of the other big stories of the time period: the sordid treatment of Native Americans by the U.S. government. Historian Jonathan Earle comments: "It is worth pondering how different the history of the postwar United States might have been had free-soil programs like free homestead been extended to ex-slaves and Indians." There is no need for pondering. The Republican Party *did* apply free-soil principles to the West and the South during Reconstruction. The "civilizing" policies intended to force tribes to adopt farming shared the exact same ideological foundations as the southern land-redistribution and education schemes. Historians generally treat land redistribution in the South as one of Reconstruction's "lost moments," while being sharply critical of federal allotment policies in the nineteenth century. My contention is that the same ideology underpinned both efforts. Republicans tried to change who would access, organize, and gain profit from land.[15]

Several individuals appear throughout the book because they show how ideas about the relationship between land use and social structure shaped mid-nineteenth-century American politics. George W. Julian, an understudied antislavery politician from Indiana, and Frederick Law Olmsted, the famous landscape architect, are the most prominent. Olmsted was a gentleman farmer in the late 1840s and early 1850s who worked to avoid soil exhaustion and improve small farm production through crop diversification, the application of fertilizers, and experimentation. He later became a fierce critic of slavery, arguing that the institution ruined valuable farmland. Julian first became involved in politics as a Free-Soil Party congressman from a rural, Quaker-dominated region of Indiana. Worried that slavery's agricultural practices would destroy western lands, leaving them useless for his agricultural constituents, Julian wanted to restrict the institution from the West and grant homesteads to landless northerners. While Olmsted and Julian came from the same intellectual milieu, the men came to blows over the establishment of nature parks. For Julian, Yosemite and Yellowstone threatened his vision of an agrarian west filled with small yeoman farmers and free of slavery. For Olmsted, nature parks helped "civilize" western farmers by exposing them to natural beauty. During Reconstruction, Olmsted moved back to New York City to finish Central Park. Julian became an influential Radical, arguing for land redistribution and granting political rights to freedmen.[16]

Samuel C. Pomeroy and Cornelius C. Cole also feature prominently in these chapters. Pomeroy, a somewhat corrupt Republican politician from Kansas, fought during the 1850s to keep the territory free from slavery. Later, he became a proponent of Radical Reconstruction and Yosemite and Yellowstone Parks. Cole helped establish the Republican Party in California and became an *opponent* of Yosemite and Yellowstone. Cole's writings show the importance of ideas linking westerners to the Union, proper land use, and civilization. The views of ordinary people are also included. Regimental histories, diaries, and letters of rural-born Civil War soldiers conveyed views on land use and slavery that were similar to those of political elites. The impressions of John Roy Lynch, a slave and later a Republican congressman from Mississippi, appear in the chapter on Reconstruction. Informative as well are letters written by Native Americans hostile to the "civilization" measures enacted by the government and by African Americans concerned about the level of violence during Reconstruction.

Evidenced by the number of students who signed up for Civil War classes during my undergraduate days at the University of California, Los Angeles, and who continue to do so where I currently teach at Lynchburg College, Americans have a thirst for knowledge about the bloody conflict. More books have been published about the Civil War than any other topic in American history, beyond the capacity of individual scholars to read and absorb. These facts beg the question of whether academia and the larger public need yet more books about the war. One trend, which I observed in graduate school, is toward greater specialization. Battle histories examine the minutiae of regimental movements during military engagements. Tomes have been dedicated to the study of President Lincoln's cabinet. Other works leave the realm of politics and war to study the home front and slavery. Recently, environmental historians have begun examining the Civil War. While great insights have come from this scholarship, I worry that the narrow focus of historians on specific themes or episodes—be it slavery, the war, politics, or the environment—prevents readers from understanding how interwoven these spheres were to the men and women of the Civil War era. The goal of this book is to illuminate such connections. While engaging in tumultuous politics, radical social change, and violence, northerners brought with them the values and beliefs cultivated through their relationship with farmland. They believed that the America of small farms and sturdy yeomen would prevail in war and continue through the nineteenth century.

A QUESTION OF SLAVERY IN THE WEST

The people of the North have examined and considered this subject,
and I think, have made up their judgments in regard to it. Their motto is,
"No slave territory, —no more slave states."—Joshua Giddings, 1849

William Henry Seward delivered his first address in the U.S. Senate on March 11, 1850. Taking note of the intense opposition to slavery's westward expansion in his home state of New York, the senator sought to capitalize on the sentiment to further his political career. Seward explained that America had a divine obligation to keep Mexico's former lands free from slavery. He claimed, in the speech's most famous passage, "It is true, indeed, that the national domain is ours. It is true it was acquired by the valor and with the wealth of the whole nation. But we hold, nevertheless, no arbitrary power over it. . . . [T]here is a higher law than the Constitution, which regulates our authority over the domain, and devotes it to the same noble purposes. The territory is a part, no inconsiderable part, of the common heritage of mankind, bestowed upon them by the Creator of the universe. We are his stewards."[1]

Both contemporaries and later historians interpreted Seward's speech as a direct attack on slavery in the South, appealing to abolitionists who ignored constitutional barriers in their quest to outlaw the institution. Yet, as the full context of the "higher law" comment shows, Seward and the majority of his supporters were more concerned with slavery's presence in the West. Historians have suggested several reasons why a northern population with strong antiblack prejudices and little abolitionist sentiment supported politicians like Seward. Eric Foner, in the classic *Free Soil, Free Labor, Free Men*, claims that the Republican Party was formed on "the precepts that free labor was economically and socially superior to slave labor."

Eugene H. Berwanger identifies antiblack prejudice as a critical element of the free-soil coalition. William W. Freehling explains how political events such as the gag rule, the Compromise of 1850, and the Kansas-Nebraska Act led Republican voters to believe that there was a "slave power" conspiracy aiming to remove their civil liberties and political rights. Michael A. Morrison's more recent *Slavery and the American West* emphasizes the importance of western expansion in the minds of many Americans. The conflict over slavery in the West was about the future of America. "Northerners," Morrison claims, "saw slavery and . . . the civilization that it had produced as un-American, not following from revolutionary principles."[2]

Most of these reasons are valid, but one that scholars have yet to explore in full detail is that after the Mexican-American War, many white northerners began viewing slavery as an impediment to the small-farm ideal once championed so famously by Thomas Jefferson. Since Jefferson's time, Americans had believed that small farms practicing agricultural permanence served as the foundation for the ideal society. This belief, however, did not have an explicit connection to the slavery controversy. Jefferson himself owned slaves and supported the institution's extension into Missouri. Only after the Mexican-American War did politicians such as Seward label slavery as the primary threat to the ideal agrarian republic.[3]

This chapter begins by exploring all the objections to slavery's extension contained in Seward's famous "higher law" speech. The source is wonderful for introducing the main antislavery ideas later conveyed by the Republican Party. The main contention is that while the Jeffersonian agrarian ideal and the initial critiques of slavery's expansion during the Missouri crisis influenced the Free-Soil and Republican Parties of the 1850s, there were differences between the earlier and later versions of antislavery. The type of antislavery ideology Seward expressed was something new, not the evolution of earlier Federalist, Whig, or abolitionist beliefs. Prior to 1848, promotion of smallholder settlement of the West did not have direct links to antislavery thought. Even many opponents of slavery in Missouri, such as Rufus King, were not troubled by the institution's establishment in the "Old Southwest."

Instead, from the 1780s to the early 1800s, Americans connected debates over land-use practices with "republicanism"—the dominant meme of politics at the time. Later, during Whig and Democratic Party conflict, land-use politics became a proxy for larger ideological battles over the market revolution. Favoring a mixed economy that balanced manufacturing with farming, Whigs promoted agricultural permanence so that farmers could reside in settled communities instead of seeking new land. Democrats countered that national expansion could best secure the needs of farmers by providing them with additional land. These views were not determined by sectional allegiance. Slave-owning Democrats such as Thomas Hart Benton supported the settlement of the West by small farmers. Slave-owning Whigs such as Henry Clay opposed national expansion, desiring to improve what the United States already owned. The acquisition of the Mexican cession changed everything. After repeatedly losing the debate over whether America should take new territory, Whigs had to deal with the issue of how this territory should be settled. Many northern Whigs, such as George Julian, began adopting the former Democratic Party position that yeoman farmers should settle the West. Julian and his fellow Free-Soilers thought that a West full of these people would act as a natural barrier to slavery. Likewise, northern Democrats such as David Wilmot joined Julian in the free-soil movement, claiming that slave plantations would destroy western soil, leaving the land unsuitable for small farms.

William Seward outlined six primary objections to slavery's presence in the West in his "higher law" speech. First, slave owners could outcompete free laborers because "slave labor [was] cheaper than free labor, and it would go first into new regions; and wherever it goes it brings labor into dishonor, and therefore free white labor avoids competition." Second, Seward played on the racial fears of white northerners, explaining that they had no desire to reside near the "debased African." Third, Seward implied that slaveholders had taken control of government to squelch free speech and ensure slavery's future growth—the "slave power" argument. He argued that it was high time for northerners to "firmly, but calmly assert their convictions" against such power. These three objections to slavery have been well-documented by Foner and other political historians.[4]

Historians have given less attention to three other reasons that Seward mentioned. First was the threat that slavery posed to American "civilization." Seward believed that free settlement in the West would create a "new and more perfect civilization . . . to bless the earth, under the sway of our own cherished and beneficent democratic institutions." Slavery was barbaric, incompatible with "the security of natural rights, the diffusion of knowledge, and the freedom of industry." All nations could move from "barbarism"—a society where poverty, ignorance, and vice prevailed—to higher levels of civilization. While earlier northern politicians thought about the best ways to achieve civilization, slavery was not universally considered an impediment to progress. Northerners feared that slavery's harmful effects on the soil prevented the advancement of civilization in the West.[5]

Second, Seward emphasized the potential for the conflict over slavery to disrupt the Union, not just on the Mason-Dixon Line but also between the Atlantic and Pacific coasts. He explained, "Will you say that California has no ability to become independent? She has advantages of position. She is practically further removed from us than England. We cannot reach her by railroad, nor by unbroken steam navigation. We can send no armies over the prairie, the mountain, and the desert." Seward warned of a "Republic of the Pacific," consisting of Oregon and the "western declivity of the Sierra Nevada [California]." After the crisis over Texas and Mexico, Americans stopped viewing abolitionists as the primary threat to the Union. Instead, the threat came from slaveholders and their aggressive promotion of national expansion, filibustering, and imperialism. One of the causes of southern disloyalty was land use. Poor land-use practices necessitated the constant territorial expansion that endangered the Union. Additionally, slaveholding "land monopolies," northerners alleged, made them too powerful and encouraged disloyal sentiments. Disunion would not only wreck the United States; it would also discredit democratic and republican governments worldwide.[6]

Third, underlying both of these ideas was a firm conviction that slavery threatened agricultural prosperity in the West. Without proper land-use practices, the chances for a strong union and a "civilized" population seemed remote. While a few writers in the early nineteenth century commented on the threat slavery posed to agrarian communities, they did so believing that white southerners would see the light of reason and get rid of the institution on their own. Land development became central to the slavery debate only *after* the Mexican-American War. Despite the rising urban population in the North, debates over soil fertility, exhaustion, and waste filled the pages of journals and popular books. Northern farmers believed that slave plantations exhausted the soil, creating an insatiable thirst for new land to exploit. Seward praised the North for embracing "the spirit of universal emancipation," "renouncing luxury," and embracing "commercial empire." In turn, the South, "misled by a new and profitable culture," had to "maintain and perpetuate slavery" in the face of soil exhaustion. Seward promised that he would not allow slavery's wasteful hands to touch the "genial climate of New Mexico and Eastern California" and ruin these lands as well. Tending small farms for multiple generations created yeomen dedicated to self-improvement, stable communities, and loyalty to the United States.[7]

Questions of land development in the early republic, prior to the Mexican-American War, pertained to which forms of land use best promoted national development and, to a much lesser extent, how land-use practices related to aesthetics. The question of slavery's expansion was sometimes referenced during debates over these questions, but it was insignificant compared to other concerns. Though Free-Soilers and Republicans would later praise Thomas Jefferson and the actual author—Massachusetts Federalist Nathan Dane—for excluding slavery from new territories in the 1787 Northwest Ordinance, republicanism was the real issue to the people of the time. Republicanism can be defined as the belief that government should remain small to prevent corruption and aristocracy. For a government to remain small and unobtrusive, however, people needed to be virtuous and moral, lest society descend into anarchy. Advocates of what historian Major L. Wilson calls "corporate freedom" looked to positive government action to achieve development over time. These men and women called for stemming the tide of western migration, arguing that settled communities improved morality. Public order could not be achieved in a violent, frontier society. Advocates of development over space, such as Thomas Jefferson and Benjamin Franklin, argued that the government should facilitate the rapid settlement of the West by freemen. Such a society benefited progress and republicanism by avoiding the political corruption and social decay allegedly existing in urban environments.[8]

Questions of land settlement appeared immediately after the American Revolution, when the U.S. government had to decide what to do with the vast swaths of land bordering the original thirteen colonies. While various Indian tribes and European nations laid claim to most of the trans-Appalachian West, the treaty ending the Revolutionary War presented the United States with the large amount of territory that forms the present-day states of Ohio, Indiana, Illinois, Michigan, Kentucky, Tennessee, and Wisconsin. After receiving the lands from the states that claimed them (New York, Virginia, Massachusetts, and Connecticut), the Articles of Confederation Congress created a plan to organize expansion. The first major land policy of the United States, drafted by Thomas Jefferson, passed in 1784. Once a territory had 20,000 people, it could apply for admission into the United States "on an equal footing with the . . . original states" given that its government "be in republican forms, and shall admit no person to be a citizen, who holds any hereditary title." Such a land policy, Jefferson believed, would allow the country to expand geographically while maintaining its republican character.[9]

Congress passed the second land ordinance on May 20, 1785. The law dictated that after foreign nations—including Indian tribes—gave land to the federal government, surveyors would divide it into squares six-miles-a-side called "townships" and then subdivide each square into 640-acre increments called "sections." Government land was to be sold in these 640-acre increments to the highest bidder. Why 640? Already connecting the size of land ownership to an intended social goal, authorities considered 640 acres the minimum amount for successful community. When settlers wanted to move away from established towns, Congress encouraged them to create small villages rather than live in geographical isolation. The 1785 ordinance also reflected the government's support for education, as Congress reserved the proceeds from the sale of the sixteenth section of every township to fund schools. Above all, the ordinance demonstrated sectional unity on land-use questions. Northern and southern congressmen alike agreed that hardworking settlers should be encouraged to buy land, and that these sales would provide the government with a much-needed source of revenue. Neither the 1784 law nor the 1785 follow-up discussed slavery.[10]

The Northwest Ordinance of July 13, 1787, continued many of the principles first outlined in the 1784 and 1785 laws, crafting land policy to advance the needs of small farmers, republican government, and education. Hoping to settle the territory—comprising today's states of Ohio, Indiana, Illinois, Michigan, Wisconsin, and Minnesota—with smallholders, Congress reserved one-seventh of the acreage as a reward for Revolutionary War veterans. Furthermore, as Article III of the ordinance explained, "[r]eligion, morality, and knowledge being necessary to good government and the happiness of mankind, schools, and the means of education shall forever be encouraged." Like the 1785 bill, the Northwest Ordinance dedicated proceeds from land sales to support education. While the bill jettisoned Jefferson's notion of a state deciding on its own to enter the Union, it still incorporated his idea that incoming states had the same rights and privileges as older states—a necessity for republican government. As historian Harold M. Hyman concludes, "Publicly supported education . . . would create literate free farmers who would staff the governments sketched in the 1787 law." The ordinance also banned slavery from the new territories. This part of the law, however, did not signify a grand plan to extend free institutions to the West. Both northerners and southerners, Jeffersonian Republicans and Federalists, believed that certain territories were better suited for particular crops, and that these crops were better cultivated by either slave or free labor. In fact, between 1823 and 1824, Illinois held a convention to discuss the possibility of allowing slavery in the state, with proponents arguing that "population grew and the economy developed most rapidly where slavery was legal."[11]

During the 1790s, conflict over land policy emerged as politicians presented different notions of what the ideal society should be. Treasury Secretary and Federalist Alexander Hamilton believed that the United States should have an economy that included agriculture, commerce, and industry. Selling land cheaply to small farmers hurt the development of the latter two sectors. Also, Hamilton wanted to get the most revenue possible from the sale of public lands in order to pay revolutionary war debts. He thus advocated the Land Act of 1796, which set the minimum price of government land at two dollars per acre and specified that land be sold in 5,760- and 640-acre segments to promote town formation. Hamilton's supporters in Congress passed the measure over Congressman Albert Sidney Gallatin's opposition. The Pennsylvanian had proposed an alternative: selling land in "quarter-section" segments of 160 acres. Quarter sections, Gallatin believed, would allow more people to own land, thus encouraging farming and western settlement. Gallatin and his political ally—presidential aspirant Thomas Jefferson—believed that expansion would preserve the agrarian character of the American republic. "Those who labour in the earth," Jefferson wrote, "are the chosen people of God, if ever he had a chosen people, whose breasts he has made his peculiar deposit of genuine virtue. It is the focus in which he keeps alive that sacred fire, which otherwise might escape from the face of the earth."[12]

As shown by the conflict over the 1796 Land Act, the debates over land use in the 1790s and early 1800s were about the best means to promote a virtuous citizenry that safeguarded republicanism. Linking small farms with a stable state, Jefferson believed that landowning yeomen, linked to the world through commerce, were the ideal citizens of the American republic. Expansion was integral to this vision. As historian Joyce Appleby explains, "Western lands drew off wage earners from both rural and urban areas, and wages rose as the work force grew smaller. It was a relationship well understood by the Republicans [Jefferson's party] in Congress who voted to reduce the minimum size of land purchases, extend credit to buyers, and place land offices in the areas where ordinary men and women lived." Criticizing Jefferson's ideas, the Federalists argued that the government did not have the necessary military power to defend distant territories against foreign threats. Reflecting their elitist background, Federalists also viewed settlers as a lawless rabble whose destructive tendencies could only be contained by the legal structures and institutions found in towns. They opposed rapid expansion and land distribution in quarter sections. A virtuous citizenry was more likely to develop in territory the United States already owned.[13]

Besides republicanism, Americans tied land use to "civilization." The word enjoyed wide currency in newspapers, political debate, and intellectual circles in both Europe and the United States at the turn of the nineteenth century. For people such as Jefferson, civilization meant the highest material and intellectual development human beings could achieve. Both Europeans and Americans had an environmental understanding of civilization. Where people lived and worked had an influence on their level of civilization. In the eighteenth century, for instance, famous French philosopher Georges-Louis Leclerc, the Comte de Buffon, accused Americans of being sickly, weak, and ignorant because they lived in an "uncivilized" world. The United States' built and natural environment prevented civilization from growing. Mammals and plants were smaller and less varied than those in Europe. America had no big cities that could exert a positive influence on mankind through art, education, science, and culture. Thomas Jefferson responded that the North American landscape could create a powerful civilization. Jefferson believed that this landscape provided ideal space for a rural society of landowning farmers. Europe was uncivilized, a "hopeless sinkhole of avarice, ignorance and abject poverty." The physical environment, he believed, both reflected and influenced American civilization. Jefferson celebrated the powerful animals of North America, even sending a large moose carcass to Buffon to tower over smaller French deer. Unfortunately for Jefferson, the moose's body decayed during the journey across the Atlantic.[14]

In 1803, after becoming president, Jefferson had an opportunity to put his ideas concerning land use and social structure into action. He engineered the Louisiana Purchase, doubling the territory of the United States. Jefferson believed the land would turn the United States into an "Empire of Liberty," creating space for the self-sufficient farmers he idealized. Four major issues immediately developed. First, would the government permit slavery to exist in new territories? Second, squatters began moving west and erecting houses, fences, and farms on government and Indian land. Would the claims and "improvements" of these settlers be recognized? Third, western land speculation grew in popularity. Speculators borrowed money to buy land from the government or Indian tribes, hoping that settlers would purchase the property at a higher price. Would these speculators continue to determine land prices? Finally, the amount of land available for sale remained controversial. Would land be sold in quarter sections to benefit poorer buyers, or would it be sold in 320- or 640-acre segments to promote townships? Until the Mexican War, answers to the last three questions revolved around party lines and an

East-West sectional split. For several years, these alliances contained the North-South disagreement over the first question.[15]

The potential for free-state and slave-state disagreement over western expansion came to a head in the controversy over Missouri's admission to the Union in 1819. Democratic-Republican congressman James Tallmadge Jr. of New York created a firestorm when he offered amendments banning slavery in the proposed state. Tallmadge and his allies believed that slavery's presence would harm Missouri's lands, preventing agricultural development and the establishment of small farms. For instance, New Yorker and Democratic-Republican John W. Taylor argued that slavery would cause Missouri to be "overrun with weeds" and filled with a "squalid slow-motioned, black population." Taylor claimed that "[h]ad not slavery been introduced into Maryland, her numerous and extensive old fields, which now appear to be worse than useless, would long since have supported a dense population of industrious freemen, and contributed largely to the strength and resources of the State." Slavery in the West could also destroy the Union by preventing its settlement by small farmers. The institution, Tallmadge explained, threatened the very empire of liberty that Jefferson sought. "Behold this extended empire," Tallmadge prophesied, "inhabited by the hardy sons of American freemen—knowing their rights, and inheriting the will to protect them—owners of the soil on which they live, and interested in the institutions which they defend—with two oceans laving your shores, and tributary to your purposes bearing on their bosoms the commerce of people." Tallmadge continued: "Reverse this scene; people this fair dominion with the slaves of your planters; extend slavery—this bane of man, this abomination of heaven—over your extended empire, and you prepare its dissolution."[16]

New York's Federalist senator Rufus King agreed, hypothesizing that Missouri's admission "not only has in purpose to fill the fertile regions W. of the Mississippi with slaves" but also to introduce slavery to the "extensive, fertile and happy States" of Illinois, Indiana, and Ohio. Despite membership in different parties, King, Tallmadge, and Taylor each espoused the view that permanent settlements were vital to a strong state. In order to achieve such permanence, farmers needed to carry out agricultural practices that allowed land to produce bountiful crops for multiple generations. The people who worked the land also needed to own it—an implicit rejection of slavery. John Lorain's *Nature and Reason Harmonized in the Practice of Husbandry*, published in 1825, attacked the "ruinous practices too generally pursued by Tenants in this country," advocating numerous methods to ensure agricultural permanence. One surefire way was to increase landownership, thus encouraging farmers to have a stake in the land they tended. Widespread landownership was impossible in a slave society. In Virginia, "[t]he laboring class of white and free citizens have been suppressed, discouraged, and nearly rooted out" by slave owners, Lorain contended. In fact, he elaborated, the "native [farming] talents" of slaves themselves "have been oppressed by savage ignorance."[17]

During the debate over the Missouri Compromise, Americans also began referring to slavery as hostile to Jefferson's vision of civilization. Slavery's poor agricultural practices prevented the establishment of civilized cities and towns. An associate of Rufus King wrote: "We protest, solemnly protest, against coupling the destiny of Maine, the civilized populous State of Maine (300,000 free inhabitants) with the trackless regions, the dreary wastes, the sable tribes of the Missouri beyond the Mississippi." Moreover, slavery halted the orderly development of society from barbarism to civilization by inhibiting material progress and intellectual development. For Rufus King, slavery "dishonour[ed] the hands of freemen." The government should instead promote "Higher Branches of Literature" to surround settlers with institutions of "civil and moral deportment." One of his associates agreed: "If this is not done for us in the West, a comparative barbarism will ensue."[18]

Contemporary observations of southern agriculture suggested to northerners like King, Taylor, and Lorain that slavery was wasteful. These observations planted the ideological seeds for future opposition to slavery in the West. Due to different soil types and crops, historian Steven Stoll explains that slave plantations practiced slash-and-burn agriculture. "Planters," Stoll notes, "used fire to prepare a clearing, cropped for a few years, and then let the land return to brush." The practice produced fields with "half-burned logs and stumps never removed, then halted and doubled back . . . bushy bramble and weedy pines still too stunted to be called an understory." Slave owners also focused on the profit-making crops of cotton, sugar, rice, and tobacco. These cash crops depleted soil nutrients, prompting planters to move west in search of new land. One South Carolina planter wrote: "Most of us have children, relatives and friends, who have left the state and gone westwardly, to seek for new lands. Many more, distinguished for talents and enterprises and public spirit, may be expected to follow, unless something can be done at home to afford them profitable occupation." While slave owner and agricultural reformer Edmund Ruffin responded by calling for new agricultural practices in the South, some viewed the unattractive landscape and emigration as an indictment of slavery itself. "[I] t has been urged, from the nature of the climate and soil of the Southern countries, that the lands cannot be occupied or cultivated without slaves," James Tallmadge explained, but in truth, slavery was "an evil . . . threatening, in its progress to overwhelm the civil and religious institutions of the country."[19]

In the compromise that followed Tallmadge's amendments, Congress admitted Missouri as a slave state, accepted Maine as a free state, and forbade slavery in the Louisiana Territory north of the 36°30' latitude. Rufus King's son, John Alsop King, predicted that debate over slavery's extension would resurface with every new territorial acquisition. In March 1820 he wrote, "This question tho' apparently settled for the present moment by the recent decision of Congress, is in truth far from being so, its influence will increase and its magnitude also, with the erection of every new State within the Southern limits of the United States." Others had a more restrained reaction. John Lorain still believed that emancipation was inevitable. "The time will arrive," he noted, "when Virginians (who are certainly as just, humane and hospital as are the citizens of the States where slavery has been abolished) may . . . set their negroes free." John King—not John Lorain—was right. Arguments that slavery poisoned the land, discouraged permanent settlement, and thus had the potential to fragment the Union would surface again.[20]

Yet, while the rhetoric of the Missouri Crisis appears similar to the slavery controversies in the late 1840s and 1850s, there were some important distinctions. Some extension advocates, such as Thomas Jefferson, believed that the institution would gradually die out through a process of "diffusion." "Diffusing" slaves over a "greater surface," Jefferson wrote, would "facilitate the accomplishment of their emancipation" by lessening the imagined danger of black freedom to the white population. Other proponents of slavery in Missouri interpreted restriction in light of the partisan politics of the time. A faction of Jefferson's party known as the "Old Republicans" believed that limiting slavery was just another "consolidating tendency," like the national bank, the protective tariff, and internal improvements—a Federalist plot to increase the authority of the central state. Opponents were not opposed to slavery's expansion in totality; rather, they questioned its appropriateness to Missouri in particular. Should Missouri produce cash crops for the world market using slave labor, or should the state have a balance of agriculture and commerce, with some production directed toward a domestic market? Federalists like King did not exert serious effort to stop slavery from expanding to Louisiana in 1812, believing that the state was well suited to slave labor.[21]

Debate over land development after Missouri did not revolve around notions of "republicanism," as it had in the 1790s, or slavery, as it briefly had in 1819 and 1820. Instead, politicians, citizens, and intellectuals formed new opinions on the role of land in American life in response to the market revolution. In the wake of the War of 1812 and peace in Europe, Americans witnessed improved technology, faster transportation methods, and more efficient business institutions, leading to explosive economic growth. The Erie Canal, connecting the Great Lakes to the Hudson River, was a prime example. Launched in 1817 and reaching Albany by 1823, the canal enabled farmers and producers in the Midwest to send their products to New York harbor and thus sell them throughout the Atlantic world. While President James Monroe proclaimed his 1817 to 1825 presidency as the "era of good feelings," a political group known as the "National Republicans" argued for continued economic development along these lines. Old Republicans, by contrast, feared the consequences of the market revolution for white farmers, arguing that "centralizing" institutions such as the national bank should be eliminated and more land acquired to provide space for yeomen.[22]

Old Republicans and their successors—the Democrats—believed that a nation of small white farmers would prevent the worst of the "centralizing" tendencies from becoming permanent. Corresponding to this notion, they favored giving settlers preferential rights to the land they had occupied on the frontier. They also wanted to encourage yeomen settlement of the West by selling federal land cheaply and in small sections. Tennessean Andrew Jackson, elected president in 1828, was their champion. Jackson removed Native Americans from coveted land and promoted preemption. Used haphazardly in frontier states since the American Revolution, preemption can be defined as "the occupying settler's preferential right to buy the public land he had squatted upon and the right to the value of the improvements inadvertently made on private land." In the Preemption Act of 1830, the U.S. government forgave pioneer intrusions on the public domain, allowing each squatter to claim 160 acres of unreserved land at $1.25 an acre. The act incurred opposition from Henry Clay, a Kentucky senator and National Republican, who called preemption "fraudulent, heartless, abominable speculation, a system that putrefied and corrupted all it touched." Clay believed that preemption promoted the settling of the frontier by a "lawless rabble" uninterested in creating stable towns. As a result of Clay's opposition, the 1830 Preemption Act was retroactive, applying only to people who had squatted on land since 1829. The act also did not allow preemption on unsurveyed land.[23]

The debate over the first preemption act showcased both change and continuity from Jefferson's time and the bruising clashes over Missouri. The Democratic Party of Jackson and Martin Van Buren—Jackson's vice president—claimed to follow in Jefferson's footsteps, arguing that expansion provided freedom from "wage slavery" by giving poor people land to farm. Representing the National Republican and later Whig opposition, Clay believed that Congress should work on improving the nation's existing territory through canals, roads, industry, and a national bank. These improvements would fuel market development. Land sales to the highest bidder, not the poor farmer, provided the funding for these projects. Whereas Clay looked at urban areas and saw bustling markets and enriching commerce, Jackson saw overcrowding, concentrated wealth, and the loss of independence. Unlike the Missouri clash, slave-state Whigs such as Clay opposed selling cheap land to aspiring farmers for reasons unrelated to slavery, while northern Democrats such as Van Buren favored it. The arguments revolved around what kind of country America would become. Old Republicans and Democrats conceived of the Union as a coalition of self-governing states expanding over geographical space. National Republicans and—after 1836—Whigs believed that a stable and more urban population, engaged in a wide range of economic pursuits, would lead to more progress and civilization.[24]

The ideological differences between Whigs and Democrats on the ideal society and its corresponding form of land use continued during the debates over preemption and homesteading in the late 1830s and early 1840s. Whigs blamed the ruinous panic of 1837 on reckless land speculation. They believed that making western land more expensive would have the double benefit of restricting speculation and providing money for new internal improvement projects that could end the recession. Democrats, particularly those from western states such as Missouri, came to the opposite conclusion. More western land was needed, they insisted, to provide farms for families impoverished by the bad economy. The Preemption Act of 1841, passed with Democratic support and signed by President John Tyler, sought to encourage western settlement. The act, unlike the 1830 legislation, allowed squatters to have preferential rights to buy land when the government sold it. Settlers could purchase up to 160 acres of land at $1.25 an acre. The 1841 law marked a Democratic triumph. The government no longer sought revenue from land sales and favored actual settlers—rather than speculators—in purchases. Democrats tried to pass another measure in 1844, when congressman Robert Smith of Illinois introduced the first homestead bill, providing a grant of "eighty acres of land to any settler who was the head of a family" and "unable to purchase said land." The act would have provided a free land title to settlers on surveyed government land. Senate Whigs defeated Smith's bill.[25]

National conversations about land development did not just revolve around expansion and farming. Popular authors, architects, intellectuals, and ordinary citizens also debated the ideal aesthetic for land. What did natural beauty look like? Why should Americans care about geographical wonders and lands displaying physical splendor? Did exposure to natural beauty benefit the mind and soul? Romanticism, a popular literary convention and ideology, provided answers to all these questions. As the famous environmental historian Roderick Nash notes, "'Romanticism' resists definition, but in general it implies an enthusiasm for the strange, remote, solitary, and mysterious." In a time of increasing market development, some Americans thought that people needed to experience raw nature or face moral decay. New Hampshire denizen Daniel Adams, author of the 1824 *Agricultural Reader, Designed for the Use of Schools*, wrote: "The spacious hall, the lighted assembly, and the splendid equipages do not soothe and entertain the mind in any degree like the verdant plain, the wavy field, the artless stream, the enameled mead, the fragrant grove, the melodious birds, the sportive beasts." Beginning in the 1820s, American tourists flocked to Niagara Falls, viewing the falls as a wellspring for artistic inspiration and spiritual renewal.[26]

Corresponding with these new romantic interpretations of nature, landscape painting and urban parks exploded in popularity. In 1825 English artist Thomas Cole started producing sketches and oil paintings of the Hudson River for public consumption. Poet William Cullen Bryant believed that Cole did a better job capturing the river's "scenic beauty" than any other artist. Painters such as Cole remained popular through the 1850s. Others thought that the beauties of nature could be brought to urban environments through the creation of parks. Andrew Jackson Downing, a renowned horticulturist from the Hudson River valley, believed that preserving or building an area for forests and meadows within cities provided space for quiet reflection and the "return" to nature that the romantics advocated. Before his death in 1852, Downing helped design the National Mall in Washington, D.C.[27]

Many suggested that another reason Americans should appreciate natural beauty was to take pride in their country's landscape. While white Americans believed that they had no cultural landmarks to compete with the castles and ruins of Europe, areas of pristine nature offered their own advantages. In his famous treatise *Notes on the State of Virginia*, Thomas

Jefferson described the commonwealth's Natural Bridge as one of "the most sublime of Nature's works," a structure that could rival any ancient cathedral or Roman ruin in Europe. Noted novelist Washington Irving spoke in 1832 of his desire to see the American West "while [it was] still in a state of pristine wildness and behold herds of buffaloes scouring the native prairies." Irving continued: "We send our youth abroad to grow luxurious and effeminate in Europe; it appears to me, that a previous tour on the prairies would be more likely to produce that manliness, simplicity, and self-dependence most in unison with our political institutions." The same year, painter George Catlin even went so far as to argue that the "pristine beauty and wildness" of the Great Plains should be preserved in a "magnificent park, where the world could see for ages to come, the native Indian . . . amid the fleeting herds of elks and buffaloes." Catlin's call was unusual and ignored; Niagara Falls did not become a park until 1885, and Jefferson's prized natural bridge became a privately held resort. By the 1840s, however, Americans had begun to appreciate natural beauty in land. This appreciation would influence midcentury debates about whether land should be reserved for small farmers or enshrined in public parks.[28]

While northerners and southerners alike could enjoy the Natural Bridge and hold similar views about western expansion, the issue of slavery extension could demolish partisan allegiances. The slaveholding Republic of Texas, which requested to join the United States in 1836, was one such flashpoint. Whig senator Daniel Webster of Massachusetts thundered in March 1837 that he would resist "anything that shall extend the slavery of the African race on this continent." South Carolina's rabid defender of slavery, Senator John C. Calhoun, responded by warning that "abolitionists, consolidationists, [and] colonizationists" had taken over the Whig Party. Texas had the potential to reignite the debates over slavery's extension first seen in Missouri and thus the claims that the institution harmed soil and small farms.[29]

Controversy over Texas and slavery's expansion dominated national headlines in 1844 when President John Tyler presented an annexation treaty to the Senate. This controversy would ultimately render the old Whig and Democratic positions on land development irrelevant. Land policy became intertwined with slavery. In the run-up to the presidential election of 1844, antislavery Whig congressman Joshua Giddings of Ohio warned that annexation would allow slavery to spread to new fertile grounds rather than collapse due to soil exhaustion. Giddings claimed that people should compare Virginia and New York to understand why the United States should not add another slave state. "Let us examine

[New York]," Giddings proposed. "[T]ake notice of her turnpikes, her railroads, her canals, her industrious and thriving population, her commerce and universal prosperity. Then look at Virginia! Mark her miserable highways, her deserted plantations, her dilapidated dwellings, her ragged slaves of almost every shade of complexion, her uncouth implements of husbandry . . . her extensive forests, [and] the almost total absence of all evidence of thrift and prosperity." Tyler, Calhoun, and southern politicians, in turn, warned of a dark plot by Britain to annex Texas and turn it into an abolitionist enclave should the United States fail to acquire the Lone Star Republic. Democratic newspapers also highlighted that annexing Texas would increase national glory and open up new land and markets for farmers.[30]

Henry Clay, the Whig's presidential candidate in 1844, lost to the proexpansion Democrat James K. Polk. Southern Democrats effectively charged Whigs with disloyalty to the South because of their opposition to Texas. One newspaper criticized "the coalition between the Clay Party, and the Abolitionists of the North and the Northwest." More important was the Democrat advertisement that Texas provided whites with bountiful quantities of cheap, fertile land, where nonslaveholders and small slaveholders alike could join the ranks of the elite planter class. As one southern Whig wrote in despair, "For anyone now to say that the Texas question had no influence on the presidential election only makes a fool or an ass of himself." In the North, the claims that England wanted Texas appealed to the anti-British sentiments of Irish and Canadian Catholic immigrants.[31]

On February 26, 1845, before Polk took office, John Tyler succeeded in cajoling Congress to accept Texas annexation. After assuming the presidency, Polk presented his full vision of expansion, calling for the United States to take control of the Oregon Territory up to the Alaskan border as well as to assert "by all constitutional means the right of the United States to that portion of our territory which lies beyond the Rocky Mountains." When the Mexican government refused Polk's demands, the president ordered a small army under General Zachary Taylor to take up a position "as near the [Rio Grande] as circumstances permit." Mexico, still considering Texas a "province in revolt," recognized the border at the Nueces River, while the Texans—and now the U.S. government—deemed the Rio Grande the border. After Mexican cavalry clashed with American dragoons near the Rio Grande on April 23, 1846, Polk asked Congress to declare war on Mexico. Indiana Whig George W. Julian, Joshua Giddings's son-in-law, fumed: "This robust Executive falsehood, with which the slave power compelled him to face the civilized world, must always hold a very high rank in the annals of public audacity and crime." On May 13, 1846, despite opposition from northern Whigs such as Julian, Congress issued a declaration of war.[32]

The war threatened the old party distinctions on land policy, forcing the issue of slavery expansion back into the politics of land development. Future debate over western land-settlement and agricultural practices became intertwined with slavery. When James K. Polk requested $2 million to negotiate a territorial acquisition from Mexico in August 1846, Pennsylvania Democrat David Wilmot attached an amendment restricting slavery from any land taken. As historian Jonathan Earle astutely notes, during the subsequent four-year debate over the proviso, "In every speech and letter Wilmot composed on the subject, he included a variation on the observation that slavery destroys not only its laborers but the land itself." By 1846, Wilmot had come to believe that slavery exhausted soil, forcing slave owners to constantly search for new land. This search, Wilmot believed, took land away from the northern white men who needed small farms. The West, he held, "was the great heritage of our people—the field in which our empire was to grow and to expand."[33]

In one of his more-famous speeches on the proviso, Wilmot began by disclaiming any abolitionist sentiment. "Is there any complexion of Abolitionism in this [the proviso], sir?," he asked rhetorically, then gave his answer: "I have stood up at home, and battled, time and again, against the Abolitionists of the North." Lest any listener mistake his intentions, Wilmot also pleaded "no squeamish sensitiveness upon the subject of slavery, nor morbid sympathy for the slave." Instead, Wilmot focused on the threat of slavery to the land itself. "Slave labor exhausts and makes barren the fields it cultivates," he explained. "The labor is only profitable to the master in the production of the staples of cotton, sugar, and tobacco. Crop follows crop, until the fertility of the soil is exhausted, when the old fields are abandoned, new and virgin soil sought out, to be exhausted in the same manner, and in its turn likewise abandoned. Thus, sir, sterility follows its path." The evidence of this phenomenon could be seen in a comparison of Michigan and Arkansas, Wilmot observed. "Contrast Michigan with Arkansas. Within the last twenty years, the former has assumed a high position among the States of this Union. She exhibits at this day all the elements and resources of a great State; cities, flourishing towns, and highly cultivated fields, with a population that outnumbers three or four times that of Arkansas. Yet, Arkansas has even a better soil, and superior natural advantages." The cause of this "disparity," Wilmot concluded, was "slavery" and "that alone."[34]

Wilmot connected slave labor with barrenness and wilderness. By contrast, he held that free labor would develop western soil correctly and thus assure civilization and a powerful nation. Free farmers, Wilmot argued, provided the best defense against foreign invasion. "Where the men who labor are slaves," he proclaimed, "you cannot place arms in their hands; and it is the free laboring man who constitutes the strength and defense of his country on the fields of battle." The Pennsylvania Democrat and future Republican elaborated, "I verily believe that the laborer of the North, who goes into the wilderness to hew himself a home, does more work than three slaves, while he consumes or wastes less." In a statement eerily prescient of Reconstruction, Wilmot held that only free laborers from the North could make the soil of the South fruitful. "Eastern Virginia," he said, "unrivalled in the fertility of its soil, and in the geniality of its climate, with navigable rivers and harbors unsurpassed in commercial importance, is this day but little better than a barren waste. The free labor of the North has commenced the work of regeneration, and to this alone can Eastern Virginia look for redemption and renewed prosperity."[35]

David Wilmot was not the only politician who peppered his speeches with references to slavery's abuse of the land. Bradford Ripley Wood, a Democratic representative from New York and later Republican, made similar claims in the debate over the proviso. For Wood, the physical threat of slavery in the West was real. He maintained "that slavery will be extended over any, or all territory hereafter to be acquired, unless this proviso obtains, is just as certain as that you have the territory." Like Wilmot, Wood believed that the future of a West with slaves could be seen in how Virginia managed its land. "I see a Commonwealth once powerful," he explained, "now no longer so—without commerce, without resources, and all things wearing the aspect of decay. I see fields, once fertile, now almost as barren as if the sirocco of the desert had swept over them." The barren fields created an unstable population. "I see miserable hovels," Wood noted, "filled with a miserable, degraded, and vicious population." Newspapers made similar claims. The *Liberator*, an abolitionist paper, editorialized: "In the older parts of the slave States . . . are seen . . . too evident signs of stagnation or of positive decay—a sparse population—a slovenly cultivation spread over vast fields that are wearing out, among others already worn out and desolate, —villages and towns, 'few and far between,' rarely growing, often decaying, sometimes mere remnants."[36]

American victory in the war with Mexico ensured that the controversy engendered by the Wilmot Proviso would continue. In February 1848,

Nicholas Trist negotiated the Treaty of Guadalupe Hidalgo, adding 525,000 square miles of territory to the United States. The Federalists, National Republicans, and Whigs had repeatedly lost the debate on *whether* the nation should expand; now the arguments centered on *how* the nation would expand. Foremost in the minds of many was the question of slavery and how it influenced land use. As Mississippi's Democratic congressman Albert Gallatin Brown described, "The North is opposed to slavery, and the South is in favor of it. . . . The North is for confining it in its present limits, where they fancy it will languish, and languishing, will die. The South is for leaving it unrestrained to go wherever it may be invited by soil, climate, and population."[37]

Antislavery newspapers and politicians, even those previously opposed to the Mexican-American War, celebrated the benefits of adding free states to the Union. The Democratic *Weekly Herald* proclaimed, "Free soil, free religion, free speech, and a free press are secured . . . the destiny of California is onward. The dream of Columbus is being fulfilled . . . let us hope that the proceedings at Washington will be such to extend and encourage the prosperity of California and Oregon, and identify their enterprise and success with the continued glory and prosperity of the Union." The abolitionist *Emancipator and Republican* agreed, cheering "the action of the Convention at Monterey" for settling "forever the slavery question for California. The harvest of the gold-sown slopes of the Sierra Nevada, and the valleys of the Sacramento and San Joaquin, we are permitted to hope, will be reaped by free hands alone." The paper explained that California's free-state status "has bound her with stronger ties to the free North and East, than those which connect Ohio with Kentucky, or Pennsylvania with Maryland—the ties of a common interest and a homogenous labor."[38]

In Ohio, Salmon P. Chase, leader of the small abolitionist Liberty Party, issued a call on May 17, 1848, to organize a "Free Territory Convention" for all those opposed to slavery in the new lands acquired. New York Democrats—furious at the southern scuttling of Martin Van Buren's presidential bid in 1844—agreed to attend. Chase also attracted Whigs such as George W. Julian, Joshua R. Giddings, and Massachusetts's Charles Sumner, who were angry at the results of the Mexican War and the Whig Party's nomination of slaveholder Zachary Taylor for president. All together, 20,000 people from these disparate groups gathered at the National Free-Soil Convention in Buffalo, New York, on August 9, 1848, to form a new political party. The convention adopted the slogan "Free Trade, Free Soil, Free Speech, and Free Men."[39]

The meeting at Buffalo signified a new kind of antislavery politics that focused, in part, on slavery's threat to small farmers and, by extension, the ideal society. George Julian wrote that a diverse assortment of "Barnburners [Van Buren Democrats] . . . land reformers . . . working men . . . special advocates of cheap postage for the people . . . members of the liberty party [and] antislavery Whigs" attended the first convention. These strange bedfellows nominated Martin Van Buren for president and Charles Francis Adams for vice president. The platform reflected the different interests of the attendees. All agreed that there should be "no more slave states and no more slave territory." Of critical importance, however, was the fact that the party placed a demand for free homesteads on the agenda. What previously had been an issue advocated by Democrats became a key component of an antislavery party inhabited by northerners of all political stripes. The political landscape had shifted. Free-Soilers now called for liberal preemption measures and a homestead law instead of Democrats.[40]

A homestead law, George Julian explained, provided the foundations for Union sentiment in the West. "Give homes to the landless multitudes in the country," he argued, "and you snatch them from crime and starvation . . . and place them in a situation at once the most conducive to virtue, to the prosperity of the country, and to loyalty to its Government and laws." Julian was envisioning an agrarian republic. Small farmers, creating stable communities on the western plains, would ensure the safety of the Union. Slavery produced the opposite effect, encouraging barbarism. Julian's father-in-law Joshua Giddings groused that Texas was "brought into the Union in order to uphold and perpetuate her slavery . . . the vilest system of oppression that has ever disgraced civilized man."[41]

The people who attended the Buffalo Convention opposed slavery's extension for many of the same reasons that Rufus King and James Tallmadge had in 1820. Most notable was the belief that slavery would deplete agricultural lands and thus halt economic development in new states. Henry Charles Carey, a Whig economist who penned tracts from the 1830s through the 1850s, provides a link between the objections of earlier antislavery men and later Free-Soilers like Julian and Giddings but also shows how they differed. Henry's father, Matthew Carey, did not have a problem with slavery expanding into Missouri in 1819, calling opposition to slavery a "seditious proceeding." At that time, both Careys believed that a program of national development along the lines of Henry Clay's American System would appeal to southern white planters and eventually eliminate their need for slavery. Only after 1848 did Henry Carey perceive slavery as the primary threat to farming, and thus to economic growth and the Union itself.[42]

In 1837 Carey asserted that farmers were the bedrock of society because of their ability "by the assistance of capital to acquire a constantly increasing measure of the comforts of life, with a decreasing amount of labor." In order to acquire such capital, farmers needed to reside in stable communities and continue working the same plot of land for multiple generations. Carey decried constant western migration in search of more fertile land. "In the infancy of society," he argued, "the want of capital compels [the farmer] to depend for a supply of the necessaries of life . . . upon the superior soils. . . . [H]e is therefore compelled to live apart from his fellow men. . . . [F]ertile land is abundant, but he has not the means of rendering it productive." Such settlement led to waste and misery. An isolated farmer, "if successful in his search after food . . . does not possess the means of transporting or of preserving [it]. . . . His life is therefore a constant alteration of waste and starvation. He is poor and miserable." Criticizing expansion, Carey argued that "if abundance of land were sufficient to ensure prosperity, the people of South America should be the most prosperous of all, and the people of England should be among the least so." According to Carey, the opposite was true.[43]

In 1840 Carey argued that free labor and property protection were necessary to life in permanent communities. Slaves did not own property or their labor. Thus, slave-based societies wasted land and prevented progress. A free person "would deem it essential to security that he should be free to perform all those actions which did not tend to the injury of others . . . to apply his labour or his talents in such a manner as he might judge to be most likely to produce advantage—to be a farmer, a brewer, a physician, or a lawyer, without being compelled to ask permission of any one." Free people also felt that governments should protect their investments in technology and property. Carey explained that a farmer "would desire to feel that *his property was secure* . . . that he could safely use it in such a way as he deemed most likely to promote the increase of his health or happiness—that he might invest it in ploughs, or horses—in railroads or canals—in houses or mills—in lands or stocks." Under slavery, however, a person "has no control over his actions, he cannot change his place of residence, nor can he determine in what manner his time shall be employed. He is liable to punishment at the will of his masters. He knows not in what constitutes security of person . . . for him there is no security of property." Surveying the United States, Carey found that in free and densely populated states, "there is a constantly increasing security obtained by the contribution of a constantly decreasing proportion of the product of labour, and with a constantly decreasing necessity for interference with the free employment of labour and capital." In areas where the "few are masters, and the many are slaves . . . [the] population is widely scattered, and there is no capital in the form of roads or canals by which men are enabled to perform exchanges, or even to meet together for the promotion of any object tending to improve their condition."[44]

Like Jefferson, Henry Carey believed that land ownership, sound farming methods, and community living encouraged civilization. Carey also believed that nature both reflected and influenced the level of civilization in a society. In 1837 he wrote, "As capital increases, population becomes more dense, and the inferior soils are brought into action with a constantly increasing return to labour. Men are enabled to benefit by the cooperation of their neighbors, and habits of kindness and good feeling take the place of the savage and predatory habits. . . . [A person's] moral improvement keeps pace with that which takes place in his physical condition, and thus the virtues of civilization replace the vices of savage life." According to Carey, once people resided in permanent communities with increasingly productive soil, they could achieve moral improvement through churches and schools. "With the further increase of capital," he argued, "man is enabled to obtain from inferior soils increased means of subsistence, and population becomes more dense. . . . [T]he proportion of the proceeds of labour required for the maintenance of government is still further diminished. . . . [C]hurches and school-houses are now erected with the labour formerly required for court houses—and prisons—morals are improved and habits of order and regularity become universal." Slavery was wrong because it forbade property ownership by enslaved people, prevented the accumulation of capital, produced a scattered population, and thus harmed civilization. A key point, however, is that in 1837, Carey expected southern whites to agree with him. It was only their insatiable desire to expand slavery at the expense of proper land development that prompted Carey to focus on the institution itself.[45]

Carey's opposition to slavery expansion became pronounced during the debate over the Mexican cession. This opposition marked a significant change from his earlier writings, where Carey believed that economic progress would prompt white southerners to abolish the institution on their own. In 1849 he argued that the slave South was unable to achieve the orderly society he first outlined in 1837, lamenting: "The growth of wealth and the tendency to the division of land, and freedom of man, in the Southern States, have been slow." This phenomenon, he continued, "resulted from the fact that their policy has tended to the exhaustion of the land and impoverishment of its owner, who has thus been compelled to fly to new lands to be again exhausted." Carey believed that halting slavery's expansion and raising a protective tariff could achieve abolition—the only solution allowing "harmony and good will among the various sections of the Union." "The way to the abolition of slavery is simple, it needs nothing but that we arrest the progress of depopulation by enabling men to live together," he explained, "combining their exertions, and thus rendering them more productive of the commodities and things which are required for the maintenance and gradual improvement of their condition." Carey continued: "Ten years of efficient protection *to the farmer and planter* in their efforts to seduce the loom and the anvil to take their places by the side of the plough and the harrow, would do more toward solving this great question [slavery] . . . than 'free soil' votes and Wilmot 'provisos' could accomplish in a century."[46]

Carey's ideas about land use found wide reception among Whigs, Free-Soilers, and, later, Republicans during the debate over slavery in the territories. In 1851 the *Boston Atlas*, a Whig paper, commended Carey as a "gentlemen well known to the mercantile community" and Whig congressional nominees for that year. Horace Greeley's *New York Tribune* and Philadelphia's *North American and United States Gazette* lauded the economist for large contributions "to the public enlightenment." The *Vermont Chronicle* called Carey a "gentleman of the highest reputation" for his "agricultural and horticultural" writings. Justin Smith Morrill, a wealthy Vermont Whig and later a Republican, found Carey compelling beginning in the 1840s. When Morrill became a Republican senator, he distributed Carey's writings to constituents interested in Morrill's political philosophy. Carey himself joined Massachusetts Republicans Charles Sumner, Henry Wilson, and Samuel Pomeroy to support the New England Emigrant Aid Company, founded in 1855 to promote free settlement in Kansas.[47]

Agricultural societies and journals also disseminated arguments that slavery led to economic decline, social stagnation, and soil exhaustion. During the 1840s, Justin Morrill became an active participant in Vermont's Orange County Agricultural Society. Morrill believed that Vermont farmers should be proud of their labor. In an 1847 speech to the society, he exclaimed: "No article is more indispensable to the requirements of the table—and no crop promises a more 'golden and ruddy' harvest, in purse and basket, than the fruit of the well-cultivated orchard." The farms in the slave South, however, were a different story. In an 1841 book, Morrill explained that the land in Virginia was "poorly cultivated, we only see here and there a negro hut. The roads being chiefly without fence of any sort." George Washington's Mount Vernon was a "disgrace to the whole country" because of slavery's agricultural failures. "There are 1200 acres of land [at Mount Vernon]," Morrill described, "yet, with a gang of slaves, the place does not yield sufficient income to keep it in repair." These impressions led Morrill to oppose slavery in the West. Yet, without the specter of slave expansion brought about by the Mexican-American War, these claims would not have carried the same weight.[48]

New England abolitionists Lyman and Henry Ward Beecher also wrote agricultural tracts condemning slavery for its impoverishing effects on land. For Lyman Beecher, like Henry Carey, agriculture was the most important pillar of society. "From agriculture," Lyman claimed in language echoing Jefferson, "will result commerce, science, arts, liberty, and independence." Yet, people needed to own the soil to care for it properly. "The possession of the earth in fee simple," he argued, "is the great principle of action in the moral world. Nearly all the political evils which have afflicted mankind have resulted from the unrighteous monopoly of the earth, and the predicted renovation can never be accomplished, until this monopoly shall have passed away, and the earth is extensively tilled by the independent owners of the soil." Lyman's son, Henry Ward Beecher, attacked the South for its reliance on cash crops. "It is extensively the practice of large farmers," the younger Beecher explained, "to put their whole force upon one staple article; a style of farming as full of risk, as it would be to invest a whole fortune in one kind of property. At the South, we have cotton plantations; nothing but cotton is raised." Instead, "a perfect system of agriculture should have in itself, a balancing power. There should be such a distribution of crops that a farmer may have four or five chances instead of one." Henry Ward Beecher had 160-acre quarter sections in mind when making his recommendations. "A farmer has 160 acres," he advised, "sixty [should be] in wood: of the one hundred clear acres, say *twenty* are used for home lots, pasture, corn, etc., and *eighty* in wheat."[49]

Free-soilers could also look to southern agricultural authorities for evidence of slavery's harmful impact on farmland. In 1849 Mississippian Tuttle H. Audas lamented that the "planters of the cotton growing States for years have seen their lands growing poorer." He contended, "If we intend to recover our former prosperity, and preserve even the present value of our lands and negroes, we must understand not only our present condition but what is likely to be in the future . . . no country can long continue to be prosperous where the system of agriculture practiced by its people uniformly, year by year, impoverishes the soil." Audas also believed that slavery's restriction would lead to the institution's demise. "If the abolitionists would be kind enough to wait a few years," the Mississippian lamented, "they might save themselves a great deal of trouble about our slaves, for we should free them ourselves. This is no exaggerated sketch of our landed property—the gulleyed and naked hill[s], the worn out and unenclosed old fields, and sparse population attest the truth of the picture." Several years later, leading southern agricultural scientist Edmund Ruffin worried about the "decline of the finest part of Virginia, and the impoverishment and ruin of thousands of the kindest and warmest hearted people in the world." Soil exhaustion and western migration caused this situation. "When a man's property is nearly expended," Ruffin explained, "he sells his land for less than the dwelling-house on it alone is worth, and moves with the scanty remnant of his wealth to a western wilderness."[50]

In the debate over the Compromise of 1850—the series of laws addressing the presence of slavery in former Mexican lands—Free-Soil politicians conveyed an environmental understanding of social development. Without agricultural plenty and small farms, progress and civilization were impossible. They used arguments about agricultural decline to oppose slavery's extension. Slavery opponents claimed that the West's fertile lands must be protected from the institution's poisonous touch. Questions of land development had shifted from being about republicanism, aesthetics, and the market revolution; slavery was now at the heart of the issue. Newly elected Free-Soil congressman George Julian echoed Henry Carey and Joshua Giddings in a comparison of Virginia and Ohio. The Indianan proclaimed: "In the former, the soil is tilled by the slave. He feels no interest in the Government, because it allows him the exercise of no civil rights. It does not even give him the right to himself. . . . [C]an the cultivation of the soil by such a population add wealth or prosperity to the Commonwealth?" He continued, "I need not point to Virginia, with her great natural advantages, her ample resources in all the elements of wealth and power, yet dwindling and dying under the curse of slave labor. But cross the Ohio River, and how changed the scene! Agriculture is in the most thriving condition. The whole land teems with abundance." Fierce antislavery ideologue Thaddeus Stevens exclaimed in February 1850: "Instead of attempting to renovate the soil, and by their own honest labor compelling the earth to yield her abundance; instead of seeking for the best breed of cattle and horses to feed on her hills and valleys, and fertilize the land, the sons of that great State [Virginia] must devote their time to selecting and grooming the most lusty sires and the most fruitful wenches, to supply the slave barracoons of the south."[51]

George Julian argued that slavery prevented the establishment of small farms in the West, thus threatening progress, civilization, and the Union. Lambasting a slave-state senator, Julian claimed: "The gentlemen from North Carolina tells us that less pauperism and crime abound in the South than in the North and that there never has existed a higher state of civilization than is now exhibited by the slaveholding States of the Union; and so in love is he with his 'peculiar institution,' which thus promotes the growth of civilization by turning three millions of human beings into savages, and prevents them from becoming paupers by converting them into brutes." Instead, the "foundations of empire in the yet unpeopled regions of the great West" lay in giving each "landless citizen of the country . . . a home upon its soil." Similar to Carey, Julian saw education as a key product of an agrarian society with widespread land ownership. Should the homestead bill become a law, he explained, "The poor white laborers of the South, as well as of the North, will flock to our territories: labor will become common and respectable; our democratic theory of equality will be realized: closely associated communities will be established; whilst education, so impossible to the masses where slavery and land monopoly prevail, will be accessible to the people through their common schools; and thus physical and moral causes will combine in excluding slavery forever from the soil." In powerful language, Julian showed that the free-soil vision of the West was dependent on the region being settled by small farmers.[52]

Opponents of slavery promoted homestead and liberal preemption measures as means to prevent slavery's western expansion and encourage smallholder emigration. This tactic was a change from prewar land debates, in which Whigs opposed expansion in all forms and slave-owning Democrats, such as Andrew Jackson and Thomas Jefferson, favored the distribution of land to free settlers. For example, in 1828, Missouri's Democratic senator and Jefferson disciple Thomas Hart Benton argued that "open territory, once taken from the Indians, had no other purpose than to be dispensed of by government . . . raising many indigent farmers from poverty and wretchedness to comfort and independence." In 1852 Massachusetts Free-Soiler Charles Sumner used Benton-esque rhetoric regarding the West. Sumner argued that distribution of public lands to yeomen settlers would plant the "nurseries of future empire." George Julian likewise claimed that the Free-Soil Party was the true heir to Jefferson's agrarian thought, regardless of what the third president believed in actuality. In May 1850, he argued, "the beneficent doctrine of land form is destined, I trust, at some time not far in the future to receive the sanction of Congress. . . . [T]he free-soil men in Congress desire the application of the ordinance of Jefferson, come whilst may."[53]

George Julian wanted to grant "every head of family a Homestead of one hundred and sixty acres out of the public domain" to prevent slavery's western expansion and ensure continued agricultural productivity. "I take it the clear interest of this Government to render every acre of its soil as productive as labor can make it," Julian maintained. "The measure now before us will secure this object by giving independent homesteads to the greatest number of cultivators, thus imparting dignity to labor, and stimulating its activity." Julian thus evoked the belief of Rufus King, John Lorain, and Henry Carey that land ownership was key to agricultural permanence, but he ignored their anti-expansion sentiments. Julian also labeled slavery as the prime threat to small-scale land ownership. The Indianan presented the Homestead Act as a "far more formidable barrier against the introduction of slavery than Mr. Webster's 'ordinance of nature,' or even the celebrated ordinance of Jefferson." Julian contended that "slavery only thrives on extensive estates. In a country cut up into small farms occupied by as many independent proprietors who live by their own toil, it would be impossible." He elaborated: "I think the adoption of the [Homestead] policy for which I am contending will be a much better 'settlement' of the slavery question than the one to which I refer [the Compromise of 1850]." It is important to note that Julian also believed that freed slaves could find refuge on homesteads. "The freedom of the public lands," he concluded, "is an antislavery measure. . . . [I]t will weaken the system of chattel slavery by making war upon its kindred system of wage slavery, giving homes and employment to its victims, and equalizing the condition of the people."[54]

Southern politicians, with a few exceptions, opposed the Homestead Act for the same reason that Free-Soilers supported it: the bill would carve free states out of the new territory in the West. "The slaveholders hated [homestead] doctrines as heartily as they hated 'abolitionism' itself," Julian recalled. Andrew Johnson, a homestead supporter, explained that his fellow slave-state representatives believed that there was a "much greater number of quarter sections of land in the free states than there are in the slave States" and consequently feared aggrandizement of northern power in Congress. The *Georgia Telegraph* viewed the homestead bill as an abolitionist conspiracy. "Left to an equal contest," the Macon paper theorized, "free labor cannot pretend to compete with slave labor. Hence the aid of the Government must be called to the side of free labor. . . . [F]ree labor shall have the start in the race, a part of its capital must be given it—Congress must vote it a gratuitous farm." The *Telegraph* asked,

"What dunce does not see the drift of the movements of Clay, Benton, Cass, Greely, [*sic*], and other advocates of free farms[?]... [T]he gratuity of a farm will induce an enormous immigration; a 'density of population' will be created; free labor will become cheaper than slave-labor, and thus, the negro will be freed!"[55]

Several Californians who arrived in the state during the Gold Rush agreed with the Free-Soilers in Congress that slavery threatened small-farmer settlement in the West. The threat of slavery coming to the state seemed real to many northerners. New Yorker Cornelius Cole, who moved to California in 1849, recalled: "At the beginning of the gold excitement in California, quite a number of people from the South brought their slaves with them to work in the mines. Many at that early day believed, and more were hopeful, that California would side with the South." He continued, "The adoption of a free constitution did not, by any means, abate the aggressiveness of the pro-slavery sentiment." In December 1849, Michigan farmer George Swain wrote to his brother William, a California miner, warning that "the South are said to be opposed to admitting California as a free state and . . . will try some hocus-pocus game over the North, but the North have their eyes open and will resist stoutly." George added a month later: "The State Constitution of California pleases the North, displeases the South. I hope the Californians will maintain the stand. Perhaps much of their own and the Nation's fate turns on their firmness now." He observed, "There is no doubt but many in the South hold the Union cheap and would rather be out than in it." William Swain worried that the lack of permanent settlement and established towns prevented California from achieving prosperity and Union. Echoing Henry Carey, Swain wrote: "The prosperity of any country depends mainly upon its innate and enduring ability to contribute to the happiness of a settled, abiding, and industrious population. . . . [W]ithout permanency, industry . . . is not likely to exist, and therefore its all creative power is not exerted in the conception and completion of great national arrangements."[56]

The Free-Soil Party, spawned by intense opposition to slavery's western expansion, gained significant support in 1848 but had little effect on the presidential election. Both of the larger parties did their best to steal the Free-Soilers' main campaign issue. Whigs and Democrats campaigning in the North gave speeches opposing slavery's extension, while those campaigning in the South supported it. Free-Soilers, however, succeeded in electing Salmon P. Chase and New Hampshire's John Parker Hale to the Senate. George W. Julian, Massachusetts's Charles Allen, Ohio's Joseph Root, Connecticut's Walter Booth, and Joshua Giddings served as the contingent in the House. Free-Soilers also received support from antislavery Whig William Henry Seward, who secured election as one of New York's senators. In the face of vociferous Free-Soil opposition, the compromise measures of 1850 passed. As George Julian recalled, "The adjournment [of the Thirty-First Congress] was followed by great 'Union-saving' meetings throughout the country, which denounced 'abolitionism' in the severest terms, and endorsed the action of Congress. . . . [T]he sickly air of compromise filled the land, and for a time the deluded masses were made to believe that the Free-Soilers had brought the country to verge of ruin."[57]

Despite the "Union-saving" meetings, many parts of the compromise galled northern voters. The Fugitive Slave Act, for instance, struck many as an unconstitutional abrogation of individual and state rights, interposing the power of the federal government against anyone aiding escaped slaves. Joshua R. Giddings confided to George W. Julian, "I think those who kill tyrants and negro catchers do God's service, and manly duty." The Massachusetts legislature sent Charles Sumner to the Senate in 1851 because of his dedication to stop slavery from entering free states or territories. The Free-Soil Party met again to nominate candidates for the election of 1852, choosing John P. Hale for president and George W. Julian for vice president. Again highlighting the connections between land policy and antislavery sentiment, the Free-Soil platform committee declared that "all men have a natural right to a portion of the soil; as the use of the soil is indispensable to life, the right of all men to the soil is as sacred as their right of life itself." During the campaign, Thaddeus Stevens advised Julian that the Free-Soilers needed to "stake the ground that there are but two parties, —the 'Free Democracy' & the Pro-slavery. . . . Never again speak the name Whig, or Democrat, nor never write or print such names for a party, but simply say of each, as one common party, the 'Pro-Slavery party.'" Though the Free-Soil Party fared poorly in the 1852 election, later events would prove the wisdom of Stevens's advice. They also succeeded ideologically where they had failed politically, spurring many northerners to think of slavery expansion in terms of land development.[58]

Two

FREE SOIL AND THE RISE OF THE
REPUBLICAN PARTY

The doctrines of Jefferson, the teachings of his example, the prestige of his name, are far more often cited and applauded in Republican than in Democratic assemblies. Nay, he and his principles are beginning to be scouted by the latter, while they are finding their home in the former. —Horace Greeley, 1860

Most of the men and women involved in free-soil politics became members of the Republican Party, which was established in 1854. As the Republicans grew in popularity and power, they became convinced that the future of the country depended on the wise use of soil. Conserving the soil for multiple generations on small farms created a stable population where cities and towns could develop. Small farms, by allowing for widespread land ownership, stopped the growth of an aristocracy threatening to the Union. Slave plantations, by contrast, exhausted the soil, preventing the development of civilized communities by constantly encouraging people to seek new land. The size of plantations created an elite oligarchy— the so-called slave power—that threatened the integrity of the Union. A critique of southern land-use practices—and the larger political and economic relationships they represented—thus formed a key element of Republican ideology. These beliefs are unsurprising given that farmers were the biggest supporters of the Republicans. By contrast, most northern manufacturers viewed the Republican Party as fanatically abolitionist and were the last to abandon the Whigs. Michigan and Wisconsin, sites of the first Republican gatherings in 1854, were among the most rural states in the entire North. New England was 63.4 percent rural and the Middle Atlantic States 64.4 percent rural, while the states of the Old Northwest had a rural population of nearly 86 percent.[1]

This chapter builds off the work of historian Mark A. Lause. In *Young America: Land, Labor, and the Republican Community*, Lause documents the presence of agrarian ideals in the founding of the Republican Party in 1854. Republicans, Lause proves, did not intend for their policies to create an industrial giant. They proclaimed Thomas Jefferson the ancestor of their party because of his agrarian notions of land development. Republicans also drew from the ideas of antebellum reformer George Henry Evans, who claimed that small family farms encouraged widespread land ownership and thus a more egalitarian society. Lause concludes that "agrarians favored freedom because of the real impact of slavery on the political and social health of the entire body politic as well as the inhumanity of the system." This chapter shows that another reason agrarians opposed slavery was the impact of slavery on the physical environment. Republicans believed that only yeomen farmers could properly care for the soil.[2]

The chapter also deals with northern impressions of the slave South. Susan-Mary Grant has written the most comprehensive history of how northerners viewed the South in the decades before the Civil War. "In the nineteenth century," Grant explains, "the image of the antebellum South as an agrarian, quasi-feudal society was contrasted with that of the North as a commercial, successful, forward-looking society. The North represented the democratic future; the South the aristocratic past. . . . [B]oth images drew their inspiration from, and centered on, the southern plantation." I agree with Grant that negative impressions of the South focused on the plantation, but I suggest that the northern self-image was of a rural society of small landowners who built churches and schools to enhance "civilization."[3]

The Kansas-Nebraska Act, sectional violence in Kansas, antislavery literature by Frederick Law Olmsted, the 1856 election, the publication of Hinton R. Helper's *Impending Crisis of the South: How to Meet It*, and the 1860 election show the political influence of Republican beliefs linking land use with social structure. These incidents also show that Republican opposition to slavery in the West derived, in part, from negative impressions of southern land use. While other factors—such as the 1857 Dred Scott Decision, the Lincoln-Douglas debates, and hostility toward the Fugitive Slave Act—certainly aided the Republicans' rise, this chapter will focus on the Kansas-Nebraska Act, Olmsted's writings, the two election campaigns, and Helper's propaganda. Each of these events illustrates the Republican belief that the South was different from the rest of America because of slavery's destructive farming practices. These farming practices produced "barbarism" and a lack of respect for the Union. Republicans, as has long been recognized by historians, did not organize around an abolitionist critique of slavery. William Gienapp points out that even abolitionists in the party publicly emphasized their opposition to the extension of slavery rather than questioning the morality of the institution in the South.[4]

Between 1852 and 1856, the old Whig and Free-Soil Parties collapsed, and the Republicans replaced them. The Whigs fielded their last presidential candidate—Winfield Scott—in 1852. The election did not feature the traditional Whig-Democrat divisions over the economy. The influx of gold from the California Gold Rush created an economic boom, negating the Whigs' ability to campaign on economic distress—one of their more successful strategies. Scott also took no official stance on the Compromise of 1850, attempting to gain free-soil support in the North while allowing southern Whigs to campaign for compromise measures in the South. The attempt failed. Free-Soilers still supported their own party, voting for candidates John P. Hale and George W. Julian. The result was a Democratic route, with Pierce gaining 254 electoral votes to Scott's 42. Upon hearing of Scott's defeat, Charles Sumner wrote to William Seward: "Now is the time for a new organization. Out of this chaos the party of freedom must arise."[5]

Sumner would have to wait four years for his "party of freedom" to develop a national organization and field a presidential candidate. Yet, the Whigs continued to free-fall. In 1853 Free-Soilers wreaked havoc on northern Whigs, adopting temperance and anti-immigration platforms in addition to antislavery appeals to crush the party in off-year elections in Maine, Ohio, and Connecticut. William H. Seward—though still a Whig—grasped the power of antislavery sentiment in the free states. In an 1853 speech, he praised James Tallmadge for opposing slavery expansion. "If the counsels of James Tallmadge had completely prevailed," Seward lamented, "then not only would American forests, mines, soil, invention and industry have rendered our country, now and forever, independent of all other nations . . . but then, also, no menial hand would ever have guided a plow, and no footstep of a slave would ever have been tracked on the soil . . . of our national domain." The Free-Soilers delighted in bringing the issue of slavery expansion to the forefront. George Julian exclaimed in April 1853: "The antislavery movement is so bringing forth such visible fruits that the whole land must ere long witness and acknowledge its power. The Whig party is hopelessly prostrated. Having fulfilled its mission, surrendered its doctrines, and outlived its honor, it has been consigned by the fates to an ignominious ground. Let us rejoice!!!"[6]

The Kansas-Nebraska Act of 1854 led to the final collapse of the Whigs and the creation of the Republican Party. Kansas-Nebraska formed from the fertile mind of Illinois Democrat Stephen A. Douglas. A strong proponent of white male equality, Douglas believed that western settlement preserved democratic government by "preventing the growth of an unpropertied pauper class." He thought that a transcontinental railroad could easily transport poor immigrants westward and benefit his hometown—Chicago. In early 1854, as chairman of the Senate Committee on Territories, Douglas wanted to organize the territories west of Missouri to start construction on the railroad. Southern senators James Mason, Robert M. T. Hunter, Andrew P. Butler, and David Rice Atchison responded by demanding that these lands be open to slavery. Since the territories fell in the Louisiana Purchase, the senators were calling for the repeal of the Missouri Compromise. Douglas's solution was to declare the 1820 compromise void and organize Kansas and Nebraska under popular sovereignty. Popular sovereignty dictated that the people of the territory would decide whether or not to allow slavery.[7]

Free-Soilers Salmon P. Chase, Charles Sumner, and Joshua Giddings became apoplectic when Douglas introduced the bill. They responded with *An Appeal of the Independent Democrats*, a powerful antislavery pamphlet that Chase claimed achieved a circulation of 500,000. The pamphlet demonstrates how issues of land development were central to Free-Soil thought. The *Appeal* first argued that slavery would harm agriculture in the West and prevent yeoman farmers from owning small plots of land. "If this bill shall become a law," the Free-Soilers stated, "the blight of slavery will cover the land. The homestead law, should Congress enact one, will be worthless there." Second, as a result, slavery would threaten the establishment of permanent towns and roads, two necessary components of civilization. "What will be the effect of this measure, should it unhappily become a law, upon the proposed Pacific railroad?" the *Appeal* asked. The answer followed: "If slavery be allowed [West], the settlement and cultivation of the country must be greatly retarded. Inducements to the immigration of free laborers will be almost destroyed." Finally, the extension of slavery could destroy the Union by separating the East and the West. "We beg you, fellow-citizens," the Free-Soilers implored, "to observe that [the bill] will sever the East from the West of the United States by a wide slaveholding belt of country." The effect of this separation would compel "the whole commerce and the whole travel between the East and West to pass for hundreds of miles through a slaveholding region, in the heart of the continent, and by the influence of a Federal Government, controlled by the slave power, to extinguish freedom and establish slavery in the States and Territories of the Pacific, and thus permanently subjugate the whole country to the yoke of a slaveholding despotism."[8]

The *Appeal* reflected the concerns of farmers in the 1850s. Many northern farmers believed that the "slaveholding despotism" prevented them from getting farms in a time when property was becoming scarce. Throughout most of the nineteenth century, the process of farm acquisition had been twofold. Sons of farm owners usually worked as laborers during early adulthood, then either inherited land from their fathers or saved money to acquire plots themselves. But as the existing land in the North began filling up, farm prices increased. A 40-acre estate cost $1,000 in the Midwest and over $2,000 in the Northeast. Farms 160 acres in size, increasingly rare, fetched almost $3,000 in the Midwest market and nearly $4,700 in New England. In the 1850s, these escalating costs meant that there was a new step in the process of acquiring a farm: tenancy. Many tenants and laborers saw the West as a region to acquire land and slavery as a threat to this dream. The slave power, described Edmund Morris in a multiple edition book entitled *How to Get a Farm and Where to Find One*, "being itself a huge landed aristocracy . . . saw with instant alarm the prospect of a multitude of small freeholdings being established, knowing that in such a community an aristocracy could not exist."[9]

Despite Sumner's and Chase's resistance, the Senate passed the Kansas-Nebraska Act on March 4, 1854. In late May, the House concurred. Debate over the bill, however, prompted a fusion between Free-Soilers and antislavery Whigs in Congress. Joshua Giddings wrote of the Nebraska bill: "Our friends now feel more confident [that] the Whigs are coming up [into] the work. They at first felt delicate about being in with us free-soilers. It was humiliating for them to be compelled to come into the very position, which they have so long condemned. . . . [O]ur position is now enviable. We lead the hosts of freedom." Echoing Giddings's experience in the capitol, Whigs and Free-Soilers in Michigan and Wisconsin called for a new fusion party to oppose slavery's western expansion. Following the advice of antislavery newspaper editor Horace Greeley, the Michiganders and Wisconsinites chose the name "Republican" for their party. The choice was not accidental. By adopting the name of Thomas Jefferson's party, the new Republicans could claim to follow in his ideological footsteps, promoting yeomen settlement of the West and an agrarian republic. As the Madison, Wisconsin, *Daily State Journal* explained: "We . . . in the defense of freedom will cooperate and be known as *Republicans*, pledged to . . . exclude slavery from all the territories over which the General Government has exclusive jurisdiction."[10]

Others chose more-direct routes of action. Massachusetts Free-Soiler Samuel Pomeroy, upon meeting President Franklin Pierce, allegedly shouted: "Sir! This measure, which has passed, is not the triumph you suppose. It does not end, but only commences hostilities. Slavery is victorious in Congress, but it has not yet triumphed among the people. Your victory is but an adjournment of the question from the halls of legislation at Washington to the open prairies of the freedom-loving West; and there, sir, we shall beat you." While this story may be apocryphal, Pomeroy did join the New England Emigrant Aid Company founded by abolitionist Eli Thayer to send 20,000 free-state settlers to Kansas. Pomeroy opposed slavery because of its influence on land. "Above all," he wrote, "I am anxious to have the right impetus given to [Kansas's] early settlement. That the best principles of our resting fathers may be transplanted there! And that thus our untold domain may be saved from the blighting—withering—deadening—damning—influence of American Slavery!" The descriptors "blighting," "withering," "deadening," and "damning" had been part of the antislavery lexicon that focused on the institution's farming practices. The Emigrant Aid Company also wanted to establish civilization in Kansas, directing Pomeroy to erect "School Houses and Churches, and thus carry to the extreme borders of population the advantages of an advanced civilization."[11]

In response to the Emigrant Aid Company's efforts, Missourian David Atchison advocated "using whatever force necessary to prevent abolitionists from seizing control of the territory." As historian Kristin Tegtmeier Oertel points out, "Many white southerners viewed Kansas as the 'key to the southwest,' connecting the future success of slavery with westward expansion. They worried that if slavery stopped in Missouri, there would be no hope of it expanding elsewhere in the West." Atchison led thousands of voters across the Mississippi River in March 1855 to ensure the election of proslavery legislators. The new legislature passed measures to threaten Pomeroy's free-soil settlement in Lawrence, Kansas. This government mandated capital punishment for people aiding escaped slaves, struck free-soil settlers from jury rolls, made voicing antislavery opinions a felony, and banned the distribution of antislavery tracts. "We will soon get the quarrel into Congress and before the country," Pomeroy predicted.[12]

The Kansan was correct. Local Republican parties began forming state by state, calling attention to the outrages in Kansas and pledging opposition to slavery expansion. Kentucky abolitionist Cassius Clay wrote in

September 1854: "The Republican party seems to go well and is significant of our principle. . . . I think things are [portentous] for a large increase of action [by the] antislavery element." The rise of the anti-immigration Know-Nothing Party produced further divisions among northern Whigs, prompting some, such as Abraham Lincoln and William Seward, to abandon the Whigs for the Republicans. The rising violence in Kansas, in turn, divided the Know-Nothings over slavery's expansion, leaving the new Republican Party to pick up the pieces. At the 1855 American Party (Know-Nothing) convention, antislavery members bolted after the platform committee accepted the Kansas-Nebraska Act. In distant California, Sacramento attorney Cornelius Cole noticed the "aggressiveness of the pro-slavery sentiment. . . . [I]ncited, it may have been . . . by a lively hope of extending slavery to the new territories of Kansas and Nebraska." In response, Cole gathered with eleven other men in Sacramento on November 8, 1855, to found the California Republican Party. The party promised "to oppose the aggressions of slavery." Cole gained support from Know-Nothings angry at the party's acquiescence in slavery's expansion and from prominent businessmen Collis P. Huntington, Leland Stanford, and Mark Hopkins—each of whom would achieve later notoriety as corrupt railroad magnates.[13]

In Vermont, newly elected congressman Justin Morrill declared his opposition to "the admission of any more slave States to the Union." Morrill deserted the Whigs and embraced the Republican Party. He was outraged that the Kansas-Nebraska Act had overturned the Missouri Compromise. The Vermonter was "in favor not only of restoring the restrictions of slavery up to the Missouri Compromise line, but also of extending that restriction to territories belonging to the United States." The reason slave states wanted more territory, Morrill surmised, was that "in Virginia, and in parts of the Carolinas[,] the system [slavery], and its crops had exhausted the soil. . . . [N]ew slave territory had become indispensable to its longer prosperous continuance. There must be [a] vent or slavery would be stifled in its home." Such a system of agriculture could not be permitted to continue.[14]

Republicans also gained support from a series of antislavery writings published between 1852 and 1854. These publications highlighted the danger that slavery presented to small-scale agriculture and, by extension, to civilization and the Union. The most famous is Harriet Beecher Stowe's *Uncle Tom's Cabin*. Stowe took pains to show that the South's physical landscape reflected slavery's misuse of the soil. At the plantation of cruel owner Simon Legree, "What once was a large garden was now all grown over with weeds. . . . The place looked desolate and uncomfortable; some windows stopped up with boards, some with shattered panes . . . all telling of coarse neglect and discomfort." Near the slave quarters, "broken machinery, piles of damage cotton, and other rubbish . . . accumulated." By contrast, the cabin of the slave Uncle Tom, being a "small log building," had a "neat garden-patch, where, every summer, strawberries, raspberries, and a variety of fruits and vegetables, flourished under careful tending." George Julian realized the importance of *Uncle Tom's Cabin* to the antislavery cause. "Mrs. Stowe," he wrote, "has not only lit up the fires of agitation to an unexampled degree throughout the whole extent of this country, but she has carried the torch to the ends of the earth, never before has slavery been compelled to pass through such fiery trials."[15]

The antislavery tracts by Frederick Law Olmsted were also influential. In the 1850s, this wealthy New York farmer cultivated ties with powerful antislavery journalists Henry J. Raymond of the *New York Times* and *New York Tribune* editor Horace Greeley, publishing several books and articles under their tutelage. Before, as head of the Richmond County Agriculture Society, Olmsted had argued that by practicing agricultural permanence, farmers could "increase the profit of our labor—enhance the value of our lands—throw a garment of beauty around our homes, and above all . . . materially promote Moral and Intellectual Improvement." Living on the same piece of land for multiple generations led to community formation, the construction of roads, public schooling, and a morally enlightened population—the essence of civilization for Olmsted. As one scholar explains, "Part of [Olmsted's] mission as a gentleman farmer in the late 1840s and early 1850s had been to instruct others in ways to improve their lands and to create farms that were both productive and permanent. In that way, a stable society might be created wherein the work of one generation laid the basis for a higher level of civilization in succeeding generations." Olmsted thus inherited earlier thinking by Henry Carey and John Lorain on the importance of agricultural permanence in creating a civilized society. Like them, Olmsted came to believe that proper land development could not happen in a slave society.[16]

Olmsted authored his first book, *Walks and Talks of an American Farmer in England*, after an overseas voyage to Britain in the early 1850s. Ignoring arguments presented by an abolitionist friend and abhorring the rise of the Free-Soil Party, Olmsted justified slavery by arguing that the institution civilized Africans. In the book, he also lauded London's public parks for their influence on civilization. "Five minutes of admiration," he wrote, "and a few more spent in studying the manner in which art had been employed to obtain from nature so much beauty, and I was ready to admit that in democratic America, there was nothing to be thought of as comparable with this People's Garden." Such parks converted supposedly unused land "from worthless wastes" to assets of "priceless value . . . most favorable for the production of thorough, sound, influential manhood, and especially for the growth of the right sort of legislators and lawgivers for the people." The book sold well enough that Raymond, the antislavery editor of the *Times*, asked Olmsted to go south and investigate slavery. The erstwhile farmer agreed, writing that he hoped "to make a valuable book of observations on Southern Agriculture & general economy as affected by Slavery."[17]

When Olmsted applied his standards of civilization and sound agriculture to the South, he was horrified. His observations did not reflect actual conditions in the South, but they are invaluable for how they represented northern impressions. Writing under the pseudonym "Yeoman," Olmsted described Virginia in unflattering terms. He pronounced, "The ordinary stock of the region is . . . the most miserable, dwarfish, ugly kine that I ever saw. I do not believe all the Northern States could produce such a scurvy drove." Tobacco cultivation had turned "thousands and thousands of acres" into a "wilderness of pines." A community of small farmers in Fairfax, "occupying from fifty to one hundred and fifty acres of land, and tilling it mainly by their own labor . . . in the old New-England Way" offered the only hope for the commonwealth. These yeomen purchased abandoned land, cleared the pines, and erected "neat farm houses and barns, with smiling fields of grain and grass," rehabilitating what slavery had destroyed. Olmsted hoped that such observations could convince the South of the "evils of Slavery." His observations provided critical evidence in support of the Republican agenda. Slavery destroyed the land, while a homestead bill—by offering 160 acres to each head of family—could create agricultural productivity and prosperous communities. Echoing Henry Carey, Olmsted argued that slavery had negative effects on agriculture because the black men and women who worked the soil did not own it. "Labor is the creator of wealth," he asserted. "There can be no honest wealth, no true prosperity without it."[18]

According to Olmsted, no possibility for agricultural improvement existed under slavery. He recognized Virginian Edmund Ruffin's writings as the "most valuable original agricultural work[s] ever published in the United States." Yet, even when planters followed Ruffin's advice, the "wretched and uneconomical labor system" still prevented profitable harvests. Olmsted lamented, "The land has very generally passed out of the families of the ancient proprietors, whose descendants are now in a large part to be found among the low whites; low because poor—poverty and degradation being synonymous in slave country." Only New Englanders, "with steady, preserving, working habits," could "rear healthful families," "settle in communities," and thus correct the damage of slavery. Instead of progressing to higher levels of civilization, "Virginia [had] gone backwards, particularly where the slave system [had] operated most freely and purely—so that, in the midst of the first settlements, on lands that were once cultivated and richly productive, you may now be invited to hunt, with assurance that there is no lack of wild-turkeys and venison."[19]

In Georgia, Olmsted witnessed further environmental damage from slavery. The "central region of the State," he explained, "has formerly been a very important cotton-producing region, but with the wretched and most un-husbandman-like agriculture—cotton being grown every year, without any cessation, until the profits of raising it would no longer pay for the labor expended upon it—the soil has been all washed from the hilltops, and, in years of low prices, a great many planters have been ruined and obliged to move to Alabama and Texas." Just as in Virginia, Olmsted found that after the soil was "deprived of its original fertility . . . pines have sprung up, and now cover a large portion of the region." Olmsted's message was clear: slavery's cash crops exhausted the soil. Instead of replenishing the earth, slave owners escaped westward, where their ruinous practices would convert more land to waste. Slavery had to expand, he believed, in order to survive. Connecting southern land use with imperialism, Olmsted quoted one slaveholder who explained that the South "*must* have more territory. It was a necessity upon the South, which every one saw. He thought California would be a Slave State. He also looked to the Amazon as a promising field for Slave labor."[20]

Olmsted also came to believe that slavery posed a threat to the Union. He believed that the United States was a democratic beacon. Valuing free speech, free elections, and universal white male suffrage, Olmsted argued that the United States was one of the "free and enlightened" countries in the world. European autocrats had crushed the revolutions of 1848, but the strength of American republicanism would encourage future efforts. Yet, American slavery in the Deep South exposed the shallowness of American ideals, harming the republican cause worldwide. "The laws of the South," he explained while in South Carolina, are designed for "restricting, holding down and keeping dark the minds of the dangerous class." These statutes "are of precisely the same title, purport, tendency and effect with those of Russia, Germany, Italy and France." Olmsted lamented that "it would be equally dangerous for me to publish and circulate [antislavery] letter[s] in Charleston, Paris, or Naples." Simply put, Olmsted was implying that wealthy slave owners shared more with Russian, Prussian, and French aristocrats rather than the average American farmer. Slave owners were foreigners, while northerners were the real Americans.[21]

The threat of slavery to farming (and thus to the Union and progress) led Olmsted to oppose the institution's extension westward. Visiting west Texas in March 1854, Olmsted was happy to find Prussian immigrants farming small tracts of land without slave labor. These Germans shared Olmsted's antislavery convictions, having escaped to America after the failed revolutions of 1848. He was "glad to say that the Prussians, and all Protestant Germans here, seem by no means to undervalue the advantages of Education, as a security for the continued safety and welfare of the State." Unlike the "aristocratic," slave-owning planters in east Texas, the Germans had created a "farming, democratic, and free labor community." Citing the Texas Act of Annexation, Olmsted informed northern Republicans that up to five states could be carved out of Texas. He hoped that the Germans and Mexicans of western Texas would create a new state prohibiting slavery, serving as a buffer against further expansion. The future state could also lead to emancipation. In the "new Western State . . . it would be required that all slaves subsequently introduced . . . should be educated and held subject to be made free after their labor should have paid their value and the expenses of their support and education."[22]

Olmsted joined the Emigrant Aid Society in the summer of 1854. For Kansas, the New York journalist raised enough money to purchase a howitzer. He broke the weapon into pieces and secretly forwarded it to Pomeroy's free-soilers in Lawrence. Olmsted urged northerners to pay attention to the Texas Germans as well. In October 1854, he began collecting funds. In one pamphlet, Olmsted explained that "a strong party has lately formed among the Germans, distinctly and avowedly hostile to the extension of Slavery. It includes in it many brave men who previous to the revolutions of 1848 had gained European reputations as Statesmen, lawyers, scholars, Merchants and Proprietors." Olmsted urged northerners to send money to save the community from the grasp of "Slaveholders and Hunkers [pro-slavery Democrats]." In another call to arms, Olmsted avowed that "Texas, by the terms of the joint resolution of annexation may be & probably ere long will be, divided into *five states*. There are reasons to hope that one or two of these states may be *secured to free labor* & real republicanism. The same system that is relied on to preserve *Kansas*—the organized introduction of free laborers—has already been silently at work in the Western part of Texas."[23]

As Olmsted sent money and weapons to west Texas and Kansas, cultivating ties among New York Republicans, conflict in Kansas became more violent. In October 1855, Samuel Pomeroy and the other free settlers established a government in Topeka in direct competition with the proslavery legislature in Lecompton. Free-soil allies in the North, such as Olmsted, formed committees to save "Kansas from the grasp of the Slave power" by sending additional free-state immigrants. By December of that year, tensions ran high on both sides. Hiram Hill, a settler in the free-soil stronghold of Lawrence, wrote: "One thing is certain[:] Thare is a grate Excitment here[.] [T]he Missourians tell terible Stories about the Abolitionest[s.] [T]hey say the abilitionest[s] are Driving out pro Slavery families & Burning thare houses." Proslavery settlers in Weston, Missouri, seized a free-soil man, tarred and feathered him, and pretended to "sell" the free-soiler as a slave.[24]

Seeking to unify the various Republican organizations and capitalize on "Bleeding Kansas," Salmon P. Chase and antislavery newspaper editor Gamaliel Bailey called for a Republican organizing convention in the winter of 1856. On February 22, hundreds of delegates representing both free and slave states gathered in Pittsburgh. George W. Julian, Owen Lovejoy, David Wilmot, Joshua Giddings, and Horace Greeley were among those who attended. Julian, who chaired the National Executive Committee, suggested the convening of a meeting in Philadelphia four months later to select candidates for president and vice president. As Mark Lause explains, "While a broad spectrum of motives inspired the new party, for the many thousands of petitioners for a federal homestead bill, the Kansas-Nebraska Act embodied their worse fears for the future imperial degeneration of the American republic."[25]

The Republicans gained momentum from two events in May of 1856: the attack by Preston Brooks on Charles Sumner and a raid on the free-soil settlement at Lawrence. In May 1856, Republican Charles Sumner delivered the most powerful condemnation of Kansas violence in a Senate speech. The Massachusetts senator drew heavily from Samuel Pomeroy's reports, calling him "an eye-witness . . . of superior intelligence and perfect integrity." After personally attacking Stephen Douglas and South Carolina Democrat Andrew P. Butler, Sumner outlined his primary objections to slavery's presence in the territory. First, Kansas had the potential to be a fertile agrarian paradise settled by yeomen farmers. Free settlers in Kansas "engaged in the cultivation of the soil, which from time immemorial has been the sweet employment of undisturbed industry. Contented in the returns of bounteous Nature, and the shade of his own trees, the husbandman is not aggressive; accustomed to produce, and not to destroy, he is essentially peaceful." Slavery threatened this peaceful world. "Hirelings, picked from the drunken spew and vomit of an uneasy civilization," aimed to destroy the territory's "peace and prosperity . . . in order to wrest its political power to the sake of Slavery." Second, Sumner defended the Emigrant Aid Company for its efforts in promoting settled communities and thus civilization. He called the company an "association of sincere benevolence, faithful to the Constitution and laws, whose only fortifications are hotels, school houses, and churches; whose only weapons are saw-mills, tools, and books; whose mission is peace and good will." The group provided the security needed for "true freedom."[26]

The speech was the last one Sumner would give for several years. South Carolina congressman Preston Brooks beat the Massachusetts Republican into unconsciousness two days later. Republicans argued that Brooks's assault showed the South's lack of civilization. Justin Morrill wrote to his wife: "The sermon [Sumner's speech] was a bold stroke at Congressional murderers, bullies, and black-guards. It . . . was terribly severe upon half-civilized self-retributionists. The excitement here is intense." Morrill argued that free-state men should show their moral superiority and manhood by bravely defending themselves against further assaults. "The Northern men," he reported, "are determined to submit to no further outrage, and scenes of great turbulence are expected. I shan't run, arm, nor kill anybody, and I don't intend to be whipt or shot." Joshua Giddings displayed similar feelings after the attack. In a letter to his daughter, Giddings wrote: "Northern men want to fight. . . . [W]hen men must show themselves, you must have no fear in regard to myself. I shall be perfectly careful to maintain my rights, say what I please." Outside the halls of Congress, common citizens expressed outrage. On May 25, an angry mob gathered in Boston to condemn the attack. George S. Hillard, who spoke at the gathering, hoped the North had "manliness enough, courage enough, civilization enough, and Christianity enough to rebuke such a proceeding as this."[27]

Brooks's caning of Charles Sumner reflected the escalating conflict in Kansas. A day before the incident, proslavery settlers attacked Lawrence, ransacking the town's hotel, burning homes, and destroying the printing press. Covering both Sumner's beating and the Kansas conflict, the *Farmer's Cabinet* claimed these outrages "on the rights and persons of American citizens" were "unparalleled in the recorded history of civilized Western communities." Abolitionist John Brown responded by dragging five proslavery settlers from their homes near Potawatomie Creek, Kansas, and hacking them to death with a broadsword. A man from Oskaloosa, Iowa, wrote to Boston abolitionist Thomas Wentworth Higginson to call for additional action. "I believe the time is now at hand for us to fight," he fumed. I can think [of] nothing else. I believe that the importance of this crisis deserves an effort of every free man & every free woman.... As long as there is a Ruffian in Kansas, my plan is not to show any quarters, and consequently take no prisoners.... Butcher them clean by the board."[28]

"Bleeding Kansas" and "Bleeding Sumner" galvanized support for the Republican Party in the election of 1856. In June 1856, following the recommendation of the February meeting, delegates from the various state Republican parties met in Philadelphia to draft a platform and nominate a candidate for president. The speakers at the convention highlighted the Republican belief that slavery needed to be restricted from the West to promote the right kind of land development and therefore safeguard the Union. Illinoisan Owen Lovejoy asked, "What was the mission, the manifest destiny of the American people? Was it to chase negroes? Was it to go filibustering over the world?" No, he answered, the mission was to show the despots of Russia and Europe "the fact that people could maintain civil and religious liberty" in a Union. Showing the extent to which the Republicans has shed the antiexpansion sentiments of their Whig predecessors, New Jersey Judge Joseph C. Hornblower predicted that the future of America was in the West. "I am a *Young American*," he exclaimed, and "I will go for the man whose star comes from the west, and is now rising in beauty over this mighty nation." A California delegate explained the importance of a transcontinental railroad to the future of the Union. He termed the railroad that "great measure of measures—that measure of both peace and war—that measure which, more than all, furnishes to the country the material guarantees for the preservation of the Union." New Hampshire Republican John P. Hale rejoined, "You have assembled not to say whether the Union shall be preserved, but whether, being preserved, it shall be a blessing to the people, or a scorn and a hissing the world over."[29]

Hale also used language alluding to slavery's negative impact on land. "We are living in the harvest-time of a pro-slavery Democracy," he lamented. "They have sown their seeds; they have germinated, budded, blossomed, borne fruit; and now the historian is writing his history in the blood of our fellow citizens on the plains of Kansas." The upcoming election, Hale proclaimed, would be fought between one "host that has sworn to extend the mildew of slavery over the whole land" and the "army that opposes them." Connecticut delegate Judge Tyler echoed his sentiments. "Stephen A. Douglas," Tyler claimed, "with his Nebraska bill, had subsoiled half a continent." Massachusetts Republican Henry Wilson agreed that slavery was uncivilized. He proclaimed: "You have preferred a platform that embraces freedom, humanity and Christianity." Buchanan—the Democrat nominee—would disgrace "America in the face of the civilized world."[30]

The convention adopted resolutions affirming opposition to slavery extension as the most important goal of the Republican Party. "As our Republican fathers," one resolution stated, "had abolished Slavery in all our National Territory, [and] ordained that no person should be deprived of life, liberty, or property, without due process of law, it becomes our duty to maintain this provision of the Constitution against all attempts to violate it for the purpose of establishing Slavery in any territory." Showing their belief that slavery was harmful to civilization, the Republicans also avowed: "It is both the right and duty of Congress to prohibit in the Territories those twin relics of barbarism—Polygamy and Slavery." Seeking to capitalize on the Kansas controversy, the Republicans demanded that "Kansas should be immediately admitted as a State of the Union, with her present Free Constitution." Finally, to connect East and West in the Union, the Republicans recommended "a railroad to the Pacific Ocean by the most central and practical route."[31]

Republican convention delegates decided to nominate John C. Frémont for president. Frémont's nomination reflected the party's concern for the future of the West. Samuel Pomeroy, who had traveled from Kansas to attend the convention, declared: "All Free Kansas would pray that the man who tracked our prairies to California may be the next President of the Union." Frémont had achieved acclaim for leading expeditions to the Rocky Mountains and California during the 1840s. In 1846 Frémont helped organize the Bear Flag Revolt against the Mexican government in California. He also served as California's senator for a brief term between September 1850 and March 1851. "His past course is the best guarantee in the world that we may safely trust his present professions," the *Dayton Gazette* commented. "To him, more than any other man, or dozen men, we are indebted for the fact that California, first born of the Pacific Empire, is a free white child instead of being, as was anxiously desired in the South, a feeble, black skinned creature, with the mark of Slavery burn[t] in his bosom." The *New York Mirror* celebrated Frémont's explorations westward, proclaiming that his "whole life has been devoted to the interests of civilization and the glory of the American Union." The *Steubenville Herald* predicted that Frémont's election would unite East and West. "It will be then," the paper lauded, "throughout the expansive North—the East and the West, that the 'Rushes and the willow-wand, will bristle into axe and brand, and every tuft of broom gave life, to freedom's warriors armed for strife.'"[32]

Frémont, in accepting the nomination, promised to reserve Kansas for yeomen farmers. "The only genial region of the middle latitudes left to the emigrants of the Northern States for homes cannot be conquered from the free laborers," he proclaimed. Settlers "will look to the rights secured to them by the constitution of the Union, as their best safeguard from the oppression of the class which—by a monopoly of the soil, and of slave labor to till it . . . reduce them to the extremity of laboring upon the same terms with the slaves." He also put out a call to "the great body of non-slaveholding freemen" in the South, explaining that the Republican Party's advocacy of free land distribution in the West would "advance their interests and secure their independence." The campaign began in earnest. Republicans forwarded campaign literature to state committees nationwide. In California, Cornelius Cole received 2,000 copies of the *Kansas Report*, 5,000 of the *Border Ruffian Code*, 3,000 of Sumner's "Bleeding Kansas" speech, 2,000 of *The Life of Fremont*, 2,000 of *The Life of Buchanan*, and an additional 6,500 copies of speeches by Indiana Republican Schuyler Colfax and New Yorker William Seward. Edmund D. Morgan of the Republican National Committee advised, "See that these documents are put in circulation immediately on their reaching you."[33]

The *Border Ruffian Code*, one of the main pieces of Republican propaganda, focused on the threat that slavery's extension posed to democratic government and the Union. In this pamphlet, hatred of aristocracy was the main theme. Assembled by Republicans Jacob Collamer, Galusha A. Grow, and Schuyler Colfax, the pamphlet labeled the nation's slaveholders an "iron-willed oligarchy" that enforced its rights to "human flesh and blood" by violence. The North, the pamphlet lamented, was full of "white slaves" who performed the oligarchy's bidding. The fact that the Senate "sanctioned and legalized . . . the work of an armed mob [in Kansas], in open violation of the laws and constitution of the United States," violated the "great fundamental principle upon which rests our whole political fabric, popular sovereignty or self-government." If Congress excluded slavery from the West, "the confidence of the people in the perpetuity and strength of free governments [would be] stimulated and confirmed, and the bonds of the Union strengthened and established upon the rock of eternal justice."[34]

The Life of Fremont argued that land monopoly created the slaveholding aristocracy so threatening to white northerners. Freemen, the book claimed, "will look to the rights secured to them by the Constitution of the Union as the best safeguard from the oppression of the class which, by a monopoly of the Soil and of Slave Labor to till it, might in time reduce them to the extremity of laboring upon the same terms with the slaves." Government land grants could ensure that farm ownership was widespread and provide smallholders with independence. "The great body of Non-Slaveholding Freemen," the book explained, "including those of the South, upon whose welfare Slavery is an oppression, will discover that the power of the General Government over the Public Lands may be beneficially exerted to advance their interests and secure their independence." Frémont promised that public lands would be disposed "in such a way as would make every settler upon them a freeholder."[35]

Frederick Law Olmsted published *A Journey in the Seaboard Slave States* in 1856, expanding on his earlier articles in the *New York Times*. An ardent backer of the Republican Party, Olmsted hoped his book would influence the election. Slave labor caused the beautiful Virginia countryside to whither and decay. Olmsted reported countless "Old Fields," containing a "course, yellow, sandy soil, bearing scarce anything but pine trees and broom-sedge. In some places, for acres, the pines would not be above five feet high—that was the land that had been in cultivation, used up and 'turned out.' . . . [A]t long intervals, there were fields in which the pine was just beginning to spring in beautiful green plumes . . . and was yet hardly noticeable among the dead brown grass and sassafras bushes and blackberry-vines, which nature first sends to hide the nakedness of the impoverished earth." The impoverished environment also produced a decrepit society. Near Petersburg, Virginia, Olmsted found a "log-cabin, with a door in one of the gable-ends, a stove-pipe, half-rusted away, protruding from the other . . . closed by a wooden shutter. This must have been the school house, but there were no children then about it, and no appearance of there having been any lately." This school was amid "a continuation of pine trees, big, little, and medium in size, and hogs, and a black, crooked, burnt sapling." The very presence of pines seemed to Olmsted as proof of inferior cultivation. In a section entitled "A Tobacco Plantation," Olmsted noted: "An oak forest had originally occupied the ground where [the plantation house] stood; but this having been cleared and the soil worn out in cultivation by the previous proprietors, pine woods now surrounded it in every direction, a square of a few acres only being kept clear immediately about it."[36]

According to Olmsted, the nonslaveholding whites of the South struggled to make a living because of the inferior soil. Traveling in South Carolina, Olmsted's driver reported: "Rather poor soil, I should say. It's the cussedest poor country God ever created. . . . You have to keep your horses on —*Shucks! damn it*." The cause of the inferior soil was not natural; it was slavery. "Put the best race of men under heaven into a land where all industry is obliged to bear the weight of such a system," Olmsted explained, "and inevitably their ingenuity, enterprise, and skill will be paralyzed, the land will be impoverished, its resources of wealth will remain undeveloped, or will be wasted." Olmsted warned that more land could look like the "un-cultivated and unimproved—rather, sadly worn and misused" farms of eastern Virginia if slavery expanded further. He even reported that Virginia's governor wanted California to be a slave state despite the compromise measures of 1850. Olmsted did not understand that ultisols, the most common soil type in the South, encouraged the shifting cultivation that he noticed.[37]

Farmers and settlers in the West found the Republican message of 1856 appealing. C. C. Andrews, a Massachusetts journalist, visited the Minnesota and "Dacotah" territories in the fall of that year. He reported that "there is much more political excitement during this campaign than there was in 1840. Flag-staffs and banners abound in the greatest profusion in every village. Every farm-house has some token of its politics spread to the breeze." The West, for Andrews and the people he met, presented a vast amount of land on which sturdy yeomen could gain material wealth and independence—provided that government policy promoted proper land development. "I have wondered," he wrote, "at the contrast presented between the comparatively small number who penetrate to the frontier and that great throng of men who toil hard for a temporary livelihood in the populous towns and cities of the Union." Andrews believed that if "this latter class were at all mindful of the opportunities for gain and independence which the new territories afforded, they would soon abandon . . . their crowded alleys in the city, and aspire to be cultivators and owners of the soil." In order to achieve these gains, farming communities needed permanent settlers and positive moral influences. Andrews was not surprised that among the "lusty yeomen . . . there was an overwhelming majority for Frémont." Farmers in Minnesota and Dakota favored the government distributing small plots of land to freemen and excluding slavery from the West.[38]

Despite the overwhelming support for Frémont that Andrews found in the Old Northwest, James Buchanan still came out ahead. Frémont won every free state except California, Illinois, Indiana, Pennsylvania, and New Jersey. He also garnered 33 percent of the total popular vote. More impressively, Frémont gained 45 percent of the popular votes within the North.

He would have done even better without the presence of nativist Millard Fillmore, who carried 21 percent of the popular vote. Taken together, Frémont and Fillmore votes would have beaten Buchanan in California, New Jersey, and Illinois and come close in Pennsylvania and Indiana. For the 1860 election, Republicans only had to add Pennsylvania and either Illinois or Indiana to their column in order to win. Despite the ignominy of having "obnoxious nests of 'Buchaniers'" inhabit the White House, Republicans were encouraged by the initial success. James Buchanan, in turn, looked to destroy Republican chances by putting the slavery issue to rest once and for all.[39]

"Old Buck," as friends called Buchanan, believed the Supreme Court could make a final pronouncement on the expansion of slavery. In March 1857, during the inauguration ceremony, observers noticed the president whispering with Chief Justice Roger B. Taney. A few minutes later, Buchanan declared that the court would "speedily and finally" settle the question of whether Congress could regulate slavery in the territories. Two days afterward, on March 6, Taney delivered just such a pronouncement, claiming that Congress had no regulatory power over the institution. Taney argued that the Constitution's Fifth Amendment—preventing seizure of "life, liberty, and property, without due process of law"—forbade Congress and territorial legislatures from barring slavery. Taken to its logical conclusion, the ruling seemed to question whether any free state—even the Republican strongholds of Wisconsin and Massachusetts—could constitutionally exclude slave property. The decision was important for two reasons. First, for many Republicans, Buchanan's actions at the inauguration proved the existence of a slave-power conspiracy to use the power of government to promote the institution's interests. And second—the focus of this study—the decision spurred new fears about slavery's western expansion, continuing the debate about whether the lands in the West would be settled by small farms or large plantations. Republicans even worried that the institution could take hold in states such as California and Oregon, where it had previously been excluded.[40]

Republicans and abolitionists believed that the Dred Scott Decision threatened to make slavery national. "As they claim the whole country for Slavery, we claim the whole country for Freedom," abolitionist William Goodwell wrote to George Julian. Julian himself observed that Republicans interpreted Dred Scott "as the distilled diabolism of two hundred years of slavery, stealthily aiming at the overthrow of our Republican institutions, while seeking to hide its nakedness under the fig-leaves of judicial fairness and dignity. They branded it as the desperate attempt of

[the] slave-breeding Democracy to crown itself king, by debauching the Federal judiciary and waging war against the advance of civilization." He warned that slaveholders would soon "attempt to divide California for the purpose of introducing slavery into the southern portion." Cornelius Cole, the California Republican, agreed with Julian's interpretation. "The adoption of a free constitution did not, by any means, abate the aggressiveness of the pro-slavery sentiment in California," he recalled. "In the South it was constantly growing more virulent, incited, it may have been, by disappointment engendered by the action of California and by a lively hope of extending slavery into the new territories of Kansas and Nebraska in the Northwest." Cole filled his diary with newspaper editorials opposing Dred Scott. One asked: "What is the inevitable deduction which flows from this statement of facts? THE CURSE OF SLAVERY, IF IT BE A CURSE—THE BLESSING OF SLAVERY, IF IT BE A GOOD OR A BLESSING—MUST BE ALIKE ENDURED OR ENJOYED BY THE PEOPLE OF A TERRITORY."[41]

Republicans reported that Buchanan's strategy had backfired. Instead of making the slavery issue disappear, the court's decision drew thousands more to the Republican ranks. "Everything seems to look pretty well politically," Salmon P. Chase wrote in May 1857. "So far as I can see, the antislavery sentiment and principle [take] a deeper & deeper hold upon the masses." Only a month later, Republicans scored another propaganda coup with the publication of Hinton R. Helper's *The Impending Crisis of the South: How to Meet It*, which they believed could convert nonslaveholding southern whites to the Republican cause. The book demonstrates how land development was at the heart of the Republican message.[42]

Hinton Helper came from a prosperous family in Davie County, North Carolina, a region in the piedmont unreliant on slave labor and hostile to slaveholder power. In 1860, as a recent biography of Helper points out, "slaveholders accounted for 85.8 percent of the state legislature." Economic opportunities proved scant in the piedmont, and Helper blamed slaveholders for the increasing numbers of landless whites in North Carolina. Having a touchy and vitriolic personality, Helper also felt personally aggrieved when a southern editor forced him to remove passages marginally critical of slavery in a book about the California Gold Rush. After this incident, Helper began work on a book demanding an immediate end to slavery in the South. The North Carolinian, however, had no sympathy for enslaved black people. Playing the role of Jeffersonian agrarian, not abolitionist, Helper attacked slavery for its negative effects on the southern environment. "The soil itself," he argued, "soon sickens and dies beneath the unnatural tread of the slave."

Quoting an Alabaman, Helper wrote: "I can show you, with sorrow, in the older portions of Alabama, and in my native county of Madison, the sad memorials of the artless and exhausting culture of cotton. Our small planters, after taking the cream off their lands, unable to restore them by rest, manures, or otherwise, are going further West and South, in search of other virgin lands, which they may and will despoil and impoverish in like manner." Free settlers, owning small tracts of land, were prosperous. Helper wanted slaveholders to "see how much more vigorous and fruitful the soil is when under the prudent management of free white husband-men, than it is when under the rude and nature-murdering tillage of enslaved negroes."[43]

Under slavery, the South, "so great and so glorious by nature," trampled its own fields and forests. "At the South everything is either neglected or mismanaged," Helper explained. "Whole forests are felled by the ruthless hand of slavery, the trees are cut into logs, rolled into heaps, covered with the limbs and brush, and then burned on the identical soil that gave them birth. The land itself next falls prey to the fell destroyer, and that which was once a beautiful, fertile, and luxuriant woodland, is soon despoiled of all its treasures and converted into an eye-offending desert." He concluded with a plea to poor southern whites: "Slavery has polluted and impover-ished your lands; freedom will restore them to their virgin purity."[44]

As a result of slavery's land-use regime, *The Impending Crisis* argued, civilization did not take root in the South. First, the institution denied education to poor whites. "The lords of the lash," Helper fumed, "are not only absolute masters of the blacks, who are bought and sold, and driven about like so many cattle, but they are also the oracles and arbiters of all non-slaveholding whites, whose freedom is merely nominal, and whose unparalleled illiteracy and degradation is purposely and fiendishly per-petuated." Second, slavery prevented material progress. Slavery, "the direst evil that e'er befell the land," was the reason "that the South bears nothing like even a respectable approximation to the North in navigation, com-merce, or manufactures, and that, contrary to the opinion entertained by ninety nine hundredths of her people, she is far behind the free States in the only thing of which she has dared to boast—agriculture." The absence of proper land development inhibited progress and brought the South "under reproach in the eyes of all civilized and enlightened nations."[45]

Helper believed that the Union could find perpetual peace only when the South abandoned slavery. "Patriotism," he proclaimed, "makes us a freesoiler; state pride makes us an emancipationist. . . . [W]ith the free state men in Kanzas and Nebraska, we sympathize with all our heart.

We love the whole country, the great family of states and territories, one and inseparable." Helper implored northerners to "organize yourselves as *one man* under the banners of Liberty, and to aid us in *exterminating* slavery, which is the only thing that militates against our complete aggrandizement as a nation." The Republicans had a "*duty* to make a firm and decisive effort to save the States which they fought to free [during the American Revolution], from falling under the yoke of a worse tyranny than that which overshadowed them under the reign of King George the Third."[46]

Helper provided ammunition to the Republican demand that slavery be excluded from the West. Like David Wilmot and Abraham Lincoln, Helper believed that slavery restriction would lead to emancipation because slavery depended on new lands to survive. "Slave society, pent up, withers and dies," he wrote. "It must continually be fed by new fields and forests, to be wasted and wilted under the poisonous tread of the slave." That desire, he believed, explained why slaveholders stopped at nothing to extend the institution to new states. Helper warned: "Consider well the aggressive, fraudulent and despotic power which they have exercised in the affairs of Kanzas [*sic*]; and remember that, if, by adhering to erroneous principles of neutrality or non-resistance, you allow them to force the curse of slavery on that vast and fertile field, the broad area of all the surrounding States and Territories—the whole nation, in fact—will soon fall prey to their diabolical intrigues." The North Carolinian concluded that the expansion of slavery would destroy Jefferson's vision of an agrarian republic: "Not content with eating out the vitals of the South, slavery, true to the character which it has acquired for insatiety and rapine, is beginning to make rapid encroachments on new territory; and as a basis for a few remarks on the blasting influence which it is shedding over the broad and fertile domains of the West, which in accordance with the views and resolutions offered by the immortal Jefferson, should have been irrevocably dedicated to freedom."[47]

New York Republicans published Helper's book on June 26, 1857. *New York Tribune* editor Horace Greeley declared that it provided "the southern masses with [a] fearless, blunt spokesman." Helper's "rolling volleys and dashing charges of argument and rhetoric," Greeley claimed, showed the inferiority of slave agriculture and an opening for the Republican Party in the South. William M. Chace, the Republican National Executive Committee secretary, argued that the remaining money from Frémont's failed election bid should be used to circulate 50,000 copies of *The Impending Crisis* for the 1858 midterm elections. Despite Greeley's initial support, Helper's first edition failed to gain traction in either the North or the South.

When Helper handed a copy to North Carolina governor John W. Ellis, the executive lit the book on fire and used it to light his pipe. Helper and other southern dissidents such as Cassius Clay asked New York Republicans to finance a second release. In June 1859, a New York publisher released *The Compendium of the Impending Crisis*, a pamphlet smaller and cheaper than the original but containing much of the same content. The smaller edition sold many more copies, and sixty-eight Republican politicians officially endorsed it. Helper himself noted that 137,000 copies had been sold by May 1860, making the book, in the words of his biographer, "the most important campaign document of the 1860 election."[48]

Schuyler Colfax, Owen Lovejoy, Edwin B. Morgan, Joshua R. Giddings, Henry L. Dawes, Justin S. Morrill, and John Sherman were among the Republicans supporting Helper's book. William Seward reportedly commented, "I have read the 'Impending Crisis of the South' with deep attention. It seems to me a work of great merit, rich, yet *accurate*, in statistical information, and logical in analysis." The fierce southern reaction to these endorsements highlighted the book's popularity and the threat of the Republican Party to slavery. Daniel Worth, an aging North Carolina preacher, attempted to distribute Helper's book to poor whites in 1860. Authorities responded by throwing the old man in jail and charging him for "circulating books deemed incendiary" and exciting in "slaves and free negroes a spirit of insurrection, conspiracy, or rebellion." The penalties for the first charge were imprisonment for more than a year and "whipping and pillory at the discretion of the Court." A North Carolina judge could recommend capital punishment for the second offense. Fearful for his life and terrified by the "horrid oaths and blasphemies" of fellow prisoners, Worth wrote to George Julian for help. "The book, Helper's *Impending Crisis*, is the greatest danger," the preacher explained. "My lawyers rely on the fact that the book was never offered to a slave or free negro, and therefore cannot fill the statute." He pleaded for "letters of Christian feeling and sympathy." Two months later, the court sentenced him to two years in prison. The old man worried that even this light sentence would lead to death "in a felon's cell, amidst oaths, curses, and blasphemies . . . in the land of 'whips and chains.'" Worth somehow escaped to New York City after posting bail and relied on his antislavery friends to keep him free until the Civil War.[49]

Proslavery southerners would not let the Republicans who endorsed the book get away so easily. On December 5, 1859, the House of Representatives met to determine the next speaker of the House. The Republicans' first choice was John Sherman of Ohio, brother of William Tecumseh Sherman. John Clark of Missouri responded by authoring a resolution declaring that "the doctrines and sentiments of a certain book, called 'The Impending Crisis of the South—How to Meet it' . . . are insurrectionary and hostile to the domestic peace and tranquility of this country." Clark argued that any man who endorsed the book could not become speaker of the house. The Republicans, who needed five votes from outside their ranks to win the speakership, failed to elect John Sherman on multiple ballots. Democrats then forced the Republicans to select William Pennington, whose only qualification was that he had no stated opinion on *The Impending Crisis*.[50]

For proslavery Democrats, Republican support for *The Impending Crisis* unveiled the party's threat to slavery. First, Republican restrictions on slavery in the territories prevented slaveholders from taking advantage of the riches of the West. Virginian Samuel M. Wolfe claimed that slave owners needed southern California. "The propriety of dividing the State into Northern and Southern California," he argued, "has already occupied the attention of the Legislature. . . . [I]t is universally conceded that, in case of its adoption, the Southern portion will establish the laws and institutions of Virginia and Louisiana." Second, and more important, proslavery southerners worried that through patronage and the disbursement of Helper's book, the Republicans could build a southern wing of their party that would outlaw slavery. Georgia senator Robert M. Toombs warned that should a Republican win the 1860 election, "It would abolitionize Maryland in a year, raise a powerful abolition party in Virginia, Kentucky, and Missouri in two years, and foster and rear up a free labor party in the Whole South in four years." Wolfe claimed that the "*Black* Republican Party's" endorsement of a book "advocating treason, rebellion, civil war, insurrection, murder, arson, rapine and bloodshed" proved the party's abolitionist intentions.[51]

As Toombs and Wolfe observed, the election of 1860 carried high stakes. Republicans believed that victory would secure a West for free white farmers using sound farming practices. Permanent towns and villages inhabited by white people best promoted the Union and "civilization." Proslavery Democrats worried that a Republican administration could strike at slavery where it existed, despite fervent promises to the contrary. Among other slavery-related issues, the Republican campaign focused on the threat the institution posed to land development. The party met in Chicago in May 1860 to select a presidential candidate and determine a platform.

Edwin D. Morgan, Cornelius Cole, and other members of the Republican National Committee welcomed all "those who are opposed to the policy of the present administration . . . to the extension of slavery into the territories, to the new and dangerous political doctrine that the Constitution of its own force carries slavery into all the territories of the United States." Reflecting the party's focus on restricting slavery, Republicans selected the author of the Wilmot Proviso to give the opening speech. David Wilmot believed the violence in Kansas and the restrictive free-speech laws championed by slaveholders violated civilization and made a mockery of the American Union. "Need I remind this intelligent and vast audience," he proclaimed, "of tyranny such as the world never saw in a civilized and Christianized land that is manifested with the spirit of slavery. Whose rights are safe where slavery has the power to trample them under foot? Who to-day is not more free to utter his opinions within the empire of Russia, or under the shadow of despotism of Austria?" Wilmot concluded with a rhetorical question: "Shall we support this blighting, this demoralizing institution throughout the vast extent of our borders?"[52]

The convention also featured speakers alluding to the link between land monopoly and disunionist sentiment. Like Hinton Helper, former Democrat Chauncey Cleveland believed that the Republican Party could save the Union by liberating the majority of white southerners from slaveholder oppression. Patronage and increasing land ownership could build a Republican Party in the South. "The disunionists are in a small minority in the slave states, and they keep down the majority," he asserted. "[I]f we treat them kindly and hold our hand out to them, as men competent to fill the high offices of the United States, we shall have the majority out from the heel of the slave oligarchy." At the next convention, Cleveland predicted, "We shall probably have the entire slave states represented."[53]

Fred Hassaureck, a German delegate from Cincinnati, Ohio, gave one of the most popular speeches on the meaning of union. Hassaureck defined "Americanism" in Republican terms. Alluding to his own experience in Prussia, Hassaureck began: "Gentlemen, I have seen the nations of Europe smarting under the arbitrary rule of despots." He proclaimed, interrupted by loud cheers from the gallery, that "if it is Americanism to believe that this glorious Federation of sovereign States has a higher object and a nobler purpose than to be the mere means of fortifying, protecting, and propagating the institution of human servitude—if it is Americanism to believe that these vast fertile Territories of the West are forever to remain sacred, to remain as free homes for free labor and free men, I shall live and die an American." Hassaureck's speech equated American national identity with free speech, union, and opposition to slavery extension—all northern, Republican values. The achievement of these values depended upon the government securing "free homes" in the "vast fertile Territories of the West."[54]

The 1860 Republican platform highlighted the importance of homestead promotion, slavery restriction, and the West to the party's appeal. To extend the benefits of civilization westward and bind far-off regions to the Union, the platform offered support for a "complete and satisfactory homestead measure" and a "railroad to the Pacific Ocean." The paramount Republican plank, however, was the ban on slavery in the territories. Absent from the platform was a moral condemnation of slavery. Joshua R. Giddings had tried to insert such a plank into the platform, but Republicans concerned with avoiding the charge of "abolitionism" defeated the proposition. Giddings fumed afterward: "A few . . . worthless doughfaced tricksters managed to get the committee arranged so as to strike out . . . the immediate rights of man." Despite their disappointment, both Julian and Giddings felt confident that Republican nominee Abraham Lincoln would support antislavery measures. "As to Lincoln," Giddings wrote, "I would trust him on the subject of slavery as soon as I would Chase or Seward [Lincoln's rivals for the nomination]. I have been well acquainted with him and think I understand his whole character."[55]

Even before the convention, Republican National Committee member Cornelius Cole worked hard to secure Republican victory in California. The construction of the transcontinental railroad and the passage of a homestead bill were the major campaign issues in his state. In a letter to Edward Morgan discussing the 1860 convention, Cornelius Cole argued: "We think here that the energies of the government should be directed towards the construction of a Pacific Railway in order to divert them [the South] from the acquisition of new slave markets. That we should thus build up more free states, rather than purchase additional lands for slavery . . . shall not this great question [factor] largely into the next campaign? In it we have something positive and progressive." Future Civil War martyr and Oregon politician Edward Baker agreed. In a speech to a Republican mass meeting in San Francisco, Baker stated: "The interest of the South is identical—the slave interest belongs to the whole of it in common and alone. . . . Whatever great measure comes before the nation, develops the hostility of the South, because it conflicts with their one interest. The Pacific Railroad is a striking example." He added: "What is true of the sentiments of the South toward a railroad, is true also of a homestead. What does she care for a homestead? She never expects to use it. . . . [S]he is in another line of business. See Virginia, once the mother of Presidents and of statesmen, now engaged in slave breeding!—rearing little niggers to send South! She cares nothing about a homestead." A vote for Abraham Lincoln, Baker concluded, was a vote for the railroad, free homesteads, and freedom in the territories. Erstwhile Democrat Harvey S. Brown told voters that only the Republicans could deliver on promises for a transcontinental railroad and a homestead law. "The Republican party," he proclaimed at a rally, "is for a Homestead law—for giving 160 acres of the public domain free of cost to the actual settler. It is for the immediate construction of an Atlantic and Pacific railroad. . . . [T]hese are Republican principles."[56]

Over 1,800 miles eastward in Indiana, George W. Julian ran for Congress in 1860, hoping to capitalize on popular support for the Republicans. Just three years earlier, Julian had complained that fellow Indianans considered his antislavery sentiments too "ultra" for election. During a speech at Raysville, Indiana, Julian lamented: "The sad truth is, that Indiana is the most pro-slavery of all our Northern States. Her Black Code, branded upon her recreant forehead by a majority . . . tells her humiliating pedigree far more forcibly than any words I could employ. Our people hate the negro with a perfect, if not a supreme hatred, and their antislavery, making an average estimate, is a superficial and sickly sentiment, rather than a deep-rooted and robust conviction." By the time of the election, the racial views of average white Indianans had not changed, but antislaveholder sentiment and concern about land development in the West had increased dramatically. Caleb B. Smith, a conservative former Whig, wrote to Julian explaining the change in public opinion. "You are regarded as ultra in your antislavery notions," Smith began. But he added: "I do not know that you have [observed] our opinion in regard to Slavery. . . . There is nothing I so much desire as to see the insolence of the slave power rebuffed and its pride and arrogance humbled." Smith concluded: "I most earnestly desire to see Indiana occupy a position of hostility to the pro-slavery democracy in the contest of 1860." Julian, claiming that the "Slave-breeding Democracy" was "waging war against the advance of civilization" and attempting "to divide California for the purpose of introducing slavery," was triumphant in 1860. Salmon Chase, congratulating Julian on his election, remarked: "So our principles prevail."[57]

Frederick Law Olmsted continued to publish books highlighting slavery's danger to agriculture and progress in the West. He hoped his work would persuade people to vote Republican and take action to stop slavery's spread. In his 1860 work, *A Journey through Texas*, Olmsted argued that slavery prolonged the "frontier condition"—wild nature—and hence prevented the growth of civilization. "I believe that the prosperity of Texas," he wrote, "measured by the rapidity with which the inconveniences and discomforts, inevitable only in a wilderness or an uncivilized state of society, are removed, would have been ten times greater than it is, had it been, at the date of its annexation, thrown open . . . to a free immigration, with a prohibition to slavery." The effects of slavery on the land were readily apparent in Texas. "Nowhere," Olmsted wrote, "in any broad agricultural district, does such waste appear to have taken place, without a present equivalent existing for it. Nowhere is the land, with what is attached to it, now less suitable and promising for the residence of a refined and civilized people." Challenging slaveholders, he asked: "What do you say to the fact that, in the eastern counties, that spectacle so familiar and so melancholy in your own State, in all the older Slave States, is already not infrequently seen by the traveler—an abandoned plantation of 'worn-out' fields?"[58]

Due to poor soil-management practices, Olmsted warned that slaveholders would never cease expanding in their quest for more land to exploit. The evidence for this claim was on display in western Louisiana: "A good part of the land had, at some time, been cleared, but much was already turned over to the 'old field pines,' some of them even fifteen years or more. In fact, a larger area had been abandoned, we thought, than remained in cultivation. With the land many cabins have, of course, also been deserted, giving the road a desolate air. If you ask, where are the people that once occupied these, the universal reply is 'gone to Texas.'" The converse, however, was also true. If free white farmers settled the West, the environment would blossom. Visiting German settlers in Texas, Olmsted wrote: "The greater variety of the crops which had been grown upon their allotment and the more clean and complete tillage they had received contrasted favorably with the patches of corn-stubble, overgrown with crab-grass, which are the only gardens to be seen adjoining the cabins of the poor whites and slaves." He concluded: "Waste of soil and injudicious application of labor is common in the agriculture of the North, but nowhere comparably with what is general at the South."[59]

During the 1860 campaign, newspapers also commented on the threat slavery posed to agricultural lands in the West because of the institution's harmful effects on soil. A self-proclaimed farmer by the name of C. Robinson wrote a letter to Senator Henry Wilson in February 1860 that the *Emancipator* reprinted. Slavery, Robinson fumed, "degrades the non-slaveholding whites to nearly the level of the blacks—all slave soil to a habitation of cruelty and crime—pollutes everything it touches—smites the soil with barrenness on which it treads." Theodore Parker wrote a similar letter to the *New York Herald* in April 1860, noting that the "live lands" of the West would not benefit from the "slovenly farming" under slavery.

Echoing an earlier claim by Henry Carey, Edward Bates wrote a letter in the *Milwaukee Daily Sentinel* in October 1860 suggesting that slaves did not care for the soil properly because they did not own it. Bates praised Republicans for being "strongly opposed to the admission of *blacks* (slaves) into the Territories, and firmly resolved to reserve . . . the virgin lands, to be settled and cultivated and made valuable by the free white voluntary labor of American citizens, and thus build up communities of white people." Bates theorized, italicizing for emphasis: *"Labor ought to own its Land."*[60]

Voters went to the polls in huge numbers in November 1860. Four candidates competed for their attention. Abraham Lincoln faced Democrat Stephen Douglas in the North, while southern Democrat John Breckinridge competed with Constitutional Unionist John Bell of Tennessee in the South. Douglas, the only national candidate, still campaigned on popular sovereignty, claiming that if the people of a territory did not want slavery, they could pass laws making the institution impossible to establish. The southern Democrats, who had broken with the Douglas wing of the party at the 1860 convention in Charleston, demanded federal protection for slavery in the territories. John Bell ignored the slavery extension issue altogether, proclaiming love for Union and the Constitution as the defining characteristics of his party. Motivated by a hatred of slaveholders and intense opposition to the institution's western extension, northerners turned out to vote for the Republican Party in droves. Lincoln won all the electoral votes in the free states with the exception of New Jersey and carried 54 percent of the popular vote in the North. The Illinois lawyer outpolled all three opponents combined, guaranteeing victory.[61]

South Carolinians greeted news of Lincoln's election with horror. The *Charleston Mercury* had pondered in 1859, "The question now for the South to consider is this—under whose government will the slaves of the South be most quietly kept in subjection and order? . . . If we had a government of our own, the post office, all the avenues of intercourse, the police and the military would be under our exclusive control." After Lincoln's election, the South Carolina legislature answered. In early November, the state senate and house voted to hold a secession convention on December 17, 1860. At this meeting, convention delegates unanimously approved secession. The secession ordinance declared, "If it is right to preclude or abolish slavery in a Territory, why should it be allowed to remain in the States? . . . In spite of all disclaimers and professions, there can be but one end by the submission of the South to the rule of a sectional antislavery government at Washington; and that end, directly or indirectly, must be—the emancipation of the slaves of the South." The rest of the Deep South followed, with Mississippi, Florida, Alabama, Georgia, Louisiana, and Texas all leaving the Union by February 1, 1860.[62]

Some Republicans worried that the Lincoln administration would compromise principles—most notably the party's insistence on no slavery in the territories—to prevent the upper South from seceding. They demanded that the president-elect refuse to give into southern threats. One of George Julian's supporters from Madison, Wisconsin, wrote: "I hope from the bottom of my soul no pro-slavery concessions will be made. It will ruin the Republican Party if they do. Even civil war would be better than to [denigrate] ourselves by yielding an [iota] of our principles." Indiana Republican Caleb Smith agreed, concluding: "While I am most anxious for the preservation of the Union and the enforcement of the laws, I am gratified to see increasing evidence of a determination on the part of Republicans not to abandon their principles to conciliate treason." Justin Morrill abhorred disunion, but he hated compromise more: "There can be no compromise short of entire surrender of our convictions of right and wrong, and I do not propose to make that surrender. All that can be done will not satisfy the cotton states. Nothing short of legalizing and introducing slavery in the North will satisfy them. . . . I regret the facts, but we must accept the truth that there is an 'irrepressible conflict' between our two systems of civilization."[63]

Lincoln followed the advice of the more belligerent wing of his party in refusing to compromise over the extension of slavery. As Salmon P. Chase reminded Julian, "I do not think that Mr. Lincoln will disappoint the true Republicans who voted for him. He may not be as radical as some would wish, but he is, I am confident, [perfectly] sincere." From December to April 1861, Unionists in Virginia, North Carolina, and Tennessee begged the Lincoln administration to support compromise measures to keep upper South states in the Union. The Crittenden Compromise, authored by Kentucky senator John Crittenden, guaranteed protection of slavery by constitutional amendment in the states where it existed and prohibited slavery north of the 36°30' line by the same mechanism. The sticking point in Crittenden's compromise and the other various plans, however, was that each included some provision for protecting slavery in the territories. The so-called Committee of Thirty-Three compromise proposed by conservative Republican Thomas Corwin of Ohio in January 1860 attracted the most Republican support. Unlike Crittenden's compromise, the committee's plan had no constitutional guarantee for slavery in the territories. Yet, since it still admitted New Mexico as a slave state, many

Republicans rejected the plan. Upper South delegates believed that the plan did not provide enough protections to slavery.[64]

As compromise measures failed and the nation inched closer toward conflict, Joshua R. Giddings viewed the exit of slave-state senators and congressmen as a golden opportunity to enact the Republican legislative agenda and ensure proper land development in the West. Giddings begged Julian to go with him: "Don't fail to meet me at as early a day as you can. A thousand reasons urge me to solicit your attention there. Your influence must be felt there whither there be a special session or not. . . . I go to make my influence felt on the great subject that has occupied my life. . . . Come to Washington and I will aid you as far as possible." The Republican Party had defined the future of America in anti-southern terms. Small farmers, by practicing agricultural permanence, could build civil society in the West. Owning land encouraged independence and loyalty to democratic institutions. Tending a farm for multiple generations allowed the formation of schools and churches, building "civilization." The slave South, if allowed to expand, would only bring land monopoly, destructive farming practices, and barbarism.[65]

LAND-DEVELOPMENT POLITICS AND

THE AMERICAN CIVIL WAR

Just, Sir, as you are the representative of an honorable Order, just as our flag is the
embodiment of a mighty nation, so, Sir, has it become the representative, the embodiment,
of an honorable nation of agriculturists.
—*Rev. John A. Anderson, "Address, Delivered at the Laying of the Corner Stone of the*
San Joaquin Valley Agricultural Society's Hall, in Stockton, August 6, 1861"

Early in the morning on April 12, 1861, Virginia agricultural reformer and rabid secessionist Edmund Ruffin stood on Cummings Point in Charleston Harbor. Ruffin had been waiting for this moment for years. Republicans, he believed, had revealed their true governing intentions in Hinton Helper's *Impending Crisis of the South*, aiming to make "all federal property into centers for abolitionist operations" and to build an antislavery party in the South through patronage and incendiary literature. The South could only preserve its institutions and culture in a separate nation. Ruffin, disgusted with Virginia's wariness toward secession, skedaddled to South Carolina, the first state to leave the Union. As the crisis over federal soldiers stationed at Charleston's Fort Sumter mounted, Ruffin went to sleep on the night of the eleventh with his clothing on, waiting for word of an attack. Before rays of sunshine hit the fort on the morning of April 12, Ruffin pulled the lanyard on a hefty Columbiad gun, sending a cannon shell crashing into U.S. soldiers garrisoned there.[1]

Ruffin's shot, and President Abraham Lincoln's subsequent call for 75,000 volunteers to suppress the rebellion, started the Civil War. In April and May 1861, Virginia, Arkansas, Tennessee, and North Carolina joined Texas, Louisiana, Mississippi, Alabama, Georgia, South Carolina, and

Florida in the Confederacy. Belying the image of the "urban" North and the "agrarian" South, a majority of the soldiers who fought in the Union army came from farming communities. With the exception of Massachusetts's John Andrew, governors of rural states in the Union, such as Wisconsin's Alex W. Randall, were *more* bellicose than governors of urban areas. On May 3, 1861, Randall urged the government to "transport an army down the Mississippi, and blaze a broad track through the whole South, from Montgomery to Charleston. Charleston should be razed, till not one stone is left upon another, till there is no place left for the owl to hoot." By contrast, as historian Thomas H. O'Connor explains, "The American manufacturer was among the most powerful and influential forces consistently working to prevent the disruption of the Union," fearing economic instability and the loss of valuable resources like cotton.[2]

Students of the Civil War often ask why the North responded so strongly to secession. The main reason is that the people of the North believed strongly in the Union; preserving it meant supporting democracy in a world where oligarchs ruled. Victory, as historian Gary W. Gallagher explains, also meant "affirming the rule of law under the Constitution and punishing slaveholding aristocrats whose selfish actions had compromised the work of the founding generation." These aristocrats, Republicans believed, derived their power both from slavery and land monopoly. Beyond victory on the battlefield, Republicans thought they had to shape the West and the South in the image of the agrarian North to prevent secession from occurring again. The beliefs about land development forged during the political conflict of the 1850s had convinced northern Republicans that they resided in a separate and superior agricultural society to the slaveholding South. Only free farmers who practiced wise land-use practices could produce a powerful and united nation.[3]

Showcasing how notions about proper land use were foremost among people's reasons for supporting the Union, this chapter will first investigate the debate over secession in California. As the scholar Ian Tyrrell explains, California, with its "rich natural resources, grand scenery, mild climate and Pacific position," seemed the best opportunity for turning the myth of an agrarian republic into a reality. Highlighting the evils of slave-based agriculture and the concomitant harm to union and civilization, California's Republican Party used agrarian rhetoric to secure the state's support for the Union. Meanwhile, illustrating the influence of agrarian thought on national policy, the incoming Republican majority created the U.S. Department of Agriculture, the Pacific Railroad Act, the Land Grant College Act, and the Homestead Act. Regardless of the consequences of these bills, northern politicians framed them as measures intended to create stable farming communities in the West and thus preserve the Union. Finally, agrarian notions connecting proper land use with union and civilization were not limited to people living in the far West or walking the halls of Congress; common soldiers had them as well. These soldiers blamed plantation agriculture for the South's lack of productivity and aristocratic society.[4]

California presents a unique case study for analyzing how politicians used agrarian ideas to garner support for the Union war effort. While politicians mostly cited union, the pending construction of a transcontinental railroad, and battlefield victories to convince Californians to stay loyal to the United States, they also warned that a Confederate takeover would prevent the development of small farms and agricultural improvement. Although the state voted for Lincoln in 1860, it differed from other free states because of its large pro-Confederate political minority. John Breckinridge, the southern Democrat candidate for president, received just over 28 percent of California's vote in 1860. While California had outlawed slavery because of gold-miner opposition in 1849, expatriate slave owners comprised a powerful political faction nicknamed the "Chivalry," or "Chivs" for short. Mississippian William M. Gwin, leader of the Chiv faction, became one of California's senators when the state entered the Union in 1850 and would remain in the position until 1861. In April 1852, Gwin ally Henry A. Crabb authored a fugitive slave law in California to supplement the national act passed earlier. The statute labeled escaped slaves who had come to California before statehood as fugitives, imposed heavy fines on anyone aiding escaped slaves, and even allowed slave owners to reside in California with their human property for an undefined time. Cornelius Cole, the Free-Soiler from New York, launched his political career defending three slaves from deportation to Mississippi in 1852.[5]

The Chivs became more powerful during the 1850s, defeating the free-soil wing of California Democrats led by feisty Irishman David C. Broderick. Broderick had broken with the Chivs over the Kansas-Nebraska Act and the Dred Scott Decision, arguing that "slavery is old, decrepit, and consumptive; freedom is young, strong, and vigorous. The one is naturally stationary and loves ease; the other is migratory and enterprising." Broderick also embraced homestead rights. California Supreme Court justice and diehard Chiv David S. Terry responded by tarring Broderick with abolitionism. Broderick's faction, Terry alleged, were "black Republicans" and "negro lovers." He elaborated: "Perhaps they do sail under the flag of Douglas, but it is the banner of the Black Douglass whose name is

Frederick not Stephen." Outraged, Broderick challenged Terry to a duel, and on September 13, 1859, Terry murdered the free-soil leader. California Republicans reported that Broderick's last words were: "They have killed me because I was opposed to the extension of slavery and a corrupt administration." Cornelius Cole wrote to William Henry Seward in frustration: "Our sky is now gloomy . . . we are not in despair though sad. Mr. B[roderick] could hardly be spared in the Senate. California was in need of such men there."[6]

Fresh off their elimination of Broderick and anticipating sectional conflict, the Chivs moved to split the state in two, with the southern half becoming the "Territory of Colorado." This territory would permit slavery. California's Democratic governor John B. Weller and Los Angeles delegate Andrés Pico began promoting the plan in the spring of 1858. In response, Los Angeles, San Bernardino, San Diego, Santa Barbara, San Luis Obispo, and Tulare Counties each voted to separate from California. The southern Democrat-dominated legislature agreed to the plan in April 1859. Slaveholders in the East were inclined to support them. Mississippi Democrat Henry S. Foote remarked that the South would gain a slave state in southern California thanks to the Pico bill. Henry Wise, the governor of Virginia, thought that California would provide new lands for plantation owners whose eastern holdings were no longer productive. As historian Leonard Richards describes, "Slavery, as Wise viewed the institution, was just not profitable on the worn-out fields of Virginia. . . . [A]nd California? No place, in Wise's judgment, came close to matching California. It was the solution to his—and every Virginia slaveholder's—problem." Cole remarked bitterly to California judge Stephen J. Field: "The Kansas difficulty is now beautifully 'localized.' Is it not?"[7]

Though the U.S. Congress never agreed to California's proposed division because of Republican opposition, this action underscored the divided loyalties of Californians on the eve of the Civil War. In the secession winter of 1860–61, Republicans in California and across the United States fretted over the state's loyalties in the sectional controversy. For them, the possibility that California would join the Confederacy or become an independent country was very real. Even before Lincoln's election, California governor John Weller had warned that "if the wild spirit of fanaticism which now pervades the land should destroy this magnificent Confederacy . . . [California] will not go with the South or the North, but here upon the shores of the Pacific found a mighty republic which may in the end prove the greatest of all." Milton Latham, one of California's Democratic senators, echoed Weller's sentiments. "We in California," he explained, "would have reasons to induce us to become members neither of the southern confederacy nor of the northern confederacy, and would be able to sustain ourselves the relations of a free and independent state." Cole worried that slaveholders could conquer California and ally the Bear Flag State with the South. "Slavery had been long in power and has so well fortified itself that the issue is extremely doubtful," he explained. "[W]e are quite as likely to turn up a slave empire in a generation or two as to come out a free republic."[8]

The stakes grew higher when the lower South seceded. In January 1861, the *San Francisco Herald* published a letter from California congressman Charles L. Scott exhorting the state to form a separate republic if the Union fractured. The next month, William H. Brewer, a scientist working for the Geological Survey of California, noted in his diary that southern California could become a slave state. Eastern newspapers agreed. A Boston journal commented, "There is at present here a well-defined and strongly marked anxiety in regard to the loyalty of the Pacific States. . . . [A]rtful, designing, unscrupulous, treacherous, Southern-born, Southern-bred, Southern taught, and Southern-purchased, educated in all the rules of the demagogue . . . men, ex-senators Gwin and Lane, are avowedly in connection with all the secret ramifications of the disunion party." San Francisco's *Daily Evening Bulletin*, a pro-Union paper, openly worried in late April 1861 that the Chivs' plan to divide the state would come to fruition.[9]

Violence was also a distinct possibility. Confederate sympathizers in San Francisco formed a secret society in early 1861 called the Committee of Thirty. The leaders of this group suggested to Albert Sidney Johnston— then in command of the U.S. Army's Department of the Pacific—that he seize San Francisco and stop all gold shipments to the East. Johnston disapproved of the committee's plan but fled the state—followed by several Chiv politicians—to become the second-highest-ranking general in the Confederacy. Johnston's replacement, Brigadier General E. V. Sumner, reported in March 1861 that "the Secessionists are . . . the most active and zealous party" in the state. Sumner requested soldiers for southern California, warning: "The disaffection in the southern part of the state is increasing and is becoming dangerous, and it is indispensably necessary to throw reinforcements into that section immediately." A group of San Franciscans told Secretary of War Simon Cameron in August 1861 that "about three-fifths of our citizens are natives of slave-holding states and are almost a unit in this crisis. . . . Our advices, obtained with great prudence and care, show us that there are about 16,000 Knights of the Golden Circle [a paramilitary pro-Confederate organization] . . . in the state, and they are still organizing even in our most loyal district." These Unionists received little aid from Governor Weller's successor, John B. Downey, who commented: "I did not believe, nor do I believe now, that an aggressive war should be waged upon any section of the Confederacy, nor do I believe that this Union can be preserved by a coercive policy."[10]

For many inside and outside the state, California seemed to have the ideal conditions for a society of yeomen farmers. Governor James Nye of Nevada, a Republican appointed by Lincoln to lead the territory, spoke to the California Agricultural Society in September 1861. "Here," Nye proclaimed, "government lays no restraint upon agricultural or other pursuits, but by its fostering care bids them all leap onward to perfection." A society of farmers and free laborers, Nye continued, would be the most loyal to the Union: "I believe there are no classes of people more interested than the farmers and mechanics of America in retaining intact this old national emblem." If California sided with the Confederacy and slavery arrived, however, the state's agricultural potential would be wasted. The famous political economist Henry George moved to California in 1858 and started working for the *Alta California* newspaper in 1861. During his time in California, George started believing that the "absence of a garden landscape of small farms linked with towns in agrarian harmony had . . . divisive consequences," including "land monopoly and environmental decay." An 1871 speech by George suggests that he had viewed slavery as threatening to this vision: "The evils of land monopolization are showing themselves in such unmistakable signs that he who runs may read. . . . [I]t has already impressed its mark upon the character of our agriculture—more shiftless, perhaps, than of any State in the Union where slavery had not reigned."[11]

From the winter of 1860 to the successful culmination of the war, Republican stalwart Cornelius Cole and a Boston preacher named Thomas Starr King worked hard to safeguard California for the Union. While King and Cole were not solely responsible for the state's loyalty, their speeches show many of the reasons that Californians allied with the North. These speeches focused on the value of union, the benefits of a free agrarian civilization, and the harm that would come if southerners transported slaves to the state. Cole argued that if California stayed in the Union and supported the Republicans, the state would receive the economic and social benefits of a transcontinental railroad. King's speeches glorified the Union and focused on the evils of slave agriculture. For the preacher, union signified not only a united America in peace and prosperity but also the best hope of democracy worldwide. Union and the transcontinental railroad, each tied to a vision of California as an oasis for small farmers, could unify both California Democrats and Republicans in support of the war effort.

America was a unique place, King believed, and provided an example for other nations to follow. Mourning the death of Daniel Webster in 1852, King explained: "He [Webster] saw an immense overbalance of good—benefits more various, more substantial, and more precious, than any polity on earth had ever secured to men. These the word Union represented; these to his mind, the blotting of that word annihilated, and in their place introduced discord, contention, and bloody strife." In another sermon, popularly reprinted during the Civil War, King exclaimed that patriotism and loyalty to the Union were one and the same. "Patriotism has learned to pronounce with emphasis the word Union," he asserted. "The world waits to see the quality and energy of our patriotism." Yet, to fulfill America's true mission, the government needed to keep slavery out of the West because the institution threatened the Union. "If the time is to come when a large section of our land insist that human bondage is to be sanctioned and extended wherever our banner and our eagles go," King warned, "that the haggard genius of oppression must sit with equal privilege and honor with the spirit of freedom[,] . . . I utter only the simplest lesson of science—then there can be no unity." Union signified democracy, defined as the freedom to choose one's government, occupation, and residence in a world where these qualities were rare. If America failed, the democratic experiment and its benefits for humanity would be lost forever.[12]

Allied with the abolitionist community in Boston, King decided to go to San Francisco to establish a Unitarian church in January 1860. The work was supposed to be temporary. Yet, after hearing of the secession crisis and California's danger, King resolved to stay in the state. Speaking to both friendly and hostile audiences, King conveyed the importance of union through allusions to American icons such as George Washington, Daniel Webster, and the battles of Lexington and Concord. Celebrating Webster's famous "Reply to Hayne," King proclaimed:

Mr. Webster's thought breaks out afresh in the proclamation of the president that America is one and cannot be broken. . . . [I]t leaps forth and brightens in the sacred steel which patriots by the hundred thousand are dedicating, not to ravage, not to murder, not to hatred of any portion of the southern section of the confederacy, but to the support of the impartial Constitution, to the common flag, to the majestic and beneficent law which offers to encircle and bless the whole republic; it utters itself in the thunder-voice of twenty millions of white citizens of the land, that in America the majority under the Constitution must rule.

King then urged military action to save constitutional government and rule by the people, concluding: "When every man within the present limits of the immense republic shall have restored to him . . . representation on common terms in the National capitol . . . and the Constitution vindicated in its unsectional beneficence, and the doctrine of secession be stabbed with two hundred thousand bayonet wounds[,] . . . then the debate between Mr. Calhoun and Mr. Webster will be completed."[13]

While the Union represented democracy and its armies marched to defend the Constitution, King believed that the Confederacy, with its large landholdings, stood for oligarchy and aristocracy. "Doom to the traitorous aristocracy whose cup of gilt is full!" he declared. "Let him [the president] say that it is a war of mass against class, of America against feudalism, of the schoolmaster against the slave-master, of workmen against the barons, of the ballot-box against the barracoon. This is what the struggle means." Cole agreed, warning: "The American slave oligarchy within a few years past have made many inroads upon the citadel of Liberty. . . . [O]ne after another of the pillars of the temple of Liberty fall and the dust of the ruins passes on the wings of the breeze. The doctrines of Washington are ignored, Thomas Jefferson is never quoted, and Madison is openly repudiated." William Brewer, the aspiring geologist, went to a King speech in June 1861. Brewer fretted that European monarchs would rejoice in the collapse of the American Union. "We are doing and reaping," he wrote, "as monarchists have often told us we would do—put designing, immoral, wicked, and reckless men in office until they robbed us of our glory, corrupted the masses, and broken us in pieces for their gain." A "Republic of the Pacific," he asserted, was "sheerest nonsense. A republic of only about 900,000 inhabitants less than a million, spread over a territory much larger than the original thirteen states, scattered hostile Indians and worse Mormons on their borders—what would either sustain or protect such a country?" King's sermon, however, gave him hope that a "very strong Union sentiment" was prevailing.[14]

Besides Union, King and Cornelius Cole harped on the rebellion's threat to civilization. Rebellion, King stated in a speech, "strikes for barbarism against civilization." He elaborated: "It sins against the ballot-box; it sins against oaths of allegiance; it sins against public and beneficent peace; and it sins, worse than all, against the corner-stone of American progress and history and hope, —the worth of the laborer, the rights of man." Education, refinement, the appreciation of natural beauty, and, above all, opportunities for intellectual and material advancement signified civilization. The North, King believed, possessed "the shrine of learning, where the principles of freedom may be perpetuated in cultivated minds." Cole agreed, arguing that in all standards of civilization, free states outperformed slave states. Echoing Hinton Helper's comparisons, Cole explained: "In soil, climate, natural scenery, position in the republic, in wealth, and fame, Virginia had altogether the start of her future rival [New York]. . . . [S]uch were her advantages, but New York today commands more than forty-five times the commerce of Virginia. In schools, churches, libraries, manufactures, and all enterprises, public and private, in fact in every thing . . . the contrast is alike remarkable." Virginia also lacked a system of education. "More than a fourth of the adult white population of Virginia are unable to read or write," Cole noted. "In the middle of the nineteenth century, the home of Washington, Jefferson, Madison, and Henry . . . is enveloped in ignorance, poverty, and misery." The sole reason for these differences in development was slavery. California had a choice. "Do we follow in the wake of New York or Virginia?" Cole asked. If it stayed in the Union and voted Republican, he implied, California would become more like New York than Virginia.[15]

Cole and King also argued that if slaves crossed California's borders, the state would face agricultural decline. California's agricultural bounty would remain undeveloped. In one sermon, first given in 1857 but presented again during the war, King warned: "The slave-system works on minds in our politics just as slavery works on the soil: it sucks the generous juices out of it, withers it, dries it into the sand, and leaves it fit only for nettles and weeds." In early 1861, Cole claimed that "slavery blights the prosperity of a State. Land in the slave communities is not worth on the average more than one third as much as lands in the free States, and the welfare of a people in all other respects is in an equal degree retarded." The ideal for Cole and other Californians was for small farmers to settle the state, as slave owners would monopolize the land and exhaust it. Neither Cole nor King predicted the large-scale industrial agriculture that came to dominate California.[16]

One of the most illuminating episodes showing the importance of negative impressions of southern land use in Californian Unionism came in 1863, when both Governor Leland Stanford and Thomas Starr King spoke at the California State Fair. Stanford, a man not known for either rhetorical brilliance or living on a small farm himself, urged farmers to tend small plots rather than large estates. Alluding to ancient Rome, Stanford reminded his audience: "In those days large farms were not regarded as a *sine qua non* to happiness and success. In fact, it was remarked by a orator of that time that he was not to be accounted a good citizen, but rather a dangerous man to the State, who could not content himself with seven acres of land." Stanford promised a future of agriculture should a transcontinental railroad reach California: "Of the varied interests of California, none will reap richer benefits from a railroad across the continent than those depending upon the pursuit of agriculture."[17]

King was even more direct. An ideal civilization and strong economy depended on proper care of the land. "The Creator," he theorized, "who gave the globe to Adam with the command to dress it and keep it has connected economy with its fertility. Economy lies at the base of high and permanent civilization." King continued: "We know very well that decay in the productiveness of the soil through false methods of tillage, wrought the ruin of some of the immense empires of antiquity." The slave society of the South was one such example of "false tillage." "One of our counts in the great indictment against slavery," King argued, "is, that it sucks the juices out of the soil, that it blasts the landscape, that it finds a garden and leaves behind it a nettle bed. We point to the farms of Eastern Virginia, of North Carolina, of Western Tennessee, whose bounty has shriveled, for our proof and illustration. And it is true." The result of these poor land-use patterns was "barbarism"—the opposite of civilization. "Barbarism in the tillage leaves barbarism on the face of nature. Slavery, except on river bottoms, quickly 'skins the land,'" King concluded.[18]

Cole further promoted Californian Unionism by associating the Republican Party with the construction of the transcontinental railroad and slaveholders with obstructing the plan. Slaveholders, Cole alleged, "were ready to purchase Cuba, or conquer Mexico, but nothing could obtain their countenance that had not a direct tendency to enhance the value of slaves, and a Pacific railroad promised no such result." He also believed that slaveholders instigated violence in Kansas to stop the railroad: "The settlement of Kansas and the organization of a state government therein, though hampered for a long time by border-ruffianism, were further events favorable to the Pacific railroad scheme: Antagonism to the project was one of the chief incentives to the barbarous practices in that country." He continued: "The slave mongers well know that a line of free states would follow the railway all along to the Pacific, and they fought it desperately." Now that the Republicans had gained control of Congress, "freedom at last prevailed and one branch of the Pacific Railroad will soon be constructed over the dark and bloody ground."[19]

Cole extended his analysis to the homestead and land-grant-college bills, asserting that slaveholders opposed both laudatory measures. "No question," he claimed, "can come before Congress, not even a Homestead

Act or an Agricultural College Bill, which is not discussed and settled in reference to its bearing upon the price of negroes. . . . But how is it with [the] Republican party—what are its aims? It is the natural antagonist of the Democratic party. . . . [E]very advantage gained by owners of slaves for the benefits of that property is equally to the disadvantage of . . . the entire body of free laborers North and South."[20]

The words of Cornelius Cole and Thomas Starr King fell on receptive ears. In April 1861, San Francisco's *Daily Evening Bulletin* asked: "Is it too much to say that Mr. King has done more than the press, more than all the lawyers in the State, more than the politicians in quickening into activity the Union sentiment in California and preserving us here from civil war?" The paper even suggested that Mr. King occupy one of California's Senate seats. King, in a more muted tone, scribbled in his diary: "It is lucky I am sound on the Government question; for, ten days ago, the people mobbed a suspicious, half Union, half Jeff. Davis, Southern minister. . . . [T]he Union sentiment is strong." Reacting to the outburst of Union support, the California legislature passed a resolution in late April 1861 affirming the state's loyalty. Five senators and twelve assemblymen, however, demurred. "The Secessionists are watchful and not in despair," King noted.[21]

While Republicans in California continued to fret about the state's allegiance throughout the war, Lincoln's reelection in November 1864 ended the last chance for Confederate victory. The *Daily Evening Bulletin* reported that the reelection of "Lincoln will assure them [the Confederacy] and the world that the North is substantially a unit for the prosecution of the war to the utter extinction of the rebellion, and that there will be no abatement of the energy with which all the power of the nation will be brought to work for the one consummation—the perfect preservation of the Union." While a belief in the Union, battlefield victories, and the passage of the Pacific Railroad Act were probably the key factors ensuring California's loyalty, California farmers also feared the agricultural harm that would come from a Confederate victory. Cornelius Cole, Leland Stanford, and Thomas Starr King used this fear to garner support for the Union. Slavery seemed to threaten the agrarian dream of a fertile land teeming with small farmers.[22]

The Pacific Railroad Act, so critical to California's loyalty, serves as a key example of how agrarian ideals influenced Civil War politics. This bill, plus the passage of the Homestead Act, the Land Grant College Act, and the creation of the U.S. Department of Agriculture, shows how ideas linking land use with civilization and union influenced federal policy. Free-Soilers and later Republicans had attempted throughout the 1850s to pass these laws, each time facing opposition from southerners such as Jefferson Davis and northern "doughfaces" like James Buchanan. Now that they had powerful majorities in Congress, Republicans could implement their vision for America's future. This vision focused on turning the West into an agrarian society of white farmers who, by tilling small plots of land for many generations, would build "civilized" communities and develop loyalty to the Union. As Phillip Shaw Paludan explains, Americans thought that railroads complemented farming, giving "farmers access to markets outside their locale [and] more potential buyers for farm goods, while at the same time providing factories and shops that could supply tools, clothing, and other household and farmyard goods." The preeminent historian of transcontinental railroads, Richard White, supports Paludan's assessment. Railroad magnates such as Leland Stanford "recognized that the most profitable traffic came from a thickly settled country of small freeholders. Railroads desired an agrarian landscape." Small farmers in the West needed to be connected to eastern markets.[23]

Nearly all congressmen, North and South, desired a transcontinental railroad in the 1850s. Indeed, the main reason that Democrat Stephen A. Douglas authored the Kansas-Nebraska Act was to organize the lands west of Illinois so that a transcontinental railroad could begin in his hometown of Chicago. Disagreement centered on whether the federal government could constitutionally fund such a project and—more important— where exactly the road would go. Southerners desired a southern route, while northerners demanded a central or far-northern route. From 1853 to secession, Jefferson Davis called for the construction of a railroad going from New Orleans to southern California. The final congressional debates on the transcontinental railroad before secession highlight how the issue had become intertwined with conflict over the expansion of slavery. In one debate, Texas Democrat Andrew Jackson Hamilton threatened secession if Congress did not construct the railroad in the South. "Do you desire to pave the way for a dissolution of the Union of these States?" he asked. "Then ignore the trade of the South in the same manner you are now doing—say that your great system of railroads shall be for the benefit of the northern, and, to a certain extent, the middle section of the Union; but that the South shall be disregarded in forming this great connection with the Pacific ocean."[24]

Unable to come to an agreement in the spring of 1860, congressmen tried again in January 1861 after South Carolina had left the Union. This time, Iowa Republican Samuel Ryan Curtis, chairman of the Committee on Pacific Railroad, introduced a bill that would have constructed three transcontinental railroads—a southern, central, and northern route. Northern Republicans and Democrats viewed the measure as one that might forestall secession and promote union. William Henry Seward proclaimed on January 5: "Every man appeals to every other man for a compromise of sectional difficulties, and for the devising of some new bond of union to hold together these states. . . . [I]t is railroads and canals and connections and facilities for communication, commerce and affection, that bind together and assimilate disconnected and ill-assorted communities. This is a great measure of conciliation, of pacification, of compromise, and of union." In addition to appealing to the South, Seward was concerned that California might separate from the Union. But with the construction of transcontinental railroads, "You will make the Pacific coast American, and you combine the energies of the East and West, extending the civilization of the world westward in its proper way, with American habits, American sentiments, and American interest, across the great continent of America."[25]

Other politicians shared Seward's concerns. Vermont Republican Solomon Foot called a transcontinental railroad "a strong, and I trust, an enduring and indissoluble bond of Union between the Atlantic and Pacific sections of the country." Milton Latham, the California Democrat of dubious loyalty, asked: "What other measure is better calculated to increase the faith of the people in the permanency of our institutions? What stronger proof can we give to the civilized world of our determination to remain united than to fasten an iron girdle round our loin, which shall be both emblematic and indicative of our indissoluble nation?" Latham then warned that if Congress continued to dither on the railroad, California and Oregon could split off from the rest of the United States. "It is to prevent this gradual alienation of sentiment," he claimed, "this growing diversity of interests in State and national affairs . . . which, more than all other national considerations, ought to prompt Congress to accelerate, by all legal and constitutional means, the construction of a railway to the Pacific." Even Jefferson Davis of Mississippi backed the compromise measure, explaining: "I have thought it an achievement worthy of our age and of our people, to couple with bonds of iron the people of the Pacific with the valley of the Mississippi."[26]

Despite support from many as a measure to save the Union, the impending crisis and continued opposition from proslavery Democrats prevented the bill's passage. Before Davis had a chance to vote in favor, Mississippi seceded, and the erstwhile southern advocate of a transcontinental railroad became president of the Confederate States of America. On January 9, the day Mississippi left the Union, Oregon Democrat Joseph Lane—another westerner with questionable loyalties—gave his reasons for opposing the railroad's construction. Lane claimed that "this country is about breaking up . . . this railroad bill cannot save it, or restore peace." The only way to prevent secession, Lane explained, was for northerners to recognize that "the idea of putting slavery in course of ultimate extinction shall be abandoned." In other words, the Republicans had to allow slavery in federal territories. "Would the senator have a railroad at the expense of the Union?" Lane continued. "Would he place it in the power of that party who disregard the Constitution; who trample upon the decision of the Supreme Court . . . who would inaugurate and bring about negro equality in this country; who would free the negroes of the South, and bring them to New York and the other northern States, and introduce them there upon an equal footing." Kentucky Unionist John Crittenden gave a less-passionate explanation for his opposition, remarking: "I will vote for no railroad bill while the country is in the condition in which it now is."[27]

Republicans began crafting a new Pacific railroad bill in late 1861 and early 1862. With southern Democrats gone, Lincoln's party quickly agreed on a central route. The House began formal debate on April 8, 1862. Republicans claimed that the measure promoted proper land development in the West. Pennsylvania Republican James H. Campbell, who introduced the bill, proclaimed: "This grand undertaking will do more to unite us as one people, will accomplish more by extending civilization over the continents . . . than any other enterprise of modern times; civilization of that high type which shall spread the cultivated valley, the peaceful village, the church, the school-house, and thronging cities, through the mighty solitudes of the West." Fellow Pennsylvania Republican William D. Kelley concurred, explaining: "Irrigate and stimulate, with all the influences of modern science, the wide space between the Pacific and the Mississippi, whereby America was to be and was made the great central figure in the civilization of the world, so that her arts, her language, her institutions, and her religion, flowed in easy channels with her commerce to the people of all nations, and made her the benefactor, the civilizer, the republicanizer, and the Christianizer of the world."[28]

The rebellion gave additional impetus to the measure. Republicans believed the bill promoted union by showing European powers that a democratic government could still function in wartime. "As we are about to suppress a rebellion by which perfidious traitors have sought to overthrow and destroy our Government," Indiana Republican William Dunn declared, "and thus demonstrate our great military power, and the stability of our institutions, it seems to me to be an appropriate time to organize this great enterprise." He added: "When all the nations of Europe are agitated with political complications, which it may be that the sword alone can cut, it is most appropriate for us to assert our true position in the world . . . [and] become, as I trust it is our destiny to be, the greatest nation of the earth." Union had become important to Milton Latham because he knew that "the popular nature of our institutions is a standing cause of disquiet to the feudal aristocracy of the Old World. Their leading reviews, journals, and parliamentary discussions, breathe a tone almost of animosity toward us, and indicate their yearning hope that this intestine war may end in overthrow and ruin a great nation." By passing the Pacific railroad bill, Congress could avert this unhappy fate. "We ask not to be dealt with as a broken or dismembered part of this great empire," Latham implored, "but that our unity with the eastern half of the American continent be maintained by the means which the nation can so easily command."[29]

Worries about secession in the Pacific West were another impetus for the measure. "From the geographical face of the country," New Hampshire Republican Thomas Edwards cautioned, "when the great region of the distant West shall have grown to the size to which it is rapidly tending, when it shall begin to feel its sense of independence, unless the relations between the East and West shall be the most perfect . . . the empire will be in danger of breaking, on the crest of the Rocky mountains." Maine Republican Samuel Clement Fessenden added: "I take the ground that the war is an additional reason, and makes it still more imperative . . . that this railroad should be constructed. Why, sir, we hear time and again upon the floor of this House that there is imminent danger that a war with foreign nations may be involved in the issues of this civil war, and the question arises what, in such an emergency, is to become of the Pacific States?" Aaron A. Sargent, a California Republican, provided ample testimony on the threat of California secession: "The long isolation to which they will have been condemned by a failure to construct a Pacific railroad on the part of the Government, may entirely banish from their hearts all sympathy with this side of the Government. . . . [W]e cling to the Union; but a generation will grow up there who know you not."[30]

Hostility to slavery and fear that southerners would return to Congress formed another dimension of the wartime debate over the transcontinental railroad. President Abraham Lincoln did not signal to his cabinet his intention to issue an emancipation proclamation until July 22, 1862, and he did not announce emancipation publicly until September. Before this action, some congressional Republicans moved to strike against slavery. In August 1861, Congress passed the First Confiscation Act, freeing fugitive slaves who had been in the service of the Confederacy. In March and April 1862, Congress began discussing a second confiscation act, which, when passed in July 1862, would emancipate slaves whose masters backed the Confederacy. The Pacific railroad debate proceeded concurrently in the spring of 1862 and displayed similarities to the other pieces of antislavery legislation. Indiana Republican Albert White argued: "I . . . hail the great Pacific measure as a salvatory measure, as a means by which we shall, as it were, outflank cottondom, and by which . . . we shall bind ourselves by a golden cord to the great Pacific." Missouri Republican Francis P. Blair Jr. reminded his colleagues that "the opposition to the Pacific railroad bill came from a certain side of the House that was obnoxious to the East as well as the West," and that they had better act before the "southern men and disunionists" stalled the project again. Pennsylvania firebrand Thaddeus Stevens agreed, commenting: "When in process of time . . . our amiable Government shall have restored the Constitution as it was, and shall have given to our warm embraces in Congress our well-beloved brethren, who have robed the nation and murdered our brothers[,] . . . we shall find them with the same arrogant, insolent dictation which we have clinged to for twenty years, forbidding the construction of a road that does not run along our southern border."[31]

The House passed the Pacific Railroad Act 79 to 49 on May 6, 1862, and the Senate concurred on June 20, 1862, by a vote of 35 to 6. President Lincoln signed the bill on July 1. Union general and future chief engineer of the Union Pacific Railroad Grenville Dodge recalled that "Lincoln advocated its passage and building, not only as a military necessity, but as a means of holding the Pacific Coast to the Union." The name "Union Pacific Railway," Dodge added, had its origins in "the sentiment that the building of the railroad would hold the Union together." The Civil War Congress, motivated by the desire to halt slavery and build a West filled with white yeoman farmers, had succeeded where even Stephen Douglas had failed: in the creation of a transcontinental railroad. Cornelius Cole understood this point well. "The work of building the road," he recalled in his memoir, "had devolved upon the Republican party. The war, instead of impeding, added arguments in favor of its early completion . . . to unite more firmly our Pacific coast possessions with the Atlantic States." Yet, as Cole later discovered, the railroad did not support small farmers in the West. Federal contracts provided opportunities for unprecedented graft and corruption. Railroad land grants created the very monopolies Cole and the Radicals abhorred. But in the triumphal spirit of 1862, these problems resided in the future.[32]

Similar to the Pacific railroad bill, Congress first contemplated creating land-grant colleges before the Civil War. Historians have cited several motivating influences for the land-grant college bill. First, the United States had a long history of granting land to states and corporations for public works. Second, one scholar cites "the broadened social vision of certain educational leaders, and the growing class consciousness of farmer and labor groups." Third, agricultural societies had long advocated vocational training to complement classical education. Yet unrecognized by most historians were concerns about continued agricultural sustainability or "improvement" in the face of widespread soil depletion in the North and South. Land-grant college advocates, from the late 1850s until the bill's passage in 1862, also argued that agricultural and mechanical schools benefited union and civilization by supporting stable farming communities.[33]

Vermont congressman Justin Smith Morrill introduced a bill on December 14, 1857, "donating public lands to the several States and Territories which may provide colleges for the benefit of agriculture and the mechanical arts." Morrill had strong views on the evils of slavery and ignorance. He also came from a state suffering agricultural decline. As the scholar Paul Wallace Gates discovered, "one half the counties and 147 towns out of 246 [in Vermont] lost population" in the decade before the Civil War. More radical than his quiet demeanor suggested, Morrill spent his time in Washington, D.C., with the vociferous Benjamin Wade, whom he nicknamed "Brave Old Ben," and Thaddeus Stevens. Stevens used his biting wit to defend Morrill on the House floor. "Uncle" Thaddeus, as Morrill's family called him, also enjoyed Justin's son Jimmy, whom the Pennsylvania Radical brought with him to congressional debates, raising the boy's hand on important committee votes.[34]

Above all else, concerns about agricultural decline and Henry Carey's teachings motivated Morrill to introduce the bill. Opening debate on the measure in April 1858, Morrill borrowed from Carey in explaining that "the prosperity and happiness of a large and populous nation depend . . . upon the division of the land into small parcels [and] the education of the proprietors of the soil." Sarah T. Phillips, the only scholar to cite concerns about land use as a motivating factor behind the Land Grant College Act, explains that Carey inspired northerners like Morrill to believe that "small farms and improved agricultural methods would eventually replace the southern plantation system."[35]

Concerned with America's unceasing thirst for more land and imperial conquests, Morrill continued: "Our agriculturists, as a whole, instead of seeking a higher cultivation, are extending their boundaries. . . . [I]f it be true that the common mode of cultivating the soil in all parts of our country is so defective as to make the soil poorer year by year, it is a most deplorable fact." Citing several southern agricultural scientists and drawing from his own observations, Morrill noted the widespread evidence of soil exhaustion and a corresponding decline in productivity in the slave South. "In Virginia," Morrill claimed, "the crop of tobacco in 1850, was less than that of 1840. . . . [N]o crop has proved more destructive to the fertility of the soil than the tobacco crop. . . . Little has been done to elevate the character of Virginia farming, and Mount Vernon itself, losing the eye of its master, has lapsed into the general degeneracy." The vast lands to the West offered no succor. "We bring forth new States by the litter," Morrill said, with a touch of sarcasm, "and when we want more, like our Norman ancestors, we commit 'grand larceny,' and annex them. This progress seems wonderful, but with it appears the bitter fact that these new States in half a century . . . become depleted and stationary. This early maturity is followed by sudden barrenness." He concluded: "The nation which tills the soil so as to leave it *worse* than they found it, is doomed to decay and degradation."[36]

A desire to promote union and civilization also motivated Morrill. From his overseas travels, the Vermont congressman had grown very sensitive to European impressions of America. "While we may be in advance of the civilized world in many of the useful arts," he proclaimed, "it is a humiliating fact that we are far in the rear of the best husbandry in Europe." Morrill lamented: "Concerted effort is necessary to educate and elevate whole nations. That effort is being made abroad with governmental aid in the lead. Here in the 'model Republic,' where a free republican government is installed to guard the general welfare, *no* such effort is being made." Democratic America needed to prove its merit in comparison with European monarchies. "All over the highest civilized parts of Europe we find the different Governments alive to the wants of agriculture," he noted. "They have established ministers of instruction, model farms, experimental farms, botanical gardens, colleges. . . . Young Americans should have some chance to study agriculture as a profession and be attracted to it as to a learned, liberal, and intellectual pursuit. Is it true, as our detractors assert, that science can flourish only under the patronage of royalty?" James Harlan, an Iowan Republican, agreed. Alluding to the lack of civilization in the slave South, he argued: "It may be that it is a blessing to Virginia that she is now more largely represented by adult white people who are unable to read and write. . . . [I]t is a blessing, however, that the people of my State do not covet. They prefer a different condition of things. They prefer that the mind of the laborer should be developed."[37]

Finally, Morrill believed that the colleges established under his bill would increase a romantic appreciation for nature and further scientific knowledge. These desires followed his personal interest in landscape architecture and agricultural permanence. The Vermonter enjoyed reading Sir Walter Scott and James Fenimore Cooper as a teenager. After becoming wealthy through a dry-goods business, Morrill built a cottage and garden based off the designs of renowned architect Andrew Jackson Downing. Downing had promoted an aesthetic appreciation of nature, picturesque architecture, and scientific farming. He not only instructed farmers on how to cultivate soil for many generations but also suggested that farms match their surrounding landscape. Furthermore, Morrill cultivated ties with George Perkins Marsh, a fellow Vermonter whose 1864 book, *Man and Nature*, was one of the first American works advocating conservation and forestry.[38]

In defending the Land Grant College Act, Morrill explained the need "to test the natural capability of soils and the power of different fertilizers; the relative value of different grasses for flesh, fat, and milk-giving purposes; the comparative value of grain, roots, and hay, for wintering stock; the value of a bushel of corn, oats, peas, carrots, potatoes, or turnips, in pounds of beef, pork, or mutton; deep plowing as well as drainage." He added: "These and many more, are questions of scientific interest even beyond their economic importance." As for aesthetics, Morrill claimed that the bill would "increase the loveliness of the American landscape" because "scientific culture is the sure precursor of order and beauty." Looking back in 1874 on the reasons he backed the bill, Morrill explained: "The very cheapness of our public lands . . . tended to a system of bad-farming or strip and waste of the soil . . . which would not be likely to be arrested except by more thorough and scientific knowledge of agriculture and by a higher education of those who were devoted to its pursuit."[39]

Agricultural societies, farmers, and professors added their voices in favor of the bill. Jonathan Baldwin Turner, an antislavery professor at Illinois College, blamed existing schools "for the pettifogging lawyers, political hacks, and sectarian bigots infesting the nation." He thought that "the establishment of an industrial university would save young men from becoming the 'starving scavengers' of a learned profession." Turner secured the support of Illinois congressman Elihu B. Washburne, who backed

Morrill's bill in the House. Bronson Murray, representing the "Fourth Industrial Convention of the State of Illinois," pointed out: "In monarchial Europe, through their polytechnic and agricultural schools, some successful effort has been made. . . . [B]ut in our democratic country, though entirely industrial and practical in all its aims and ends, no such effort has been efficiently made. . . . [O]ur common schools are . . . inefficient and languishing.[40]

The Board of Education of the State of Michigan and the Michigan Faculty of the Agricultural College, two education groups, believed that a land-grant college bill would make free labor more dignified and lead to a higher civilization. Education, they claimed, was "inseparably connected with a system of labor." Agricultural colleges would "afford ample and thorough education of the student physically, morally, and intellectually; to ennoble the calling of agriculture, and teach men to increase the productions of the earth." The group continued: "No more legitimate and no wiser disposition can be made of [the public lands] than for the instruction of men in multiplying the productions of the earth, and thus conducing to their comfort, prosperity, and higher civilization." Alexander W. Randall, governor of Wisconsin from 1858 to 1862, compared agricultural colleges to farmer's clubs and lyceums, which met "once each week during the winter season" for "lectures, readings from agricultural works and papers, discussions, and a mutual interchange of opinions."[41]

In 1857 both the Senate and the House passed the Land Grant College Act by slim majorities over southern opposition. Slave-state representatives had opposed the bill on the grounds that free public schools would be foisted upon the South, threatening slavery. If the bill was passed, Virginian James M. Mason surmised, "[w]ould it not be in the power of a majority in Congress to fasten upon the southern States that peculiar system of free schools in the New England States which I believe would tend . . . to destroy that peculiar character which I am happy to believe belongs to the great mass of the southern people." Mason was likely pleased when President James Buchanan vetoed the bill. The Pennsylvanian rejected the bill on constitutional grounds, arguing: "Congress does not possess the power to appropriate money in the Treasury, raised by taxes on the people of the United States, for the purpose of educating the people of the respective States. . . . Should Congress exercise such a power, this would be to break down the barriers which have been so carefully constructed in the Constitution to separate Federal from state authority." The Montgomery, Alabama, *Daily Confederation*, associating the measure with Republicans, lauded the president's veto "of a very obnoxious piece of legislation."[42]

The Republicans tried to pass an agricultural college bill again in May 1862. Morrill's friend, Ohioan Benjamin Wade, introduced the legislation to the Senate on May 2. Morrill had made three changes. First, recognizing the effectiveness of the Confederacy's military academies in producing skilled officers, Morrill mandated that military tactics be a required subject at new land-grant colleges. Second, he excluded states in rebellion from receiving the benefits of the act. Finally, he increased the size of the grant, donating 30,000 acres of federal land per senator and representative for the construction of colleges. Unlike in the late 1850s, disagreement over the second bill centered on whether it would limit the effectiveness of the Homestead Act, which was being debated concurrently, and whether it would take away too much land from new states. Morrill responded to these claims by asserting that without education, land was "at best a bauble, and often a curse" to future homesteaders. He also claimed that colleges could end wasteful farming techniques, increasing the value of land in new territories. The bill passed both houses of Congress with ease. Abraham Lincoln signed it on July 1, 1862.[43]

Included in Morrill's original agricultural college bill was a reference to an "agricultural department of the patent office." As opponent James Mason astutely noted in 1858, no such department existed in the U.S. government, though the nongovernmental United States Agricultural Society had long agitated for one. Morrill had intended the department to work with the new colleges in diffusing agricultural knowledge, following Henry Carey's dictum "to secure knowledge and profit and dignity to agriculture" through "the application of science." On April 27, 1860, Ohio Republican John Carey introduced a similar bill establishing an agricultural division of the Department of the Interior. This division aimed to disseminate the most productive crop varieties, soil-fertilization techniques, and technology to American farmers.[44]

In introducing the bill, John Carey used the language of union, civilization, and proper land use to call for its passage. "It is well known to every man upon this floor," he began, "who has reflected for one moment, that agriculture lies at the foundation of civilization, and of all other interests of the country." Quoting Daniel Webster, the Ohioan continued: "Without cultivation of the earth, [man] is a roaming barbarian." Connecting civilization with agricultural permanence, Carey argued that farmers needed to educate their children in "the culture of the soil" to develop settled communities in the West. Slavery, however, "was degrading to [the] white man who works," threatening farmers' interests in new territories. Carey was proud "of being a farmer—a laborer." He despised "the man who will declare that labor is disgraceful. It is blasphemy. God said that man should earn his bread by the sweat of his brow." A department of agriculture would aid the workingman instead of the lazy planter. Slavery also challenged the Union that Carey prized. "Now," he asked, "supposing that, on the subject of this disturbing question of slavery, the South should secede. . . . [T]hat very moment will the grandeur and magnificence that have been portrayed in such glittering and glowing terms fade away, and we will become a ruined, broken down, and destroyed nation." The government needed to focus on improving agriculture and dignifying free labor to save the nation from destruction.[45]

Though Carey's bill failed, Republican congressmen, agricultural societies, and government bureaucrats continued to call for the creation of an agency that promoted agriculture. In early 1861, the patent office urged private agricultural societies to have "a more intimate Union and a more decided cooperation on their part with the general government in the great work of agricultural improvement." Many, including the Philadelphia Horticultural Society, agreed and urged that the government expand its agricultural activities. The U.S. Agricultural Society recommended "the establishment of a department of agriculture by the government" in January 1861. One New England farmer believed that such a government department would encourage more young men to take up farming as a profession, thus avoiding "eminently artificial" city life. Men could find "true happiness . . . busying themselves in the advancement of the science of agriculture." He explained: "The science of agriculture, or book farming, is now becoming the guide, and the true one, to all desirous of improving."[46]

On February 17, 1862, Radical Illinois Republican congressman Owen Lovejoy introduced a bill to create a Department of Agriculture as a "distinct bureau," which differed from previous suggestions. While lacking a cabinet position, the department would function as an independent agency separate from the Patent Office or the Department of the Interior. Primarily, Lovejoy believed that the scientific knowledge disseminated by the department—later known as the U.S. Department of Agriculture (USDA)—would prevent agricultural decline and restore exhausted land. According to Lovejoy, the land between the Mississippi River and the Sierra Nevada was uninhabitable. Americans could not solve soil exhaustion simply by moving West. "The laws," he asserted, "which control the operations of nature in the productions of the earth are so uniform that we need only to know them to calculate with approximate exactness the result of our toil." Scientists in an agricultural department could determine "the nature of different soils, to which particular crops they have special or peculiar adaptation, the amount and character of nutriment abstracted from the soil by any particular crop," and "the adipose and muscular tissue which the different grasses, cereals, and vegetables will place upon the beeves, swine and sheep." Armed with this knowledge, farmers could improve their "modes of culture" and bring back land "to its pristine vigor." After all, he concluded, "we cannot for very many years depend upon virgin soils, and must look to some mode of restoring or retaining their original strength and productiveness."[47]

Lovejoy's bill passed the House by a large majority—122 to 7—on February 17, 1862. The *Country Gentleman and Cultivator*, an agricultural magazine, called for the Senate's agreement. An agricultural department, the magazine claimed, would "be of incalculable good to the agricultural portion of the people of the United States." The *Cultivator* urged "farmers from every part of the country . . . to suggest to their senators the great importance of this bill, and the necessity of putting it forward." Indiana war Democrat Joseph Albert Wright argued that the establishment of the Department of Agriculture would strengthen the Union and help crush the rebellion. "The great agricultural interests of the Union underlie its prosperity," Wright explained. The United States depended upon agricultural exports for revenue and good relations with foreign countries. Exported breadstuffs, he highlighted, "saved us from national bankruptcy, enabling us to fill the warehouses of Liverpool, Havre, and Bremen with wheat and corn . . . aiding us to crush the rebellion." Wright concluded: "Hence the great importance of proper legislation upon this subject at this time." The USDA could also prove the viability of democratic government. "The object of a democratic Government is the regulation of the public affairs of the country in accordance with the wishes of the people," Wright proclaimed. "[T]he scientific investigation of our national resources, for example, is a matter affecting the very foundation of our national greatness and prosperity." European nations had agricultural schools and colleges, Wright elaborated. Why not America? Despite a few objections in the Senate that only elite farmers could appreciate scientific agriculture, the bill passed 25 to 13. Abraham Lincoln signed it into law on May 20, 1862.[48]

Although the creation of the USDA received some notice by agricultural publications like the *Country Gentleman and Cultivator*, the general public paid much closer attention to the Homestead Act. As discussed in the first chapter, Democrats initially championed homestead measures to aid small farmers in the West. Democrats believed that westward expansion aided by government land grants allowed for republican liberty and prevented feudalism. Whigs argued for what one historian calls a "controlled and gradual development" of the West, where settled communities and agricultural production complemented the nation's manufacturing industries. After the Mexican-American War, however, Free-Soilers began promoting a homestead bill as a means of settling the West with free white farmers instead of slaves. By and large, southern Democrats—much to the chagrin of southern homestead advocate Andrew Johnson—began opposing the bill for the exact same reason. Historian Daniel Feller notes that "Americans stopped perceiving [homestead promotion] as a land question and began treating it as a slavery question." In truth, the relationship between slavery and land development was at the heart of the debate.[49]

Andrew Johnson tried throughout the 1850s to pass a homestead bill. His last attempt, during the Thirty-Sixth Congress of March 1859 to March 1861, foundered on free-state and slave-state discord. Alfred O. P. Nicholson, a Tennessee Democrat and senator, warned his colleague: "I cannot shut my eyes to the fact, that the public domain, to be peopled under the operation of this bill [the Homestead Act], is inevitably destined to be free territory." He elaborated: "I am bound, further, to know that every new State thus formed and admitted into the Confederacy, will increase the preponderance of political power against the South. . . . [I]f the sectional spirit that now predominates in the free States shall then prevail, an attempt will be made to destroy the institution of slavery." Louis Wigfall, a cantankerous Texas Democrat, made a similar point. "The whole object of this thing is sectional," he proclaimed. "It is to free-soil the Territory. Massachusetts . . . has organized a society to fill up Kansas with a free-soil population. Having kept that up until Kansas has ceased to bleed or freedom to shriek, now comes in this homestead bill."[50]

James Mason, the Virginia senator who opposed the land-grant college bill, asserted that the object of the Republican Party's homestead bill was "to get the control of this Government, that they may act directly on the condition of African bondage in the southern States." Democratic senators Robert W. Johnson of Arkansas and James S. Green of Missouri added their voices. "I do not entertain any respect for this homestead bill," Johnson said. "I believe it to be a mere abolition measure." Green concurred, stating: "If, unfortunately . . . this bill should ever be enacted into a law, it will result as a monopoly in the hands of Eli Thayer and such men, sending out the creatures of their emigrant aid societies. . . . [I]t will be a means of abolition." The Missourian even threatened secession if the bill passed, warning: "There is a point beyond which even the South, humble as we are . . . will not go; there may come some event to make us take a stand."[51]

Republicans gave credence to the southerners' charges, angering Andrew Johnson, who hoped for bisectional compromise. Republicans argued that the measure would improve land cultivation and prevent the expansion of slavery, thus safeguarding the Union and extending civilization westward. Minnesota Republican Morton Wilkinson argued that furnishing land to western immigrants would bind them to the United States. When given land, pioneers would "pitch their tents, build their houses, br[eak] up and improve the soil, and open the broad acres to occupancy and culture." They, Wilkinson asserted, furnished "a more sure and perfect protection to our western frontier than can be given by all the armed soldiers along the borderline. Coming mostly from the different States of the Union, they bring with them a deep and permanent attachment to the institutions of our country." He continued: "Open up your domain to him [the settler], give him a home out of the vast abundance of your lands, and you will have found the surest method for the perpetuation of your Government." Providing homesteads also furthered civilization by encouraging people to settle in fixed communities. Men would build "schoolhouse and churches . . . establish roads, and construct bridges; in short . . . start and create everything that is essential and necessary to the happiness of a civilized people." John Parker Hale, the New Hampshire Republican, agreed: "We in New England are, and have been, the great bee-hive of this country; we have a small territory; we have a sterile soil; we have a severe climate; but against all these we have contended, and we have sent out from the beginning of our history our young men, and they have carried with them the principles of civilization, of liberty, of knowledge, and of science."[52]

In the last quote, Hale alluded to the belief that scientific cultivation and hardworking small landowners could create agricultural prosperity even in areas of "sterile soil" and "severe climate." James Rood Doolittle, a Republican senator from Racine, Wisconsin, gave more testimony on this point. Doolittle attacked large plantation agriculture, blaming slavery for ruining land. Only free landowners owning small plots of land could manage the soil for multiple generations. In the debate on the homestead law, Doolittle relayed his observations of George Washington's Mount Vernon: "Plantation cultivation with slaves has done its work. The laws of nature asserted their supremacy. Everything fell into decay; and within the last ten years . . . that very church, which cost Washington so much labor to locate and to erect, ha[s] become a stable for cows and oxen: the country all around it growing up to those pine barrens where the very wolves are returning to howl." Doolittle said that this example showed that "the system of slave labor" and the "cultivation of the lands in large estates" exhausted soil and transformed beautiful farmland into wilderness. Mocking southern opposition, Doolittle invited slave owners to Wisconsin, where they could compare "happy homes filled with brave sons and blooming daughters, with well-tilled fields and orchards and gardens, to the broad uncultivated wastes" of the slave South. Doolittle also parroted Hinton R. Helper's arguments, explaining that he supported the homestead measure because "it will enable the poor non-slaveholding white men of the slave States to escape from the crushing burden" of slavery. The speech left Andrew Johnson muttering, "All at once, it has got a 'nigger' in it—slavery has crept into the question."[53]

Despite southern opposition, the Republicans passed the Homestead Act in the spring of 1860 by a vote of 114 to 66 in the House. Eighty-one Republicans voted for the measure, as well as 29 northern Democrats. All the "nay" votes came from slave states, with the exception of one William Montgomery, who, as a Kansas newspaper explained, "vote[ed] against granting the boon of a Homestead to the poor man, in order to gain favor with the South." The paper suggested sending the Pennsylvania Democrat "back to that obscurity from which he never ought to have emerged." The *Georgia Weekly Telegraph* interpreted the bill's passage as a sign of free labor's weakness: "We look upon the bill as one of the worst and most fatal achievements of abolitionism—it will amount in the end to supporting Northern pauperism out of the National Treasury." While in the North, "all is strife and antagonism," in the South, "all is harmony—servants never so valuable—never so well cared for—never more contented and happy; masters never so prosperous."[54]

President James Buchanan rejected the bill on June 22, 1860. Buchanan quoted large passages from his veto of the agricultural college bill. First, Congress did not have the power to make donations of land to states and individuals. Second, Buchanan argued that the "offer of free farms would probably have a powerful effect in encouraging emigration from States like Illinois, Tennessee, and Kentucky, to the west of the Mississippi and could not fail to reduce the price of property within their limits." The president concluded with a mysterious warning that the bill "will go far to demoralize the people, and repress [the] noble spirit of independence. It may introduce among them those pernicious social theories which have proved so disastrous in other countries." He may have been referring to socialist promotion of agrarian communes or the potential for abolitionist ideas to enter the South. Indiana Republican George Julian asserted that Buchanan vetoed the bill "at the bidding of his Southern masters; and the friends of the policy had learned in the struggle of a dozen years that its success was not possible while slavery ruled the government."[55]

When the Republicans secured a majority in Congress following the 1860 election and the South's secession, they gained an opportunity to pass a homestead bill. Wisconsin's Republican Senator, John Fox Potter, explained on December 4, 1861, that "no bill . . . will come before this Congress at its present session of more importance than this homestead bill." Just as in the previous debates, Republicans defended the measure by making explicit links between proper land use and the ideal social structure. George Julian argued that Union veterans could help establish civilization in the West by taking advantage of the homestead bill. The bill promoted small farms "tilled by their occupants, who will build villages, school houses, and churches, and establish free homes and organized civil communities in the wilderness." Pennsylvania Republican Galusha A. Grow, the speaker of the House, added: "While we provide with open hand for the soldier on the tented field, let us not heap unnecessary burdens upon these heroes of the garret, the workshop, and the wilderness home. They have borne your eagles in triumph from ocean to ocean, and spanned the continent with great empires of free states, built on the ruins of savage life. Such are the men whom the homestead policy would save."[56]

William S. Holman, a war Democrat from Indiana who voted with Republicans on land policy, believed that the Homestead Act would make the Union stronger by cultivating a society of small farmers in the West. "In my judgment," he said, "the policy of applying the public lands in such manner as to increase the number of independent farmers, of secure and independent homesteads, decentralizing and diffusing the wealth of the nation, is of the very first importance; vital, indeed, to the ultimate stability of the Republic." Holman blamed slaveholding aristocrats for starting the war. Diffusing wealth and land ownership would prevent further upheaval. "The greatest of the English statesmen finds the causes of internal war, seditions and factions organized against the Government," he explained, "in the centralization of the wealth, and especially the lands of a nation, destroying the interest of the people in the stability of the nation. . . . Instead of baronial possessions, let us facilitate the increase of independent homesteads." The Indianan also worried that if the North failed to reunite the nation and provide for widespread material plenty, "the monarchists and aristocrats of the world would [exult] . . . that the government of the many was inconsistent with the nature of man."[57]

Wartime contingencies also had a large influence on the homestead debate. In late 1861 and early 1862, some Republicans urged rapid passage of the law to strike against slavery before emancipation and before southerners returned to Congress. Their statements show how questions of land development and slavery were intertwined. "We know the source of opposition to this bill," John Fox Potter reminded his colleagues. "We know from whence has proceeded such opposition heretofore. It is from the very men who are now engaged in a wicked rebellion against this Government . . . that is the class of people who are opposed to the adoption of this policy." George Julian believed that slavery caused the rebellion. He warned: "The mere suppression of this rebellion will be an empty mockery of our suffering and sacrifices, if slavery shall be spared to canker the heart of the nation anew, and repeat its diabolical deeds." The homestead bill, Julian claimed, "recognizes the inalienable rights of the people and the dignity of labor, and thus brands the slave power as no act of the nation ever did before." Homesteads would also end land monopoly, which Julian believed was another cause of secession. The Indianan argued that the Confederacy was a "rebellious aristocracy founded on the monopoly of land and the ownership of Negroes."[58]

Samuel Pomeroy gave the lengthiest argument in favor of a homestead bill, believing that the legislation benefited union and civilization by changing land-use practices. Large landowners, especially absentees, prevented the growth of civilization. "The greatest curse to a new country," Pomeroy stated, "is to have large tracts of unoccupied lands held by non-residents and non-occupants. It retards the growth of a community, paralyzes its industry, delays internal improvements, [and] forbids a general system of free schools . . . tending to produce a worse state of things than in Europe." He wanted to open America's doors and lands to people suffering under European aristocracy—including eastern Europeans and those with dark skin color. "I am," Pomeroy declared, "for opening these lands for the landless of every nation under heaven . . . 'no matter if he may have roamed the wilds of Siberia, or have been burned by a vertical sun.' To me he is an American, if he . . . yields himself joyfully to the molding influence of American civilization." Donating land to yeomen farmers also ensured loyalty to the government. The Kansan explained, "As surely you provide for a man comfortably to support himself, so surely you enable him to support your government." Small farms, he continued, "of a quarter section of land each will greatly promote the wealth, strength and glory of the Republic." Land ownership also provided an incentive for increased, sustainable agricultural production. Pomeroy proclaimed, referring to western settlers: "I ask senators, shall we hesitate longer about giving a homestead to such a people? They have conquered an empire and subdued it to civilization. . . . [T]hey have made the waste places glad, the silent prairie vocal, the wilderness a fruit-ful field, and the 'desert to bud and blossom like a rose.'" He recalled that in Kansas, free settlers reclaimed land "rich as the valley of Nile" from the "blighting influence of human slavery."[59]

Pomeroy also maintained that homesteads under the control of free white men prevented slave owners from moving West. At the time, Pome-roy probably had no idea that Lincoln would issue the Emancipation Proc-lamation. He worried that "marauding rebels" could invade and conquer the lands west of the Mississippi. Free-soil settlers provided a better guar-antee than congressional prohibitions that the territories would be free from slavery: "I declare, to-day, in the American Senate that to secure a country to freedom forever, I would prefer to have this homestead bill en-acted into a law and extended to the whole public domain, than to reenact the ordinance of 1787 [the Northwest Ordinance]." Recalling his violent clashes with slaveholders in the 1850s, Pomeroy declared: "Freedom was secured in Kansas by being planted in the soil, set to growing upon each quarter section of land that we were able to hold, and made permanent as the homesteads were secured." Comparing Native Americans to Confeder-ates, Pomeroy argued that a homestead act would safeguard western set-tlers from both enemies. "The savage on the one side, or the traitor on the other," he stated, "will never invade his [the homesteader's] quarters." The Kansan concluded: "Slavery has had its day and run its course . . . neither Congress, the press, or the pulpit will ever come again to the rescue."[60]

Republicans also believed that the homestead bill established agricul-ture as the predominant American enterprise. Minnesota representative William Windom explained that America was "an agricultural nation" that achieved prosperity through "the products of the soil." Pomeroy ar-gued that the "speedy settlement of the country by actual occupants of the land, though they be 'small-fisted farmers' taking a homestead . . . will produce more revenue to the country, and vastly more increase its wealth and productiveness." Real wealth, Pomeroy elaborated, "consists in flocks and herds, cultivated fields, in well-paid labor, and well-directed energy." The *Farmer's Cabinet*, a New Hampshire newspaper, proclaimed that the Homestead Act and Pacific Railroad Act together would further "the material interests of a great nation" by opening up more land to farm-ing and development. Indiana Republican Schuyler Colfax believed that a homestead bill would allow the urban poor to become wealthy yeomen "by giving them independent freeholds . . . to rear families in habits of industry and frugality, which form the real elements of national greatness and power."[61]

The House and Senate passed the Homestead Act by large majorities in the middle of May 1862. President Lincoln signed it into law on May 20, 1862. A constituent wrote to George W. Julian thanking him for backing the measure. "It seems to me that the measure is the grandest & most Statesmanlike that has ever been carried through the Congress of the United States," the man noted. "Indeed, I may say through any legislative body on the globe." Others believed the act could serve as a model for transforming southern society after the war, again linking land use to social structure. Abolitionist and feminist Lydia Maria Child "observed with anxiety" in the spring of 1864 "that large tracts of Southern confiscated lands were being bought by Northern capitalists." Child thought that "they ought to be mainly distributed among the emancipated slaves and the poor whites who will consent to become loyal." She concluded: "Wealth arising from the cultivation of the soil is what we must rely upon." The Pacific Railroad, the Land Grant College Act, the creation of the USDA, and the passage of the homestead bill all reflected the Republican vision of an agrarian society of small landholders—the opposite of the slave South.[62]

While Republican congressmen and senators cited poor southern land-use practices during debates over wartime legislation, what did average soldiers believe? Did the common Civil War soldier from the North have a negative impression of agriculture under slavery? Did they agree with Republican proscriptions for change? The answer to these questions is yes: in wartime diaries and regimental histories, soldiers argued that the Confederacy had wasteful and decrepit landscapes. These landscapes, soldiers believed, created a barbaric society. Tying the appearance of the South's urban environment to the level of civilization, soldiers cited the disheveled abodes, low literacy rates, scattered settlements, and filthy habits as "proof" of the Confederacy's barbarism. Influenced by antislavery writings criticizing poor farming practices on rural plantations, soldiers also believed that slavery destroyed the land, leaving it permanently unfit for cultivation. Moreover, the large landholdings of slave plantations created an oligarchy hostile to American democracy. Soldiers believed that slaveholders were lazy aristocrats, hostile to free institutions, free white men, and prosperous farming communities. Southern people, both white and black, could only be incorporated into the Union if they adopted the small-scale farms prevalent in the North.[63]

Soldiers who focused on the detrimental effects of slavery on agriculture tended to be white; black soldiers, who joined the army in the middle of the war, emphasized the moral evils of slavery itself. "What is the colored men fighting for[?]" one African American soldier asked in

September 1863. "[I]f the war makes us free we are happy to hear it[.] And when we are free men and a people we will fight for our rights and liberty[;] we care nothing about the union." For many, the fight became personal. Spotswood Rice had a dire warning for his former mistress: "I want you rembor this one thing, that the longor you keep my child from me the longor you will have to burn in hell and the qwicer youll get their for we are now making up a bout one thoughsand black troops to Come up." Rice planned to rescue his children from the woman. "I expect to get them," he asserted, "and when I get ready to come . . . I will have bout a powrer and authority to bring hear away and to exacute vengencens on them that holds my Child." Yet black soldiers often tied abolition to preserving the Union. A sergeant explained the link between the two. "We are fighting for liberty and right and we intend to follow the old flag while there is a man left to hold it up to the breeze of heaven," he remarked. "Slavery must and shall pass away." Wearing a blue uniform also brought respectability. Elijah Maars recalled: "I felt like a man with a uniform on and a gun in my hand. . . . I felt freedom in my bones." Still others saw paths to small-scale land ownership and education in the army. Sergeant Prince Rivers of the 33rd U.S. Colored Infantry organized an association to buy land. "Every colored man will be a slave," Rivers explained, "and feel himself a slave until he can *raise him own bale of cotton and put his own mark on it.*"[64]

Much Civil War scholarship has focused on whether U.S. soldiers focused more on preserving the Union or ending slavery. Chandra Manning argues that "few white Northerners initially joined the Union rank and file specifically to stamp out slavery . . . yet the shock of war itself and soldiers' interactions with slaves, who in many cases were the first black people northern men had ever met, changed Union troops' minds fast." Gary Gallagher disagrees, emphasizing that throughout the war, Union soldiers "believed victory over the slaveholders confirmed the nation, made it stronger in the absence of slavery's pernicious influence, set the stage for the country's continuing growth and vitality, and kept a democratic beacon shining in a world dominated by aristocrats and monarchs." With the exception of African American soldiers, detailed above, the division is overly schismatic. Antislavery beliefs blended with passionate feelings about the Union, but these beliefs, by and large, were *not* abolitionist in nature. Northern soldiers hated slave owners far more than they sympathized with those enslaved. Most important, the debate has prevented historians from taking a closer look at how negative impressions of southern landscapes influenced opinions about both the Union and slavery.[65]

George W. Driggs of the 8th Wisconsin Volunteer Infantry provides a perfect example of a soldier vehemently opposed to emancipation but holding passionate views about union and the evils of slave agriculture. "We are fighting," Driggs wrote in December 1861, "for a great and glorious cause—for the maintenance of right, and for the best Government that ever was framed." He had nothing but scorn for rebels. Writing in July 1862, Driggs wrote to his family from "the land of secession and rebellion—of lizards, snakes, and varmints, by the million—of silly, sneaking, men of puny cast, who stroll about our camps unfearful of arrest." Abolitionists, however, were no better. "Where are they?" Driggs asked, then answered: "At home by their firesides, praying for the immortal nigger. . . . They are doing their utmost to make slavery the issue of this war. We do not propose to interfere with slavery." When camped on the border between Missouri and Arkansas, Driggs gave his opinion on the southern environment: "I would not give the poorest farm in Wisconsin for the whole country we have passed through on our march, for farming purposes, and be obliged to live here."[66]

The polar opposite of Driggs on emancipation was abolitionist James T. Miller, a private in the 111th Pennsylvania Infantry. A poor farmer from rural Pennsylvania, Miller saw action at the Battles of Gettysburg, Cedar Mountain, and Chancellorsville prior to dying in 1864 at the Battle of Peachtree Creek. Miller expressed an intense moral hatred of slavery. "I dont want to see peace," he wrote in Virginia, "until every slave in the reble states is free[;] it is the most abominable institution the world ever saw." He elaborated: "I tel you that Uncle Tom's cabin bad as it was fel far short of portraying the evils of slavery in as bad a light as they realy exist. . . . [T]wo years of war have made more Abolitionists than the lectures of Wend Philips and Gerit Smith and Wm Loyd Garison would have made in one hundred years." Yet, just like Driggs, Miller also commented on the evils of slave agriculture. Both men believed in the Union and in the inefficiency of southern farms. "After we got into Kentucky," Miller wrote in October 1863, "the effects of slavery and the rebellion began to show themselves in the destruction of fences [and] burnt buildings and the curse of slavery could be seen in the whole of large plantations gro[w]ing up to brush and weeds." Similar to Frederick Law Olmsted, Miller believed that the soil was naturally fertile but had been left undeveloped because of slavery: "The country although it shows every simtom of being naturally a fertile one looks desolate and forsaken[;] there [is] not a particle of fence to be seen for miles." Soldiers in the 150th Pennsylvania Volunteers offered similar sentiments. They penned a resolution on March 11, 1863, stating:

"We believe that 'fighting for Southern rights' means nothing more than warring for the extension of slavery, which we regard alike as a *curse to the land*, and a *great moral wrong*."[67]

Most Union soldiers had beliefs on slavery and emancipation that were in between the ideological extremes of Miller and Driggs. Just as with these two men, however, one of the themes uniting northerners fighting in the war was a harsh view of the southern environment and slave agriculture. J. C. Williams of the 14th Vermont Infantry proclaimed that the "preservation of this Union is one of the noblest things to fight for. Not anywhere in the annals of the past ages do we find a government founded upon such liberal principles." When this pro-Union soldier entered Virginia, however, he was struck by its physical appearance: "The dirty, filthy condition of the streets of Alexandria is not only discoverable in all Southern cities, but exhibits very plainly the blighting effects of slavery." The Vermonter hated slavery, in part, for its effects on the land and the white people of the South. Slavery "impoverished the land, and reduced the people to the lowest state of misery and degradation, and has at last culminated in this wicked rebellion."[68]

Richard Eddy of the 60th New York Infantry made similar criticisms of both the built and natural environments of Virginia. Traveling with a fellow soldier in Fairfax County, Eddy noted: "All we saw, seemed like a barren waste. Some negroes we met thought it was very good land, however, for 'they could raise two barrels of corn on an acre!'" Stafford Court House, in Stafford County, Virginia, seemed to decay under slavery. "Stafford Court House," Eddy observed, "is one of the ugliest-appearing places one could ask to see. Settled in 1660, it appears to have had no improvements for at least a century. The Court House is a tumble-down and filthy building, and the jail, which stands in the middle of the road, is a miserable two-story affair, built of rough stone." He continued: "The lower story is occupied by hogs, and the upper is reached by stairs from the outside." Eddy connected this grim scene to the soil exhaustion found on the county's farms. "With but one exception," he explained, "the few surrounding dwellings are of somewhat similar appearance, and, like the soil, are worn out."[69]

John C. Myers of the 192nd Pennsylvania Volunteers thought that while pretty, the southern countryside was being crushed by slavery. "The country surrounding camp is very pretty," Myers wrote upon entering Maryland in late July 1863, "but every foot of it exhibits the blighting and destructive presence of the defunct 'peculiar institution.' Barren fields are everywhere visible—scarcely a garden patch has sufficient growth in it to feed an ordinary grasshopper. The soil is worn out, having been planted for years without manure; even the cattle seem half starved, and these are of the poorest stock. Agriculture is in its most primitive state." Myers hoped that with the destruction of slavery, the "land and this people [were] were soon to be released from the misery and darkness which has rested upon them for a century." If slavery disappeared, "civilization would soon dawn." The men of the 192nd Regiment were also proud of their background as farmers. The commander of the regiment gave a speech that Myers deemed important enough to record. Colonel Ferguson "remarked that they were farmers, an honorable calling which they had still more ennobled as soldiers for the defense of their government. . . . [T]hey had shown the world that farmers could be soldiers."[70]

Myers believed that free farmers—like the men in his regiment—could make the fertile southern environment prosper. While in Virginia, he observed that "slavery has kept all these vast resources, the bountiful gifts from the hands of Providence, in their primitive obscurity, contenting itself with working the soil on the surface to death with unpaid labor, while the still more valuable product was neglected and remained undisturbed below." The arrival of the Union army and the destruction of slavery offered opportunities for renewal. "The horses, mules, cattle, swine, and live stock generally," the Pennsylvanian farmer wrote, "which once so plentifully abounded on all these extensive plantations, have disappeared. The fields have . . . fallen into the original state of nature which they were found." He was ecstatic about the future. Myers proclaimed: "Who can realize the greatness of the free South, —her millions of acres of untouched, virgin lands, monopolized by a small fraction of slaveholders . . . set free and open to the industry of all."[71]

Sergeant E. J. Hart of the 40th Illinois Infantry celebrated that his company was composed mostly of small farmers. Of the 104 men in Hart's company, he listed eighty-nine as being farmers. While en route to fighting, Hart took note of the "intelligent farmer" in the fields of the North who furnished their brethren "with all the necessary supplies." However, the large farms of the South produced an "aristocracy." This "southern aristocracy," imbibed with the "spirit of rebellion," was determined to destroy the "noblest *Government* on earth." Even though Hart saw a lot of "beautiful farming country" in the South and "fine mansions," he observed that the "farm improvements did not wear the same neatness of our pretty western farms." Like Myers, Hart was hopeful for the future of the South. Hart wrote down a speech where an officer told the men of the 40th Illinois that "you should remember these farms are all to be cultivated, and may assist in augmenting our national wealth, when this cruel Rebellion is crushed."[72]

Another Illinoisan, J. R. Kinnear of the 86th Illinois Volunteer Infantry, openly mocked southern farming practices. "Farming in the Southern States," he noted while serving under General William T. Sherman, "is carried on in a very simple and seeming ignorant style. One could not refrain from laughing at their oddity in agricultural pursuits. They are a great many years behind the North in this respect, as well as in many others." He elaborated: "The improvements are usually very poor, with but few conveniences." The southerners Kinnear met reacted with astonishment when the Union soldiers told "them we break our ground with two horses, plow our corn with a plow on which we can ride; that one man can tend forty acres and raise forty bushels to the acre." Besides slave labor, one of the other problems Kinnear identified with southern land use was "single persons owning very large tracts of land." As a result, parts of the South, particularly South Carolina, were not "thickly settled" and contained a "proud chivalry" hostile to the republic. Hating this class, Kinnear observed: "From the very first they [Union soldiers] treated South Carolina as her acts of treason and atrocity deserved. Nearly every house all over the country was fed on the flames of Yankee vengeance. When their houses were burnt, the proud chivalries were obliged to seek refuge in negro shanties."[73]

The men of the 21st New York State Volunteers were horrified at the level of ignorance among white southerners. In an unsigned letter to the *Buffalo Courier*, one of the soldiers noted: "The mass of the population is ignorant to a degree that is startling to a Northerner. It knows little that transpires in the world beyond its immediate circle. . . . [T]he very dialect of the mass betrays its ignorance—differing in no respect from that used by slaves." The concentration of wealth in large estates was the reason for this ignorance. Bould Soger—likely a pen name—wrote to an upstate New York newspaper: "Ye petty princes of the South, owners of broad estates, masters of cringing serfs, *your* masters are here. . . . [Y]ou are in the way of the nation, and you must step out. You may be princes, lords, of the first families, knightly, chivalrous, and all that sort of nonsense; but 'Princes and lords may flourish, or may fade . . . but a bold yeomanry, their country's pride, when once destroyed, can never be supplied.'" In a less lyrical tone, Soger noted in the Rappahannock River basin that "the break-up of almost boundless estates into small farms would make this valley the garden of Virginia." As certain places in the commonwealth stood now, wrote J. Harrison Miles, one found "no fences or signs of cultivation, only a few stunted, dried down shrubs apologizing for the wasted forests that once stood upon the exhausted soil."[74]

As was true for Frederick Law Olmsted and Hinton Helper, many soldiers saw the appearance of pine trees on abandoned plantation land as proof of the destructive nature of slave agriculture. Twelfth Indiana chaplain M. D. Gage visited McPhersonville, South Carolina, near the end of the war. "This little town lay nestled among pines of almost a century's growth," he recorded, "which covered a large cotton plantation, abandoned on account of sterility. Tens of thousands of acres, once under cultivation, are now surrendered to the restoring hand of nature. Pines, in all stages of growth, from the short to the tall stately tree, stand among the cotton rows of former plantations." Gage was not sure why plantations were so destructive to the soil, but he advanced several theories. One was that "under the influence of slavery, the very ground [was] being cursed in consequence of the sin of the people." The second theory was that "no effort is made to recruit the waste of productive elements, in the light soil of the vast pine region of the Carolinas, by the use of fertilizers, but when old fields are exhausted they are given up to the invigorating power of nature . . . and thus the careless round of unrequited toil goes on." The "vast pine forest," Gage concluded, seemed a "curious spectacle to eyes accustomed to scenes of beauty and fertility in the vicinity of rural villages of the North."[75]

Albion W. Tourgée of the 105th Ohio Infantry came from the Western Reserve, home to Radicals Benjamin F. Wade and Joshua R. Giddings. Tourgée was proud that his county had "the lowest rate of illiteracy of any county in the Union" and was a place where "intelligence and freedom of thought" thrived. Comparing the North and the South in relative degrees of civilization, Tourgée found that "the laws, customs and institutions of the North were shaped by freemen in the furnace-heat of free-thought and free-speech. The public-school was everywhere; opportunity was untrammeled. The institutions, laws, and policy of the South were shaped by slave-owners to promote the interests of the slave-holders; the free-laborer was despised. Every official belonged to the slave-owning class; free-schools were unknown; free-speech was repressed by the law and the mob." Tourgée correlated the lack of civilization in the South with an impoverished landscape. He noticed immediately upon crossing into slave territory that "the grass was parched . . . the pools were dry; the low branching oaks showed brown and dusty under the summer sunshine; the wild wormwood grew rank and green above the stubble; the shorthorns roamed restlessly about, vexed with thirst and stung with flies." Such, he explained, "was the ineradicable stamp which slavery left upon the land."[76]

Previewing Reconstruction, many Union men argued that redistributing land to small farmers could redeem southern agriculture and society. Henry T. Jones, a soldier in the 49th Massachusetts, believed that widespread land ownership produced a more egalitarian society and a beautiful landscape. Near Baton Rouge, Louisiana, he wrote: "Take away the trees and shrubbery, and you cannot find what you would term a handsome place, in town. Few can afford plantations, [the others] live in cities[;] . . . the wealth is in the country, to which towns are the merest adjuncts; land-owning, and consequent slave-owning, is the criterion of respectability." Reflecting on the debate over the homestead bill in the 1850s, Jones continued: "Who own[s] the land will be the rulers. Hence home-power of Southerners, hence their opposition to homestead bills." Jones felt that the Civil War was a contest between "aristocratic usurpation and popular rights," a repeat of "the old contest, old as human governments." The solution, however, was clear. "[The] Feudal South can only be republicanized by impoverishing the great landlords," Jones asserted. "The war will do, is doing that. Then democracy will gravitate to the country, and the aristocracy to towns and cities." Such a society would be more productive as well. After witnessing sugar cultivation in the Mississippi Delta, Jones wrote that "the South should not attempt to raise sugar for it is a forced crop. If it cannot be raised without forced or slave labor, God never intended it to be raised at all. Small farmers will yet raise it by free labor."[77]

For men such as Jones, Tourgée, Gage, and countless others, the Civil War did not show, as one historian claims, "what the industrializing nation was capable of." Instead, in the words of nineteenth-century farming advocate Edmund Morris, the farmers who fought the war came out convinced that settlers, "mostly from the Free States . . . would not only till the soil with their own hands, but would build school-houses, establish newspapers, and diffuse education" in the South and the West. The inferiority of slavery to free labor, the soldiers believed, could be seen in the soil itself.[78]

THE CREATION OF YOSEMITE AND

YELLOWSTONE

It was during one of the darkest hours, before Sherman had begun the march upon Atlanta or Grant his terrible movement through the Wilderness, when the paintings of Bierstadt and the photographs of Watkins, both productions of the War time, had given to the people on the Atlantic some idea of the sublimity of Yo Semite.—Frederick Law Olmsted

On July 1, 1864, as William T. Sherman marched toward Atlanta and Philip Sheridan fought Jubal Early in the Shenandoah valley, President Abraham Lincoln's attention was diverted from the Civil War to the signing of a bill creating Yosemite State Park in far-off California. The law removed Yosemite valley and the neighboring Mariposa Big Tree Grove from the public domain so that California could manage the sites for "public use, resort, and recreation." In other words, Yosemite would become a state-owned nature park. The act was the first of its kind and generated a heated controversy over whether the government had the right to create parks.[1]

At this point, a reader might question the relevance of the Yosemite controversy to the topics explored in previous chapters. What does Yosemite have in common with the Homestead Act and the free-soil movement? The answer is that *opposition* to Yosemite was rooted in the exact same ideals that produced the Homestead Act and free-soilers. Union nationalism and nineteenth-century notions of civilization explain why the United States established Yosemite. Believing that small farmers comprised the ideal society, opponents such as George W. Julian argued that Yosemite valley should be reserved for yeomen farmers. Nature parks, Julian asserted, threatened their rights by challenging homestead and preemption claims. This controversy influenced the 1872 creation of Yellowstone as a *national* park under federal control. Authors of the Yellowstone legislation believed that California's mismanagement of Yosemite showed the necessity for national rather than state control. The debate about Yosemite also exposed a fissure in the Republicans' agrarian vision. Radicals such as Julian believed that private land claims were the basis of successful land stewardship, and thus civilization. Park proponents such as Olmsted, by contrast, began arguing that reserving natural beauty for the general public promoted civilization more effectively.

Yosemite supporters believed that the park provided value for an American nation undergoing sectional strife. Following Europe's failed revolutions of 1848, many believed that if the United States collapsed, republican government would be discredited and the world's aristocrats would gloat in triumph. William Brewer of the California State Geological Survey feared in April 1861 that "the prestige of the American name is passed away, not soon to return." Making areas of scenic beauty accessible to everyone highlighted the value of republican government. Everyone, not just the wealthy and powerful, needed to experience the sublime scenery provided in parks. Second, park advocates believed that the creation of a public park on the California frontier would help the region transform from barbarism to civilization. Yosemite supporters argued that making the valley's immense natural beauty accessible would improve the mind and spirit of all who visited, making them more civilized.[2]

Free-soil beliefs created the framework for opposition to Yosemite. As shown in chapters 1 and 2, Free-Soilers, and later Republicans, believed that the disbursement of the public domain to yeomen settlers allowed the poor to achieve prosperity by harvesting the fruits of nature. Encouraging western settlement also brought "civilization" to a "barbaric" wilderness. George W. Julian, after all, believed that the 1862 Homestead Act was an effective method of promoting civilization and keeping slavery out of the West. Preemption, another method of land distribution favored by Free-Soilers and Republicans, allowed settlers to claim 160 acres on the unsurveyed or surveyed public domain. When the land became available for sale, the pioneer could purchase his claim for a nominal fee. Former Free-Soilers believed the federal government could not violate preemption or homestead rights to create a public park. As one California congressman explained, "The Constitution and the laws are for the protection of citizens and not for the creation of a fancy pleasure grounds by Congress out of a citizen's farms." The dream of an agrarian West, settled by hardworking yeoman farmers, seemed threatened by nature parks. While both supporters and opponents of Yosemite believed that proper land use excluded slavery, they disagreed on how the valley should be put to use.[3]

Neither supporters nor opponents of Yosemite State Park achieved a complete victory. Yosemite advocates headed off legislative attempts by George Julian and his allies to open the park to private land claims. They also defeated a lawsuit by Yosemite residents that sought federal and state recognition of preemption rights in the valley. Nevertheless, the same Yosemite residents—through savvy political maneuvers and stubborn resistance—prevented California from effectively administrating the park. Their efforts produced a burst of commercial development in the valley. Republican politicians Lyman Trumbull and Samuel Pomeroy claimed that state control failed because of California's inability to prevent Yosemite's degradation. Future "natural curiosities," these men believed, should be placed under federal control. Trumbull's and Pomeroy's claims occurred in the context of heated debates over Reconstruction, in which the same politicians argued that federal courts needed to protect freed slaves when state governments failed to do so. Moreover, the creation of a federally administered park would have been impossible in prewar America, when the federal government was much smaller and had limited powers. While scholars have long assumed that states' rights were never germane to the Yellowstone debate because of the park's location in a federal territory, the historical evidence suggests otherwise.[4]

These arguments both challenge and build from the work of previous historians who have examined national parks. Scholars often portray the history of parks as a battle between "preservationists" who wanted to protect land for aesthetic beauty and those who advocated utilitarian resource development. "Proclaimed as a public trust as early as 1864," argues Alfred Runte in *Yosemite: The Embattled Wilderness*, "Yosemite bears the longest evidence of the tension, found in every major park, between preservation and use." A 2006 environmental history of nineteenth-century America labels the creation of Yosemite as an early example of preservationism, which only occurred because the valley "seemed to have little industrial value." The "preservation" versus "use" paradigm is insufficient in explaining the history of Yosemite and Yellowstone, however, because it ignores the historical context in which the government created both parks. The first opponents of Yosemite becoming a park did not want to see dams and mines constructed in the valley. Coming from a rural background, they urged the government to recognize small land claims intended for farming. Supporters did not want to preserve pristine nature; they wanted to make that beauty available to all. As Jen A. Huntley points out in the most recent examination of Yosemite's early history, the traditional tale of "heroic nature lovers join[ing] with a benighted government to defeat the selfish entrepreneurs standing in the way" ignores much of the "messy complexity" involved in the park's creation. Likewise, Lisa Brady notes the ties between government expansion and park preservation, explaining: "In expanding the federal government's powers and authority, the Civil War created the circumstances in which the government could set aside land from economic development, create agencies to oversee and manage those lands, and establish in perpetuity a system of parks and wilderness areas for the benefit of all Americans."[5]

Americans first found the Yosemite valley and the Mariposa Big Tree Grove appealing because of a romantic appreciation of nature, the increasing popularity of sport hunting and fishing among wealthy elites, and the moneymaking possibilities the areas offered. Yet, widespread appreciation of these qualities did not mandate Yosemite's transformation into a park. In fact, Americans had long expressed romantic appreciation and cultural pride in natural areas without arguing that they be turned into parks. Thomas Jefferson, for example, believed that Virginia's Natural Bridge was the "most sublime of Nature's works," but he did not want to establish the site as a park. In 1832, as recounted in the first chapter, artist George Catlin believed that the government should preserve the "pristine beauty and wildness" of the Great Plains in a "magnificent park, where the world could see for ages to come, the native Indian . . . amid the fleeting herds of elks and buffaloes." This plea, however, gained little attention. As the controversy over Yosemite's creation shows, many people believed romantic beauty, tourism, and sporting activities were best promoted by private—not public—land ownership.[6]

One of the earliest published accounts of Yosemite shows what nineteenth-century Americans found inviting in the area. White men first entered the valley in 1851 in pursuit of the Yosemite Indians, who were accused of depredations against gold miners residing in nearby Mariposa. Upon returning, militia captain John Boling told Mariposa residents and San Franciscans about a valley in the Sierra Nevada containing 1,000-foot waterfalls. James Mason Hutchings, editor of San Francisco's *Hutchings Magazine*, inquired with Boling about his discovery and decided to go to the area in 1855. Bringing along landscape artist Thomas A. Ayres, Hutchings publicized details of his adventure in the *Mariposa Gazette*. Hutchings proclaimed that the Yosemite valley offered "to the dyspeptic denizens of our larger cities . . . recreation and medicine . . . pure, free air, and . . . ice-cold water." Upon descending toward the valley, the party viewed a scene of "wondering admiration" filled with such "wild and sublime grandeur" that one person asked, "Can this be the opening of the Seventh Seal?"

Hutchings also found abundant sporting opportunities in the valley. For the "Disciples of Issac [*sic*] Walton," the valley provided "speckled trout in any quantity," and "the hunter" could find "plenty of geese, pigeons, and deer." Most important, he noted that the "wonderful valley will attract the lovers of the beautiful from all parts of the world; and be as famed as Niagara [Falls], for its wild sublimity and magnificent scenery."[7]

California Unionist and Unitarian minister Thomas Starr King also found solace in Yosemite valley. Awestruck by what he saw, King sent a series of letters to the *Boston Evening Transcript* between December 1860 and February 1861. "The patches of luxuriant meadow with their dazzling green," King explained, "and the grouping of the superb firs, two hundred feet high, that skirt them, and that shoot above the stout and graceful oaks and sycamores . . . are delightful rests of sweetness and beauty." King believed that beauty was the "highest use which mountains serve." He pondered: "Think of the loss to human nature if the summits of Mont Blanc and the Junfrau could be leveled, and their jagged sides, sheeted with snow and flaming with amethyst and gold, should be softened by the sun and tilled for vines and corn." King also believed that he could see God in nature, proclaiming: "The Truth of Nature is part of the truth of God: to him who does not search it out, darkness, to him who does, infinity."[8]

Reacting to these articles and other accounts printed in California newspapers, travelers soon found their way to the valley, while some Californians moved to take advantage of the tourist rush. G. W. Coulter set up a stagecoach route from Coulterville to Yosemite valley. James Hutchings and Vermont emigrant Frederick Billings also realized the opportunity for profit. In April 1859, Illinoisan James C. Lamon, a close friend of Hutchings, settled in the east end of the valley, building a home, garden, and orchard. Lamon reported to Hutchings that "he was amazed at the gentleness of the season and at the number of sunny days when he could work in the garden," encouraging the magazine editor to quit his job and live in Yosemite. After a visit in the summer of 1863, Hutchings agreed, buying Yosemite's only hotel and applying for a 160-acre preemption claim. Hutchings constructed a log cabin near Yosemite Falls, planted fruit trees, and imported livestock. He also built a water-powered sawmill and a "causeway . . . over the meadows from the hotel to make Yosemite Falls . . . more accessible to his guests." The former magazine editor took up permanent residence in the spring of 1864.[9]

Frederick Billings, an ambitious lawyer specializing in contested California land claims, made frequent trips to the valley and the giant sequoia grove in the 1850s. The beauty of these areas reminded him of landscape paintings he owned by Thomas Cole, Frederic E. Church, Asher B. Durand, and John F. Kensett. What impressed him the most, however, was the tourism potential of the natural attractions. On a trip to an alabaster cave en route to Yosemite, Billings noticed the "agreeable ride, low cost, efficient and attentive service, good food and lodging . . . and the visual pleasure of a natural landmark." The formula was successful for drawing people to visit. In fact, Billings believed that California's natural sites could draw more visitors than Europe's manmade wonders and become a source of national pride. He claimed that people would tire of "old tapestries" and "visiting a dungeon where some poor creature had been ill treated." California, instead, "was a place of wild beauty, challenge, and even adventurous folly, where all Nature's processes could be seen plain."[10]

Yet, the creation of Yosemite State Park was never a fait accompli. James Mason Hutchings, who treasured the Yosemite valley and Mariposa Big Tree Grove as tourist attractions and valued their transcendental beauty, opposed the park's creation. For Hutchings, private property ownership in Yosemite would not harm the area. Instead, the government had an obligation to uphold his land claims. Hutchings's belief was not a "beguiling hallucination," as one scholar argues. To understand why others believed that Yosemite and the Mariposa Grove should be encased in a public park, one must examine the ideas of Frederick Law Olmsted. Living through the political strife of the 1850s and an eyewitness to the carnage of the Civil War, Olmsted came to believe that America needed public parks. They provided an important "civilizing" influence on the frontier and demonstrated the power of republican government. Olmsted's writings on the value of public parks influenced Frederick Billings and a host of powerful California politicians to push for the creation of Yosemite.[11]

A main reason that Olmsted supported public parks was his fear that free states were not fulfilling their democratic potential. While, after his travels to the slave states in the 1850s, Olmsted promoted small farm ownership as a bulwark against slavery, he also believed that public ownership of natural beauty promoted civilization. These two beliefs would only cause conflict in the Republican Party after the creation of Yosemite. "Slaveholders," Olmsted wrote in 1853, were intent only on buying more land and slaves, possess[ing] few of the domestic amenities essential to civilized life." Yet, after a visit to Nashville, his acquaintance—white southerner Samuel Perkins Allison—attacked Olmsted's characterizations, claiming that the slave states displayed a higher level of civilization than did the North. Allison forced Olmsted to concede the "rowdyism, ruffianism, want of high honorable sentiment & chivalry of the common farming and laboring people of the North." Olmsted decided that to improve northern civilization and democratic equality, the government needed to sponsor parks. "I do very much [feel] inclined to believe that Government should have in view the encouragement of a democratic condition of society," he wrote to a friend. "[T]he two need to go together as they do at the North in much greater degree than at the South. . . . [T]he poor need an education to refinement and taste. . . . I believe, go ahead with the Children's Aid and get up parks, gardens, music, dancing schools[;] . . . the state ought to assist these sort of things."[12]

Olmsted aided the creation of America's first urban park, cultivating powerful allies in the process. Since 1850, architect Andrew Jackson Downing had been advocating a park in New York City modeled after the gardens that Olmsted visited in Britain. After taking office in April 1851, New York mayor Ambrose C. Kingsland endorsed Downing's vision. The plan did not get under way until 1857. But when Olmsted heard of the effort, he applied to be in charge of land clearing. Olmsted met with the head commissioner of the so-called Central Park in August 1857 and then drafted a petition to convince the commissioners of his ability. The petition included signatures by landscape painter Albert Bierstadt, famous New York City lawyer David Dudley Field, and influential *New York Tribune* editor Horace Greeley. After Olmsted received the position, the Central Park commissioners opened a competition for the park's design. Olmsted and co-designer Calvert Vaux conveyed their ideas about the function of parks in a republican society in their successful proposal. They claimed that public parks—allegedly available to all classes—provided people with the opportunity "to come together for the single purpose of enjoyment, unembarrassed by the limitations with which they are surrounded at home."[13]

Central Park served as the model for Yosemite. Horace Greeley, who knew Olmsted and supported his bid for the Central Park job, visited Yosemite valley and the neighboring Mariposa Big Tree Grove in 1859. Greeley recommended that the "big tree grove . . . be preserved from the ravages of the ax and fire" and instead become a "place of wonderful attraction." Greeley, drawing from his experience with Central Park in New York City, had a "park" in mind when he made this recommendation. Though the feisty editor never used the word, he warned after his return to New York that "if the village of Mariposa, the County, or the State of California, does not immediately provide for the safety of these trees," they would be destroyed. "I am sure they will be more prized and treasured a thousand years hence from now," Greeley continued, "should they by extreme care and caution, be preserved so long, and that thousands will then visit them, over smooth and spacious roads."[14]

Israel Ward Raymond, the California agent for the New York City–based Central American Transit Company, was the next person to advocate a park. Raymond wrote to California's Union Party senator John Conness in February 1864 calling for the creation of Yosemite State Park and giving an outline of legislation. Raymond argued that Yosemite valley and the Mariposa Big Tree Grove should be reserved "for public use, resort, and recreation" in order to "prevent occupation and especially to preserve the valley and the big trees from destruction." He further recommended that a commission be empowered to manage Yosemite valley and the Mariposa Grove for public benefit. It is possible that Raymond had tourism in mind. From 1856 to 1864, New York newspapers carried advertisements for travel from New York City to San Francisco on Raymond's steamship line. The company Raymond worked for was the largest shipowner in the nation, conducting a lucrative trade between California and the East. Perhaps the company wanted to advertise attractive destinations at the places its lines reached. Additionally, there is evidence that Olmsted provided Raymond with the idea of a public park. In his letter to Conness, Raymond recommended "Fred. Law Olmsted of Mariposa" as commissioner for Yosemite State Park. The recommendation indicates that Raymond knew of Olmsted and his promotion of public parks. Additionally, in April 1862, while working on the Sanitary Commission—the Civil War equivalent of the Red Cross—Olmsted had met the steamship company's president, William Aspinwall, and solicited donations from him.[15]

Conness also received letters from Frederick Billings and Stephen J. Field—a recently appointed U.S. Supreme Court justice—in support of the park. Billings, in particular, warned Conness that the two settlers in the valley "would need to be bought out or removed." Again, Olmsted's influence can be inferred: Billings had dined with Olmsted when the landscape architect arrived in California to manage a gold mine in 1863. Stephen J. Field may have known Olmsted through his brother, David Dudley Field. Conness quickly followed up on the requests, drafting legislation to remove Yosemite from the public domain and grant it to California. Surveyors Clarence King and Jim Gardiner established the park's boundaries. On March 28, 1864, Conness introduced Senate Bill No. 203 into Congress. Thus, a politically powerful group of men, influenced by Frederick Law Olmsted, spurred the creation of Yosemite State Park.[16]

A photograph display also aided the push to create Yosemite. Many elite easterners became familiar with the park's scenery when Carleton Watkins's photography went on display at Goupil's New York Gallery in 1862. Visiting Yosemite in 1861, Watkins had taken photos of Nevada Falls, Mount Broderick, the "Grizzly Giant" sequoia tree, and other scenes using a cumbersome camera capable of producing eighteen-by-twenty-two-inch photographic plates. Thirty of these photographs and 100 stereoviews became part of a showing following an earlier exhibition of Mathew Brady's photography of the Civil War dead. Olmsted noted how the contrast between beautiful scenery and violent death encouraged the park's creation. "It was during one of the darkest hours," he commented, "before Sherman had begun the march upon Atlanta or Grant his terrible movement through the Wilderness, when the paintings of Bierstadt and the photographs of Watkins, both productions of the War time, had given to the people on the Atlantic some idea of the sublimity of the Yo Semite." The *New York Times* added: "The views of lofty mountains, of gigantic trees, of falls of water which seem to descend from the heights of heavens . . . are indescribably unique and beautiful."[17]

In debate, Conness stated why the government should create a park. Yosemite and the nearby Mariposa Big Tree Grove were "wonders of the world," the California senator explained. "The trees contained in that grove have no parallel. . . . They are subject now to damage and injury, and this bill . . . proposes to commit them to care of that State for their constant preservation, that they may be exposed to public view, and that they may be used and preserved for the benefit of mankind." Only one person questioned the wisdom of Conness's bill. Republican Lafayette Foster of Connecticut worried that the legislation could violate California's state rights. "It str[ikes] me as being rather a singular grant," he explained, "unprecedented so far as my recollection goes, and unless the State through her appropriate authorities signified some wish in the matter, it might be deemed by the state officious on our part." Conness replied, "There is no parallel, and can be no parallel for this measure, for there is not . . . on earth just such a condition of things. The Mariposa Big Tree Grove is really the wonder of the world." Californian control of the park also satisfied Foster's objection.[18]

The main reason, however, that Conness's bill faced little resistance was his assurance that the "property is of no value to the Government" and that no one had land titles in Yosemite valley. Conness thus deliberately concealed Hutchings's and Lamon's land claims. George W. Julian, then chairman of the House Committee on Public Lands, allowed the bill to pass because he thought no white men inhabited Yosemite. Julian recalled, "It was never dreamed that any one in the occupancy of that land was a preemptor. If it had been, the committee would not have interfered with his rights under the laws of Congress." With minimal opposition, the Senate passed the bill on May 17, 1864. The House, with Julian's blessing, voted for the bill on June 29, 1864. On July 1, Abraham Lincoln signed it into law.[19]

The statute granted Yosemite valley and the Mariposa Big Tree Grove to California. Both areas would be managed by "the Governor of the State with eight other Commissioners, to be appointed by the Executive of California, and who shall receive no compensation for their services." News of the law's passage reached California on August 9, 1864, and shortly after, Governor Frederick K. Low issued a proclamation accepting it. Low appointed Frederick Law Olmsted as director of the Yosemite Valley Commission, reflecting the New Yorker's influence on the creation of Yosemite. California's governor nominated Professor Josiah Whitney, William Ashburner, I. W. Raymond, E. S. Holden, Alexander Deering, George W. Coulter, and Galen Clark as the other commission members.[20]

The commission advocated a vision of public parks that reflected Yosemite's origin as an expression of Unionism. The park paid tribute to the republican government many in the Civil War fought to uphold. Frederick Law Olmsted began the Yosemite Commission's *Preliminary Report* by claiming, "It is a fact of much significance with reference to the temper and spirit which ruled the loyal people of the United States during the war of the great rebellion, that a livelier susceptibility to the influence of art was apparent." He continued: "It was during one of the darkest hours . . . that consideration was first given to the danger that such scenes [in Yosemite] might become private property and through the false taste, the caprice . . . of their holders; their value to posterity be injured." Olmsted was manifesting pride in the U.S. government's ability to promote republican measures while facing the greatest test of its survival.[21]

Furthermore, preserving Yosemite as a public park would demonstrate the value of republican government in a time when the world seemed shrouded in tyranny. Olmsted attacked European private ownership of beautiful scenery. "There are in the islands of Great Britain and Ireland more than one thousand private parks and notable ground devoted to luxury and recreation," he observed. "[T]he enjoyment of the choicest natural scenes in the country and the means of recreation connected with them is thus a monopoly, in a very peculiar manner, of a very few, very rich people." Thus, "the great mass of society, including those to whom it would be of greatest benefit, is excluded from it. In the nature of the case private parks can never be used by the mass of the people in any country." In America, however, "it is the main duty of government . . . to provide means of protection for all its citizens in the pursuit of happiness against the obstacles, otherwise insurmountable, which the selfishness of individuals or combinations of individuals is liable to interpose to that pursuit."[22]

Tied with Olmsted's view of republican government was his notion of civilization. Yosemite, because of its beautiful natural scenery, could further civilization by increasing mental aptitude and artistic appreciation. "If we analyze the operation of scenes of beauty upon the mind," Olmsted explained, "and consider the intimate relation of the mind upon the nervous system and the whole physical economy, the action and reaction which constantly occurs between bodily and mental conditions, the reinvigoration which results from such scenes is readily comprehended." He continued: "The power of scenery to affect men is, in a large way, proportionate to the degree of their civilization." Upon visiting Yosemite, "the whole body of the susceptibilities of civilized men and . . . their powers, are on the whole enlarged." Republican governments should not allow the benefits of civilization to accrue only to wealthy elites because the absence of "means supplied in nature for the gratification, exercise, and education of the esthetic faculties . . . ha[ve] caused the appearance of dullness and weakness and disease . . . in the mass of the subjects of kings." Indeed, free governments had a duty to promote civilization. "It was in accordance with these views of the destiny of the New World and the duty of a Republican Government," Olmsted concluded, "that Congress enacted that the Yosemite should be held, guarded and managed for the free use of the whole body of the people forever."[23]

Olmsted first read this report at a meeting of the Yosemite Valley Commission on August 9, 1865. Republican Schuyler Colfax, speaker of the House of Representatives; Samuel Bowles, editor of the *Springfield Republican*; Albert D. Richardson of the *New York Tribune*; and Republican William Bross, lieutenant governor of Illinois and cofounder of the *Chicago Tribune*, also attended. These men were visiting Yosemite valley as Olmsted's guests. Bross's, Colfax's, and Bowles's recordings of the event suggest that the report was well received. Bowles recommended that all areas with beautiful "natural curiosities" should be preserved as state parks. "The wise cession and dedication [of Yosemite] by Congress and proposed improvement by California," he commented, "furnishes an admirable example for other objects of natural curiosity and popular interest all over the Union. New York should preserve for popular use both

Niagara Falls and its neighborhood, and a generous section of the famous Adirondacks, and Maine, of her lakes and its surrounding woods." Bross's *Chicago Tribune* called Yosemite "the most wonderful valley in the world," urging readers to "visit these magnificent natural curiosities before spending their time and money to see what is not half so interesting in Europe." Colfax wrote in *Hearth and Home*, "The reality [of Yosemite,] as is so rarely the case, is, in romantic beauty and wild sublimity, far beyond the mental pictures drawn by the most vivid imagination." He proudly noted: "Towns and settlements and homes are far behind you." Olmsted had convinced several powerful Republicans of the value of public parks.[24]

The *New York Tribune*, still controlled by Horace Greeley, celebrated Olmsted's plan. Greeley's paper explained that the park, while under state control, could be "national" in nature. Olmsted's "ripe taste," the newspapers explained, "and large experience guarantee that the work will be done faithfully and judiciously. This wise legislation secures to their proper national uses incomparably the largest and grandest park and the sublimest scenery in the whole world." Olmsted had helped create the national park "idea."[25]

Yet, historians assert that after Olmsted read his report, fellow Yosemite valley commissioners Josiah Dwight Whitney, Israel Ward Raymond, and William Ashburner suppressed it, fearing that the California legislature would be hostile to Olmsted's management plan. The evidence given for this claim is that in November 1865, Whitney, Raymond, and Ashburner deemed it "inexpedient at present . . . to call for an appropriation so large as $37,000, the sum demanded by Mr. Olmsted." Thus, one Olmsted biographer insists that his sweeping brief about the power of parks "gained no currency whatever." A close examination, however, proves otherwise. Olmsted, in an 1890 article explaining his time as Yosemite Commission chairman, recalled parting amiably with the commission and the governor of California. Moreover, simply because Whitney, Raymond, and Ashburner believed that Olmsted's requested budget was too large does not mean the *entire* report was suppressed.[26]

California, in fact, adopted the majority of Olmsted's suggestions. The state legislature passed a law on April 22, 1866, accepting the federal government's removal of Yosemite valley and the Mariposa Big Tree Grove from the public domain to create a state park. In the "Act of Acceptance," the state legislature gave the commission "full power to manage and administer the grant made and the trust created by said Act of Congress" and "power to make and adopt all rules . . . for . . . improvement and preservation of said premises [Yosemite]." The statute forbade people from "cut[ting] down or carry[ing] off any wood, underwood, tree, or timber, or girdl[ing] or otherwise injur[ing] any tree or timber, or defac[ing] or injur[ing] any natural object, or sett[ing] fire to any wood or grass upon said premises, or destroy[ing] or injur[ing] any bridge or structure of any kind or other improvement that is or may be placed upon." Any person violating these edicts was subject to a $500 fine and six months in jail. These provisions followed Olmsted's request that the commission needed "to prevent a wanton or careless disregard on the part of anyone entering the Yosemite or the Grove" and that the commission "should be clothed with proper authority and given the necessary means for this purpose."[27]

Frederick Law Olmsted returned to New York City to complete Central Park in November 1865. Despite his departure, the commission aimed to implement Olmsted's program, meeting on May 21, 1866, to decide how the goals set in the *Preliminary Report* could be accomplished. The commission first resolved to settle Hutchings's and Lamon's preemption claims. The group notified the men that they must accept ten-year leases at "a nominal rent" or leave the valley. They also informed Hutchings that he must cease grazing livestock and constructing buildings without commission approval. William Irvin, head commissioner after Olmsted's departure, complained: "He [Hutchings] virtually claimed and endeavored to exercise the rights of possession over the whole valley; for as early as the summer of eighteen hundred and sixty four some gentlemen on going to Yosemite found a fence run across the lower end of the valley to keep the stock that he had running loose from escaping." Hutchings insisted "upon the right of allowing his horses, cattle, and pigs to roam at pleasure all over the valley." He refused to accept the lease plan offered by the commissioners, claiming that "the Preemption Laws of the United States were a sacred compact between the Government and Citizen." Hutchings informed the commission that "to exercise authority over my house, or my horse, or anything that I possessed . . . they had [to prove] a better [title] to either than I had got."[28]

Hutchings's refusal to surrender his land claims ignited a controversy over Yosemite State Park that lasted until 1875. He gained support from fellow California settlers and former Free-Soilers who felt that the government should promote a "civilized," agrarian society in the West. The creation of parks out of the public domain threatened the doctrines of preemption and homestead, principles needed to promote proper land use and civilization. As Republican George W. Julian stated, "colonization" of the West by settlers seeking their own land was "one of the great tidal forces of modern civilization." Given that many Free-Soilers and Republicans had fought hard for liberal preemption laws and a homestead bill against a decade of slaveholder opposition, they were not going to allow diminution of the laws' legal power for a mere park. Julian, for his part, was always wary of a new conspiracy that could threaten settler rights. In 1864 he warned that the government may "go back from the Christian dispensation of free homes and actual settlement to the . . . darkness of land speculators and public plunder." The Indianan would discover such a conspiracy when James Hutchings transformed his land claims in Yosemite into an issue of national importance.[29]

In May 1867, the Yosemite Valley Commission filed suit to eject Hutchings and Lamon after the pair refused to accept a lease or surrender their property. Hutchings responded by launching a campaign against the commission and hiring lawyers to defend his claims in court. First, he started a petition "asking for favorable legislation on behalf of the Yo-Semite Settlers." The petition, Hutchings recalled, was "numerously signed by a large majority of the prominent residents of the county of Mariposa." Hutchings also wrote letters to San Francisco and Sacramento newspapers. Despite Hutchings's wealth, the former magazine editor portrayed his fight as one between a powerful central government and poor settlers. He contended that "the great United States and the State of California were for mere grandeur going to turn them out of their modest little homes that in spite of the dangers of flood and storm, and snow and avalanche, they had hitherto so bravely held in Yosemite."[30]

While Hutchings's lawyers were arguing his case in the Northern California District Court, a Mariposa state senator introduced a bill in the California assembly granting preemption rights to Hutchings and Lamon. The senator explained that the settlers had taken up claims in "good faith" and had not even received "compensation for their improvements." Hutchings traveled to Sacramento to support the legislation. He demanded that the state surrender its "right and title to each of our quarter sections." The assembly passed the bill with little debate. The legislation gave the two men preemption rights "to the extent of one hundred and sixty acres . . . under the grant made by Congress, subject to the Ratification of Congress." Democratic governor Henry Haight then vetoed the bill, alleging "it was not competent for the Legislature of California to grant relief since Congress had made the grant and, made it inalienable." Only one California newspaper supported Haight's action. The Republican *San Francisco Bulletin* explained that since the park was "national" in nature, it should never be given away to private citizens. "When the grant was made on condition that it should never be alienated but kept open to the public who visited it," the newspaper contended, "the public meant citizens from other States as well as Californians, and therefore, Congress was legislating for all Americans in placing that restriction in the grant." Unfortunately, the *Bulletin* lamented, "the press from one end of the State to the other sympathized with [Hutchings and Lamon]." The legislature passed the bill over the governor's veto.[31]

Hutchings also achieved success in district court. Despite never having paid for the land, Hutchings claimed that his preemption claims should still be recognized. He argued that the government should recognize his property rights during the whole process of preemption, not just when the government put the land up for sale. The 1850 U.S. Supreme Court case *Lytle v. The State of Arkansas* stated that if a settler had tried to register a preemption claim in the county land office and pay the government, he acquired rights to the land regardless of whether the process was complete. The California District Court Judge agreed: "I . . . decide that when a preemptioner enters upon the unsurveyed public lands, under the sanction of a public law, and makes improvements and becomes a bona fide settler, he acquires such rights as the Government cannot divest or take from him." The judge also forbade Hutchings's ejection because of the California state legislation: "[It] would operate as a great and irreparable injury to [the] defendant to be ejected from the lands in controversy before the final action of Congress upon the Act of Legislature last mentioned." The Yosemite Valley Commission appealed the decision, urging the California Supreme Court to hear the case.[32]

Meanwhile, California's 1868 act thrust the Yosemite controversy into national politics by requesting that Congress sanction Hutchings's and Lamon's land claims. The *Bulletin* urged Congress to ignore the "foolish" action of the California legislature and "preserve a greater natural wonder for the gratuitous enjoyment of men forever." George Julian, however, took up the settlers' cause. He introduced H.R. 1118 on May 26, 1868, to "provide that the act of the California Legislature shall be . . . ratified by Congress." Hutchings and Lamon, he explained, had "expended several thousand dollars in establishing for themselves a comfortable home, while encountering for all the privations and hardships incident to a life remote from society and civilization." Democrat James A. Johnson of California agreed, explaining: "There is no authority in Congress to deprive these men of their rights as settlers, and I think it a hardship and wrong upon them to compel them to fight the whole power of the State of California to protect themselves in their rights against an act unconstitutionally passed by the Thirty-Eighth Congress." For Julian and

Johnson, the creation of public parks threatened a vision of a West settled by independent, land-owning farmers who would "civilize" the region. Hutchings and Lamon, "hardy and enterprising enough to advance ahead into the unbroken wilderness and blaze out a way for civilization to follow," should be favored above all others.[33]

The House of Representatives approved Julian's land bill with little debate on June 5, 1868. The Senate then had to decide the issue. Frederick Law Olmsted, back in New York City, leapt into action. Olmsted wrote an article for the *New York Evening Post* that incorporated many of the passages from the 1865 *Preliminary Report*. Newspapers from across America carried the *Post's* article. In the piece, Olmsted claimed that "with the early completion of the Pacific railroad there can be no doubt that the park established by act of Congress as a place of free recreation for the people of the United States and their guests forever will be resorted to from all parts of the civilized world." For Olmsted, visitor access to Yosemite provided a means of protecting the region. Shortly after the *Post* and other papers published Olmsted's article, he circulated a petition in Congress opposing the bill.[34]

Olmsted also enlisted the help of the *New York Times*, whose powerful Republican editor, Henry J. Raymond, had published many of Olmsted's writings on slavery. The *Times* urged senators to reject Julian's bill, criticizing Californians' lack of appreciation for Yosemite. "Though the Yosemite Valley and its Big Trees and its marvelous sublimity are known to everyone in the world who has read anything about the natural wonders of California," the paper explained, "they seem to be considered of very little account of Californians themselves." Instead, "a few squatters . . . had erected their shanties in the valley, and . . . laid claim to all the best lands and groves between its wonderful walls." These private claims, the paper claimed, would destroy the natural beauty of the valley. "We earnestly ask senators to examine the case; and we beg them, in the interest of all that is interesting and sublime, as well as in the interest of California itself, not to give their sanction to this attempted spoliation of the magnificent valley of the Yosemite," the *Times* concluded.[35]

Horace Greeley also entered the fray. Greeley's *New York Tribune* argued that parks reflected a high level of civilization. "Let Congress absolutely refuse to acknowledge their [Hutchings's and Lamon's] right to settle upon the land itself, and so defeat the object for which the valley was ceded to the state," the editor proclaimed. "The fact that the General Government gave the land for such a purpose and that the State accepted it, showed a high state of civilization. Barbarian or half-civilized States do not so respect great natural wonders nor propose to devote them to the enjoyment of the world." Greeley argued that the park should be put under national control. "If Californians do not see their own interests more clearly, and if they will not respect the rights of the whole country, it is the bound duty of Congress to protect us in the possession of this most splendid of Nature's gifts to the American people."[36]

Fortunately for Yosemite supporters, John Conness was still California's senator and served on the Committee on Private Land Claims. The *San Francisco Bulletin* urged Conness to use "his influence to protect it [Yosemite]." In committee, Conness convinced the rest of the senators to reject Julian's legislation. Republican Charles Sumner of Massachusetts also helped defeat the bill, presenting to the Senate a memorial from Harvard Professor Louis Agassiz "protesting against the ratification by Congress of the legislation of the California Legislature in regard to the Yosemite Valley." Furious, Julian traveled to California to see the valley for himself in 1869. The *Bulletin* hoped that the cantankerous Indianan could "be convinced of the importance of keeping it wholly a public property, so that it can never be shorn of any of its natural charms." The opposite occurred. Meeting with Hutchings and Lamon in Yosemite, Julian assured them that he would continue to "warmly espouse" their interests. Julian introduced another bill (H.R. 184) when he returned to Congress in January 1870. The legislation aimed "to confirm to J. M. Hutchings and J. C. Lamon their preemption claims to the Yosemite Valley." Unlike the previous debate, Julian received aid from the California delegation. Cornelius Cole, now a Republican senator, introduced an exact copy of Julian's measure on April 8, 1870. Cole sought to deflect devastating Democratic charges in California that the Republicans cared nothing for the land claims of average settlers. California's Democratic Party platforms of 1870 and 1871 stated, "The public lands yet left to . . . the state of California should be disposed of only to actual settlers in limited quantities, and on the most favorable terms."[37]

As politicians debated both bills, supporters and opponents of the park mobilized national opinion in support of their vision of land use. Julian argued that even areas of sublime beauty should be reserved for settlement. "I think it might have been far wiser," he proclaimed, "to carve it [Yosemite] up into small homesteads, occupied by happy families, decorated by orchards, gardens, and meadows, with a neat little post-town in their midst, and churches and school-house crowning all." William Bross's *Chicago Tribune* opposed Julian. "There is only one Yosemite Valley," the *Tribune* claimed, and "it embraces the greatest variety of sublime and beautiful natural scenery that has been found in the world." Samuel K. Bowles also warned of the consequences of private property ownership in the valley: "If the best lands in the valley are surrendered to private parties, the effect will be to enable them and their heirs to prostitute to private gain this great store-house of beauty, by giving them the power to put a tax of any amount upon all visitors, and, in every other way that private greed might suggest, to hinder the enjoyment and add to the expense of an excursion to this wonderful region."[38]

George Julian used every measure at his disposal to get the bill passed. He invited Hutchings to testify before the House and Senate Committees on Public Lands. Highlighting their status as small landowners, Hutchings informed both groups that his and Lamon's livelihood depended on the preservation of their "little mountain homes." Hutchings also started a letter campaign, writing to major newspapers in defense of his cause. "I have always considered the Preemption laws as a binding contract between the Government and its citizens," he explained in the *New York Times*. "That if a citizen found a spot anywhere on the public lands of the United States as beautiful as the garden of Eden, if it were unreserved, or in any way undisposed of, there would never be an 'if' or a 'but' of question as to its title." Hutchings treasured Yosemite valley for its natural beauty and, while in Washington, D.C., gave lectures calling for an end to logging in the area. But such feelings did not lead him to support its creation as a park. Julian concurred, explaining that "the marvelous beauty of this valley can have nothing whatever to do with the right of preemption as a legal principle."[39]

Unlike the 1868 debate, Julian faced opposition in the House of Representatives. Tennessee Republican Horace Maynard offered testimony from Yosemite commissioner Josiah Whitney in opposition to the bill. Whitney warned that if the bill passed, "the Yosemite Valley, instead of being held by the State for the benefit of the people, and 'for public use, resort, and pleasure,' as was solemnly promised, will become the property of private individuals and will be held and managed for private benefit." If Hutchings and Lamon secured 320 acres of Yosemite valley, Whitney cautioned, they would "have almost a monopoly of the valley." With the two men owning much of the land in Yosemite, any regulations issued by the Yosemite commission would be unenforceable. Ohio Republican Robert Cumming Schenck argued that Yosemite would be destroyed if Congress permitted private land ownership in the valley: "It is now proposed to make two reservations within that valley to be held as private property, with no security that these reservations may not be converted into places of resort or amusement, filled perhaps with lager beer saloons . . . or if used for agricultural purposes those reservations may be covered with corn fields, or potato patches, or cow yards. I want no such destruction of that beautiful place." Republican John Baldwin Hawley of Illinois added that "there are many beautiful and magnificent trees standing and growing in the valley. . . . Yosemite valley should be given to the State of California, to be held forever as a pleasure ground, as a place of beauty for the people of the United States."[40]

Despite spirited opposition, Julian once again succeeded in passing the bill 104 to 31, with 94 abstaining. Many congressmen believed, as California Republican Aaron Sargent explained, that "a mistake was originally made in ceding this Yosemite Valley to the State of California." After the bill's passage, Julian ordered a speech printed in the *Congressional Globe* entitled "The Yosemite Valley and the Right of Preemption." Congressmen often read speeches into the *Globe* and then published them as pamphlets, circulating the tracts to the public. Julian hoped that by disseminating this pamphlet, voters would put pressure on their representatives to sign the bill. In the document, he warned of a conspiracy to deprive settlers of preemption rights in all beautiful lands. "Our great western States and Territories are full of natural wonders, as well as beauty," the Indianan reasoned. "There are many lovely valleys and beautiful waterfalls in our country besides those of the Yosemite, and we are quite sure the law has not yet established any standard of beauty and sublimity by which the rights of preemptors on the public lands shall be determined." For Republicans like Julian, the Yosemite controversy went beyond the claims of Hutchings and Lamon. Julian and his supporters believed that proper management of land by small farmers led to freedom, union, and an improved society. Since there were many "lovely valleys and beautiful waterfalls" throughout the West, Julian worried that parks could become a new tool to prevent farmers from acquiring small plots of land.[41]

Despite Julian's best efforts, Kansas Republican Samuel Pomeroy killed both the House bill and Cornelius Cole's Senate equivalent in committee. Pomeroy deemed the issue a matter of "public policy" to be determined for the greatest good. "It was a question between forty millions of people" who deserved access to Yosemite and "two men" who wanted to keep it for themselves, he alleged. While Pomeroy had promoted small farms in Kansas before and during the Civil War, the Kansan disagreed with Julian that the creation of a nature park threatened the rights of farmers throughout the country. The *New York Times* agreed, stating that "the public good overrules; the two pioneers must yield to the general welfare, and the State of California should compensate them for their improvements and pay them for their claims, and then reserve the whole for the people forever." After the Senate had repeatedly turned down Julian's legislation, the House of Representatives refused to pass another bill. On July 3, 1870, the *New York Times* celebrated the defeat: "Mr. Julian, though a great land reformer, attempted yesterday to push through the House of Representatives a bill confirming the title of a couple of squatters to locations in the Yosemite Valley. If these persons have any rights, it would be far better for the Government to compensate them outright, in money, than to destroy what should be carefully preserved as a wondrous national park. The House properly voted down the bill by a large majority."[42]

Having failed to secure his claims in Congress, Hutchings turned to the courts. The California Supreme Court heard the appeal of the Yosemite Valley Commission in July 1871. Since Hutchings's successful district court case, the U.S. Supreme Court had narrowed the scope of preemption in *Frisbie v. Whitney*, also known as the "Suscol Ranch Case." In the case, decided in December 1869, the court proclaimed that preemptors obtained land rights only when they had registered their title and paid the government for the property. Termed by George Julian "the Dred Scott decision of the American pioneer," Suscol Ranch proved disastrous for Hutchings. Because of this decision, California judge J. Crockett decided in favor of the Yosemite commission. "Under the principles announced in *Whitney v. Frisbie*," he explained, "it may now be considered as finally settled, that if a qualified preemptioner enter upon a portion of the public domain . . . the Government may, nevertheless, at any time . . . devote the land to another purpose."[43]

Refusing to give up, Hutchings enlisted George Julian to argue his case before the U.S. Supreme Court. Julian hoped that *Frisbie v. Whitney*, like the Dred Scott Decision, would become irrelevant. Unfortunately for Julian and Hutchings, former California Supreme Court justice Stephen J. Field now sat on the bench. Field was a friend and political ally of John Conness. Before Field left for the U.S. Supreme Court, the California senator had wanted the judge to be a Yosemite commissioner. Besides these personal ties with the defendants, Field had restricted preemption rights during his tenure as a California Supreme Court justice. Given Field's hostility, Julian hoped to convince the other justices of Hutchings's claims. The Indianan began by explaining the necessity of preemption rights. "The adventurous pioneer," he professed, "is generally poor and it is fit that his enterprise should be rewarded by the privilege of purchasing the favorite spot selected by him." Julian claimed that since Hutchings had "complied with all the conditions of title which were within his power," registering for a preemption claim and building improvements, he deserved rights to the land.[44]

The tactic did not work. As historian Carl B. Swisher explains, the other Supreme Court justices deferred to Field in cases involving California's "dramatic and highly controversial and sometimes malodorous land claims." Field decided for the Yosemite commission. The justice claimed that the 1841 Preemption Act "adopted for the benefit of settlers was not intended to deprive Congress of the power . . . to appropriate them [government lands] to any public use." This construction of preemption, Field continued, "preserves a wise control in the government over the public lands, and prevents a general spoliation of them under the pretense of intended settlement and pre-emption." He concluded by criticizing California's 1868 act giving Hutchings and Lamon land titles in Yosemite valley, calling it a "perversion of the trust solemnly accepted." As historian Jen A. Huntley brilliantly notes, "Preemption reflected the antebellum faith in the individual 'yeoman farmer' as the primary agent to settle distant lands. However, Field's language in the Hutchings decision illustrated the postwar shift from this older view." For Field and Yosemite supporters, the best use for Yosemite was not yeomen farming. They believed that a nature park produced the same ideals—union and civilization—that Julian and the opponents sought. Defeated in court and Congress, Hutchings returned to his home in 1873 and awaited the Yosemite commission's next move.[45]

Hutchings v. Low and the subsequent state mismanagement of Yosemite prompted the formation of a national park system instead of one predicated on state control. After the establishment of Yosemite, observers viewed the legislation as an important precedent for the creation of future state parks. Samuel Bowles's 1865 *Across the Continent* argued that parks like Yosemite could be formed nationwide. Frederick Law Olmsted noted to his father in the summer of 1865 that Yosemite was by "far the noblest park or pleasure ground in the world," an example for future states to follow. Yet, due to the controversy surrounding Hutchings's land claims, changes took place in the Yosemite environment that convinced politicians that future parks needed to be under national control. When white Americans "discovered" Yellowstone in the late 1860s, senate Republicans argued that it should be designated as a national park. Horace Greeley had foreshadowed such a plan when he called for Congress to take control of Yosemite valley to save it from Hutchings's land claims.[46]

Arguments about the need for federal administration of large nature parks took place after the federal government's expansion during the Civil War and Reconstruction. Between 1861 and 1872, the date of Yellowstone's creation, the United States passed several measures transferring authority from state governments and citizens to the federal government. During the war, the United State nationalized its currency, freed 4 million people previously considered protected property, revoked the right of habeas corpus for suspected rebel sympathizers, created a banking system, incurred a national debt, provided state aid for railroad and agricultural college construction, and established the Freedmen's Bureau (a whole new federal bureaucracy). All of these measures originated in the Republican Party. After the war, many Republicans felt that the federal government could solve problems when state governments failed. During Reconstruction, Republicans continued to use central state power. In 1866 the Civil Rights Act nullified black codes passed by southern state governments. The Fourteenth Amendment mandated that each state provide "equal protection of laws" for its citizens. The Reconstruction Acts of 1867 divided the ten unreconstructed states into military districts, subjecting them to the authority of Congress. The Fifteenth Amendment, ratified on February 3, 1870, prohibited states from denying the right to vote based on "race, color, or previous condition of servitude." The Ku Klux Klan Act of April 1871, passed less than a year before the Yellowstone Park Act, brought civil rights crimes committed by individuals under the purview of the federal government. All of these measures would have been unthinkable in antebellum America.[47]

James Hutchings's actions following his unsuccessful appeals to Congress and the Supreme Court convinced Republicans that state management of Yosemite had failed. These politicians believed that the national government would do a better job administering nature parks than the states. Even though the Yosemite commission achieved victory with Justice Field's decision, the board was unable to eject Hutchings and impose Olmsted's program. The Yosemite commissioners realized that "during the period which intervened between [1864] and [1873]," when the commission tried to eject Hutchings once more, "he had succeeded in manufacturing a large amount of public sympathy" and gained powerful friends in the state assembly. Therefore, the commission was "desirous to give him every opportunity of either applying for a lease, or else disposing his business and property in the most advantageous manner." The group submitted a report to the California assembly recommending a "special appropriation for the purpose of settling with all those parties who held claims in the Yosemite." The assembly agreed to pay Hutchings, Lamon, and one other settler a total of $60,000 in compensation. Head commissioner William Irvin also offered Hutchings and Lamon ten-year leases on their property.[48]

Stubborn, Hutchings refused and, according to Irvin, claimed "his property to be worth much more." After a year, however, Hutchings realized he could not receive more money from the legislature and agreed to the sum offered. California paid Hutchings $24,000 and Lamon $12,000 for their land claims. In November 1874, Hutchings met with the Yosemite commission to negotiate a lease on his former property. At the meeting, Hutchings changed his mind again, asserting that "he had been forced to take much less than the property was worth" and refusing to relinquish his land. Furious, the commission announced in Mariposa, Sonora, and San Francisco newspapers that they would forcibly remove the stubborn man. The group selected George W. Coulter, a commission member, as the new lessee of Hutchings's property. Coulter wanted to build a toll road to Yosemite valley and operate the former magazine editor's hotel for profit. Hearing the news, Hutchings once again leapt into action. He persuaded the attorney general of California to block the commission's order. The attorney general accused the commission of "fraud" and corruption in its handling of Hutchings's lease. Though the commission eventually succeeded in ejecting Hutchings from his old property in 1875, the triumph was short-lived. In 1880 a new board of Yosemite commissioners under state pressure decided to appoint Hutchings the "Guardian of Yosemite Valley."[49]

While there is no doubt that Hutchings cared deeply about the landscape, his agitation prevented the Yosemite commission from taking control of Yosemite valley and the Mariposa Big Tree Grove until 1875. Travelers to Yosemite witnessed degradation of the area from the lack of state oversight. In 1871 the *New York Times* printed a story from the *San Francisco Chronicle* explaining how "grazers" used Yosemite and the Hetch Hetchy valley "for summer-sheep pasturage." Hutchings's "horses, cattle and pigs" also remained in Yosemite to provide his guests with food and transportation. The livestock changed the way the valley appeared. Commissioner Josiah Whitney complained of "wanton damage to trees, shrubs and flowers" from the animals. Sheep cropped the flowers and grasses closely to the ground. They also carved "conspicuous" trails throughout Yosemite. John Muir, a Scottish naturalist who arrived in 1868 to work for Hutchings, noted that "most of the meadows were fenced for hay fields or for the confinement of domestic animals." He observed that "each night some three hundred horses were let loose to graze and trample the remaining vegetation out of existence. The only flowers were those on inaccessible ledges and recessed high on the walls."[50]

Changes also occurred because of increased visitation. The completion of the transcontinental railroad in 1869 created easier access to California and Yosemite. In 1868, 623 people visited the state park. In 1873, 2,530 people went to the area. Entrepreneurs, free from restriction, moved to profit from these tourists. Hutchings constructed numerous improvements to his hotel, using a water-powered sawmill to cut boards from the valley's pines and cedars. Travel writer Grace Greenwood (Sarah Jane Lippincott) reported seeing the sawmill. Greenwood's party stopped "for a little chat with the workmen we found grappling the great logs and putting them through" the mill. The workers told her of the "law prohibiting the felling of live trees in the valley." Greenwood, however, noticed that the trees "looked singularly sound and plump as though they had died a sudden death, not, I am sure, from heart disease." One of the workers explained: "I think the pines, at least . . . might all be cut down; they are no ornament to the valley."[51]

Other people established hotels, roads, and trails. J. C. Smith founded "The Cosmopolitan" in 1870, where visitors could experience "baths, drinks, and various unexpected comforts." James McCauley built a toll trail to Glacier Point from 1871 to 1872. He also started the first "firefall," pouring hot coals and ashes off the face of the point. The *New York Times* feared that these changes spelled "the doom of Yosemite." The paper warned: "The once majestic wilderness will be converted into a gigantic beer-garden, and in place of flowers will grow only confused, pint pots and defective whisky bottles. . . . The enterprising drug-dealer will next cover every inch of rock surface with gigantic invitations to the general public to purchase remedies for all possible diseases, and the humiliation of Yosemite will be completed by the pitching of the tents of peripatetic circuses." The *San Francisco Bulletin* echoed the *Times*'s concerns. Californians, the *Bulletin* urged, "ought to guard their finest places of resort from the exorbitant and worrying toll system that prevails at the East and in Europe—a system which puts a tax on natural beauty, on sun and air and water, and bothers the tourist with inconvenient and impertinent guidance where none is needed."[52]

As newspapers reported outrage over the improper use of Yosemite, settlers in Montana thought they had discovered a rival beauty near the Yellowstone River. If the reports of "thermal springs that leap from 50 to 200 feet into the air are true," the *San Francisco Bulletin* lamented,

"Montana will prove a serious competitor to California, with her Big Trees [and] Yosemite." Henry Washburn, surveyor general of the Montana Territory, and Nathaniel Langford, internal revenue collector for the territory, began an expedition to explore the area in 1870. To help fund the trip, Langford met with Jay Cooke of the Northern Pacific Railroad to "convince him that the wonders of Yellowstone could be a useful device for promoting the line." Frederick Billings, who now controlled a one-eighth interest in the Northern Pacific, believed that the area—like Yosemite—could be another one of "God's Greatest Creations." While there is no evidence that Billings urged Cooke to press for a park, it is probable that Billings related to Cooke the success of tourism at Yosemite. Cooke and the Northern Pacific funded the expedition to Yellowstone and a lecture series by Nathaniel Langford advertising the region.[53]

On October 27, 1871, director of the U.S. Geological Survey Ferdinand Hayden received a note from A. B. Nettleton, an agent of the Northern Pacific Railroad, recommending that "Congress pass a bill reserving the Great Geyser Basin as a public park forever—just as it has reserved that far inferior wonder—the Yosemite Valley and big trees." Hayden, the Northern Pacific Railroad, and the members of the 1870 Washburn expedition lobbied for the creation of a park. They enjoyed the benefit of close political connections. A member of the Washburn expedition, Walter Trumbull, was the son of Republican senator Lyman Trumbull. Walter urged his father to support the creation of Yellowstone Park. Kansas senator Samuel Pomeroy, who had repeatedly killed George Julian's bill in the Senate, also supported the park's formation. He introduced a bill in December 1871 that set aside Yellowstone as a national park and protected it "from preemptions or homestead claims."[54]

The Senate debated Pomeroy's bill on January 23, 1872. The Kansan explained that Yellowstone was a "great natural curiosity" full of "great geysers . . . water-spouts, and hot springs." He thought it best "to consecrate and set apart this great place of national resort for the purposes of public enjoyment" as a national park. *Hutchings v. Low*, Pomeroy believed, gave him legal justification for such a plan. "We found when we set apart the Yosemite valley that there were one or two persons who had made claims there," the senator explained. "[I]t has finally gone to the Supreme Court to decide whether persons who settle on unsurveyed lands before the Government takes possession of them by any special act of Congress have rights as against the Government. The court has held that settlers on unsurveyed lands have no rights as against the Government." With this decision, Pomeroy noted, "the Government can make an appropriation of any unsurveyed lands, notwithstanding [any] settlers [that] may be upon them." If *Hutchings v. Low* had been decided in favor of Hutchings, Pomeroy would not have been able to introduce his bill; the government would have had to recognize preemption claims in Yellowstone. H. R. Horr, who was residing near Mammoth Hot Springs prior to the Senate debate, demanded recognition of his preemption claims after hearing about the possibility of an "act laying off a portion of the Yellowstone for the purposes of a National Park."[55]

Debate on the Yellowstone bill continued on January 30. Cornelius Cole opposed the legislation, arguing that settlers should have control over the area. "The geysers will remain no matter where the ownership of the land may be and I do not know why settlers should be excluded from a tract of land forty miles square," he argued. "I cannot see how the natural curiosities can be interfered with if settlers are allowed to approach them." Lyman Trumbull responded by attacking California's management of Yosemite State Park: "I think our experience with the wonderful natural curiosity [Yosemite] . . . in the senator's own State, should admonish us of the propriety of passing such a bill as this." Yosemite's failure under state control had convinced Trumbull of the need for a federal park. He alleged: "[T]he Yosemite Valley . . . we have undertaken to reserve, but there is a dispute about it. Now, before there is any dispute as to this wonderful country, I hope we shall except it from the general disposition of the public lands and reserve it to the Government." With the backing of Trumbull, the bill passed in the Senate.[56]

The House debate also reflected the impetus for federal control. Republican congressman Henry Laurens Dawes of Massachusetts commented that the Yellowstone bill

[f]ollows the analogy of the bill passed by Congress six or eight years ago, setting apart the Yosemite valley and the "big tree country" for the public park, with this difference: that that bill granted to the State of California the jurisdiction over that land beyond the control of the United States. This bill reserves the control over the land, and preserves the control over it to the United States, so that at any time when it shall appear that it will be better to devote it to any other purpose it will be perfectly within the control of the United States to do it.

Dawes explained that the federal government could better "preserve that country [Yellowstone] from depredations" than territorial or state governments. The bill, he continued, "will infringe upon no vested rights, the title to it will still remain in the United States, different from the case of Yosemite valley, where it now requires the coordinate legislative action of Congress and the State of California to interfere with the title." The Yellowstone bill cleared the House by a vote of 115 to 65, with 60 abstaining. On March 5, 1872, President Ulysses S. Grant signed it.[57]

The *New York Times* believed that the creation of Yellowstone National Park provided an example for the "salvation" of Yosemite. The paper argued that Yosemite should be converted from a state park to a national park. "There is yet a way by which the Yosemite can be saved," the *Times* explained. "Congress is already considering the expediency of preserving the wonderful Yellowstone region from profanation, by converting it into a national park. Every argument in favor of this scheme will apply with equal force to the Yosemite Valley." If the government transformed Yosemite into a national park, the valley would "remain a place which we can proudly show to the benighted European as proof of what nature—under a republican form of government—can accomplish in the great West." A majority of Republicans had broken with the free-soil beliefs of George Julian and Cornelius Cole. Cole and Julian thought that the creation of nature parks threatened homestead and preemption laws—laws that had been achieved after decades of slaveholder opposition. Republicans such as Frederick Law Olmsted, Lyman Trumbull, and Samuel Pomeroy, however, believed that nature parks showcased America's republican government—a government, they believed, saved during the Civil War.[58]

SEEKING PEACE IN THE SOUTH AND WEST

My Policy is Peace. When I said, "Let us have peace," I meant it. I want peace on the Plains as everywhere else. —Ulysses S. Grant

Union victory in the Civil War presented the Republican Party with an unprecedented opportunity to shape the nation as it pleased. When John Wilkes Booth assassinated Abraham Lincoln in April 1865, the party enjoyed a commanding majority in both the House of Representatives and the U.S. Senate. In the proceeding years, Republicans debated answers to the tricky questions posed by the Confederacy's surrender. Would Confederate officers and the leaders of secession be punished for treason? On what terms would seceded states rejoin the Union? What would happen to the slaves who secured freedom during the war? In addition to these questions regarding the South, Americans contemplated the future of the West. In answering, Republicans turned to the agrarian ideology cultivated during a decade of sectional strife and four years of war. The best citizens, Republicans believed, were small farmers because they used the soil wisely, were loyal to the Union, and advanced quickly to higher levels of civilization. In the 1850s, however, "citizens" meant free white men. Due to the revolutionary changes brought by the war, Republicans believed that citizenship should expand to include African Americans and Indians. Colonization, the "solution" to emancipation once offered by Abraham Lincoln and Hinton Helper, seemed unviable to Republicans. The violent extermination of Indian peoples—seen at the 1864 Sand Creek Massacre, where over 100 Cheyennes and Arapahos died at the hands of Colorado militia—appeared repulsive to some.

Yet, citizenship for both African Americans and Indians hinged upon their acceptance of Anglo-American culture, religion, and—the subject of this chapter—land-use ideals. Republicans believed that once given small plots of land, former slaves and Indians could learn the latest methods of soil conservation from government schools. By using techniques that conserved the soil, people could stay on the same tract of land for many years, building communities that were loyal to the Union. Northern policy makers did not want to industrialize the South and the West. Instead, linking proper land use with a clean environment and a stable social structure, they intended to promote farming communities and strengthen the yeomanry that provided the foundation for republican government. Republicans ignored alternative visions of "civilization" and government, especially those voiced by Indians.

People usually see little connection between the South and the West during Reconstruction, traditionally defined as the years between 1863 and 1877. What, after all, links emancipation, the Freedmen's Bureau, and the federal occupation of the South with the "Peace Policy" promoted by Ulysses S. Grant? Elliott West, the great historian of the American West, presents an answer in his book *The Last Indian War: The Nez Perce Story.* West argues that the period is better termed "the Greater Reconstruction" because "far western expansion and the Civil War . . . raised similar issues." One of the key issues was how to incorporate Indian peoples, southern whites, and freed blacks into the nation after the Civil War. West notes that "Washington's answers for East and West were much the same. Freedpeople and Indians would ultimately be citizens. They would be ushered in, assimilated, via strikingly similar programs of Christian mission, common school education, and integration into the economy of agriculture and the manual arts." The main contention of this chapter is that Republicans had an environmental view of citizenship. Proper citizens, besides becoming Christian and adopting Victorian values, farmed the soil in ways deemed by white Americans to be responsible. African Americans, corresponding to their prewar desires for land, bought into the program. The violent opposition of southern whites, however, blocked land redistribution efforts in the South. Many Indians did not embrace the Republican view of citizenship, wanting to maintain a hunting-and-gathering lifestyle deemed "barbaric" by most whites. Yet, since forcing tribes to adopt farming aligned with the views of many western whites, who stood to gain land when the federal government compelled Indians to live on smaller plots, "reconstruction" continued in the West, culminating in Henry L. Dawes's allotment act of 1887.[1]

Reconstruction began in December 1863 after the United States gained control of most of Tennessee, Arkansas, and Louisiana. President Abraham Lincoln took command of the process, issuing a "Proclamation of Amnesty and Reconstruction" offering full pardons and restoration of all property except slaves to any rebel who would swear allegiance to the United States and recognize all legislative and executive orders regarding slavery. When 10 percent of the 1860 voting population accepted these terms, citizens could establish a state government recognized by the United States. These governments would have to accept emancipation in areas where the proclamation applied, but Lincoln only gave limited support for black suffrage in the affected states. He advised Louisiana's provisional governor in early 1864, "I barely suggest for your private consideration, whether some of the colored people be let in—as for instance, the very intelligent and especially those who have fought gallantly in our ranks." Early Reconstruction policy did not promote black citizenship or deal with Indian tribes; the focus, instead, was on the war. Lincoln believed that a less-burdensome Reconstruction would end the conflict sooner, giving Confederates less to fight for. Maintaining the loyalty of strategically critical border states such as Kentucky and Maryland—both hostile to any radical social change—was also crucial. Furthermore, he still believed that there was significant white Unionist sentiment in the South, sentiment that only needed encouragement to reassert itself. Finally, Lincoln had to consider the opinions of Democrats, who made up just under half of the northern population and, by and large, were hostile to emancipation.[2]

Republicans in Congress also tried to form southern Reconstruction policy. Motivated by different concerns than the president, congressional Republicans—especially Radicals such as Charles Sumner, George Julian, Samuel Pomeroy, Benjamin Wade, and Thaddeus Stevens—believed that the United States should smash the slaveholding oligarchy and remake the South in the image of the North's farming communities. Observing the long history of legislative defeats at the hands of southern Democrats, they also believed that the Republicans must become a national party with freed slaves and southern Unionists forming a southern wing. George Julian asserted that the North should "convert the rebel States into conquered provinces, remanding them to the status of mere Territories," which would allow Congress to implement sweeping social change. Though Lincoln was closer to Julian's sentiments than he was to conservative Democrats, his primary objective was winning the war. Radicals, as Julian noted, not only wanted to win the war but also aimed to transform southern society.[3]

Congressional Republicans flexed their power by refusing to seat the delegates elected by the Arkansas and Louisiana governments under Lincoln's plan. Ohio Radical Benjamin Wade and Maryland Unionist Henry

Winter Davis offered an alternative on July 2, 1864. This plan stipulated that only people who took a so-called Ironclad Oath of allegiance to the federal government could serve in constitutional conventions forming new state governments. The oath required people to swear that they had *never* supported the Confederacy and had always been loyal to the Union. In 1864 there was no chance that the southern states could fulfill this charge. Congress aimed to delay the creation of Reconstruction policy until the end of the war, when the focus would be on remaking southern society instead of winning the military struggle. Lincoln responded by pocket vetoing the legislation, citing concerns that the plan would undermine Louisiana's new government. Wade and Davis penned a manifesto on August 5, 1864, accusing Lincoln of perpetrating a "studied outrage on the legislative authority of the people."[4]

In the summer of 1864, congressional rebellion against the president reached a fever pitch. Not all of the anger had to do with Reconstruction; Republicans feared that military failures doomed Lincoln's reelection chances. They moved to replace him with a more-radical candidate: Salmon Chase, the treasury secretary. Samuel Pomeroy, future sponsor of the Yellowstone Park legislation, led the effort. "Mr. Lincoln seems to be joyful in our adversity!!!" Pomeroy complained to his close friend Anna E. Dickinson, "[a]nd approaches some of us who urged him 'against his own better judgment' as he says, to deploy negroes to help 'fight our battles'!!!! O. My God! When will he learn that this is a war for mankind[?]" The Kansan issued a "circular" outlining the reasons the Republicans should drop Lincoln. If Lincoln were reelected, Pomeroy warned, "his manifest tendency toward compromises and temporary expedients will become stronger during a second term . . . and the cause of human liberty and the dignity and honor of the nation, suffer proportionately." Pomeroy attacked Lincoln for failing to act against slavery earlier. He stated in a congressional speech: "Slavery committed the overt acts of rebellion and treason. . . . [W]hat could have been clearer than the *cause of the rebellion*? What easier than then and there to have pronounced upon the means for its overthrow? But how slow [the administration] was to learn the lesson of events, to comprehend the magnitude of the struggle."[5]

Salmon Chase's platform provided a glimpse into the Radical goals for Reconstruction. Pomeroy, in a speech promoting Chase, demanded "amendments to the Federal Constitution as shall prohibit slavery wherever the flag of the Union floats, with suitable encouragement to a general system of education, in order that suffrage shall be *intelligent* as well as *free*, thus furnishing additional guarantee for the perpetuity of our liberties." The call for education followed the theory that freed people could be assimilated into the country through public schools. Pomeroy also urged "the confiscation of the property of leading rebels, and inauguration of republican governments in all the districts of rebellion" to ensure a more equitable distribution of land in the South. The program also included a plan for the West. Pomeroy stated the need for "the extension of suitable aid for the construction of a railway across the continent, for the better union of the Atlantic and Pacific States, and their easier defense against possible foreign enemies." If America accomplished these tasks, the nation would be redeemed in the eyes of the world. "To close the war in this way," Pomeroy concluded, "will be most gratifying to mankind." Congressional Radicals wanted to impose their prewar vision of a prosperous society where families farmed small plots of land and accessed the national market through railroads throughout both the South and the West.[6]

Union victories at Atlanta and in the Shenandoah valley revived Lincoln's election fortunes and doomed Radical plans to replace the president with his own treasury secretary. In the first months of 1865, moreover, the Radicals felt that the sixteenth president was on their side. German emigrant and Radical Republican Carl Schurz recalled: "Had he lived, he would have as ardently wished to stop bloodshed and to reunite all the States, as he ever did. But is it to be supposed for a moment that, seeing the later master class in the South . . . intent upon subjecting the freedmen again to a system very much akin to slavery, Lincoln would have consented to abandon those freedmen to the mercies of the master class?" On January 31, 1865, the House, by a vote of 119 to 65, passed the Thirteenth Amendment abolishing slavery. Lincoln supported the legislation and quickly passed it on to the states.[7]

Abraham Lincoln also supported the creation of the Freedmen's Bureau, an entirely new government agency, in March 1865. First advocated by northern philanthropists in the American Freedmen's Inquiry Commission, the bureau promoted education, rebuilding, and poverty relief in the South. The bureau, though never intended to be a permanent department, also recognized freedmen as citizens with civil rights. Support for the bureau increased in Congress because of changing racial attitudes, a belief that the benefits of "civilization" needed to be extended southward, and a persistent notion that land redistribution could create a southern yeomanry. Massachusetts Republican congressman Charles Dawes Eliot relayed a message from the northern philanthropists on February 2, 1865, explaining that "we have found the freedman easy to manage, beyond even our best hopes; willing and able to fight as a soldier; willing and able to work, as a laborer; willing and able to learn as a pupil; docile, patient, affectionate, grateful." The groups demanded "the immediate creation of a bureau of emancipation, charged with the study of plans and the execution of measures for easing, guiding, and in every way judiciously and humanely aiding the passage of our emancipated" into freedom. This bureau could then apply "the sound canon of civilization"—education—"to the freedmen."[8]

Another function of the organization was to lease "confiscated and abandoned lands" to freedmen, giving them the option to buy forty acres at the end of three years. As Charles Sumner explained, "The freedmen for weary generations have fertilized these lands with their sweat. The time has come when they should enjoy the results of their labor at least for a few months." Such redistribution, Justin Morrill of Vermont believed, was the only means to provide "personal protection" and "personal security" for freedmen's rights. Freedmen sympathizer Lydia Maria Child wrote to George Julian: "The old Satanic fire will long remain in the ashes of the rebellion. If those tyrannical oligarchs have their land monopoly restored, they will trample on the blacks and the poor whites, as of old. Those mammoth plantations ought to be divided into small farms, and an allotted number of acres given to the soldiers, white and black." The consensus seemed clear. With Union victory in the war, the Republicans wanted to punish Confederates and incorporate southern blacks into the nation by offering the freedmen small farms.[9]

Lincoln's assassination on April 15, 1865, halted the Radicals' plans. At first, many believed that Andrew Johnson, Lincoln's successor, would follow the course laid out by Congress. Carl Schurz, for instance, believed Johnson's declaration that "the principal traitors should be hanged and the rest at least impoverished" to mean that large plantations would be "taken from them and sold in small parcels to farmers." George Julian was more on target when he noted that Johnson "was, at heart, as decided a hater of the negro and of everything savoring of abolitionism, as the rebels from whom he had separated." Schurz was surprised on May 29, 1865, when Johnson issued two executive proclamations outlining a new Reconstruction policy. The first proclamation restored property rights to all those who pledged loyalty to the Union and acquiescence in emancipation. High-ranking Confederate officials, men who had sworn oaths of loyalty to the United States before the war, and owners of property valued at over $20,000 dollars had to apply to Johnson individually for pardons. The second proclamation presented a Reconstruction plan for North Carolina. Johnson appointed William W. Holden, a wartime Unionist, as governor of the state and asked him to frame a new constitution that included the voting qualifications from the prewar constitution. This action meant that southern blacks would have no voting rights. Johnson's first proclamation, meanwhile, undercut the ability of the Freedmen's Bureau to lease "confiscated" land to former slaves because the lands now had to be given back to pardoned Confederates. Johnson did not share the view of Republican Radicals like Schurz and Julian that the South should be a region of small farms tended by black and white yeomen. Instead, Johnson wanted the South to revert to the social structure of the 1850s.[10]

Soldiers, journalists, politicians, judges, and presidential envoys visited the South in the months after the announcement of Johnson's policy to determine its effects on the region. The observations of these travelers were critical in sparking congressional opposition to Johnson and forming new Reconstruction plans. Republican visitors argued that the former Confederacy could only be reincorporated into the Union if the region adopted northern land-use ideals. They called for the federal government to break up the large plantations of slave owners and give the land to those men who remained loyal: former slaves and white Unionists. By giving small farms to black men, Confederates could be prevented from returning to power. By owning land, former slaves could become independent of southern whites, allowing them to better defend their political rights. While many Radicals genuinely believed in equal political rights for freed slaves, they realized that many of their constituents in the North did not. Publicly, they deemed black citizenship and land redistribution as punishments for rebels, steps toward reunion, and means to avoid a lengthy occupation. If former slaves had political power and owned land, Republicans believed, they could defend themselves without a lengthy U.S. Army presence in the South. The soil itself would also become more productive if tended by small farmers.

Securing union was the most important objective during Reconstruction. Observers tied union to land-use patterns, believing that wealthy landowners were responsible for secession. Soldiers on occupation duty often derided planters as the "chivalry." Matthew Woodruff, a Democrat serving in a Missouri Union infantry regiment, served in the South from June to December 1865. Woodruff hated southern slaveholders. In New Orleans, he observed: "The pomp & pride of southern chivalry has no charms for me." Unfortunately, the "chivalry" had yet to be crushed. In October 1865, Woodruff noted: "Go where you will & you will hear barefaced Trason uttered in the strongest terms, even the Public Press does not hesitate to pitch its vile rebukes right into the teeth of the authorities." The election in

November restored many rebels to power, sending Woodruff into a rage, leading him to support giving power to southern loyalists. "There is not 9 out of 10 of these so called 'Whiped' traitors," Woodruff fumed, "that I would trust until I saw the rope applied to their Necks, then I would only have faith in the quality of the rope." Yet, he continued, "here we see them evry [*sic*] day restored to all their former rights & privileges, put in office and other responsible positions in the North as well as South where the true patriot and loveing defender of his country and the only self deserving men of our country, is refused."[11]

John Richard Dennett, a correspondent for the *Nation*, also visited the South in the summer of 1865. The *Nation*, whose backers included Frederick Law Olmsted and abolitionist Wendell Phillips Garrison (the son of William Lloyd Garrison), had a decidedly radical agenda. The magazine strived to report on "the progress made by the colored population in acquiring the habits and desires of civilized life," "to promote 'true democratic principles' in government and in society," and to support "popular education." Dennett told readers that only "secessionists" believed that "the Negro was not fit to vote." He found lazy *whites* "loafing about the streets, without any ostensible means of making a living." To Dennett, black freedmen had a better chance of becoming ideal yeomen. "It is to the custom of the country," he elaborated, "which throws all work upon the Negroes, that the general idleness must in great part be attributed." The poorest whites, Dennett implied, were lower in civilization than black people. He commented on two women who "both seemed the poorest of whites, dirty and wretched to the last degree," concluding that "[i]t would have been useless, I suppose, to counsel [them] to cleanliness or industry or decency of manners and morals." The journalist contrasted these scenes to a political gathering of "colored citizens" at the "African Methodist church" in Raleigh, North Carolina. The well-dressed and eloquent men discussed their desire for "education for our children" and to "to have all the oppressive laws which make unjust discrimination on account of race or color wiped from the statutes of the State." Above them was a "large plaster bust of Lincoln" with the words "with malice toward none, with charity for all, with firmness in the right" inscribed. Compared to the "unintelligent, as well as uneducated; narrow-minded men" in control of the government, these loyal black people deserved the vote.[12]

Sidney Andrews, a correspondent for the more-moderate *Boston Advertiser* and *Chicago Tribune*, reported on conditions in North Carolina, South Carolina, and Georgia in the fall of 1865. Andrews was shocked at the "prevalent indifference to the negro's fate and life. It is a sad, but solemn fact, that three fourths of the native whites consider him a nuisance, and would gladly be rid of his presence, even at the expense of his existence." Former rebels were threatening to regain control of the region and reestablish what Andrews called an "aristocracy." South Carolina was, he explained, "republican in name, but not in fact; while the whole under-current of her society set toward monarchical institutions. Everybody, even now dreads popular elections." Andrews complained that the Johnson-appointed administration "was not a republican form of government" and the state "will not soon be, a republican community."[13]

Evidence for these assertions came from Andrews's observation of the state legislature's proceedings. One delegate, a Mr. L. W. R. Blair, wanted to "enact such laws as are needful to prevent negroes and persons of color from engaging in any business or pursuit but such as involves manual labor." The provisional governor attacked congressional leaders for forgetting "that this is a white man's government, and intended for white men only; and that the Supreme Court of the United States has decided that the negro is not an American citizen under the Federal Constitution." Andrews concluded that the group had "no special love for the Union" and planned to "repeal" rather than "annul" the state secession ordinance, thus surreptitiously affirming secession. Just like Dennett, Andrews found black men to be ideal material for a southern yeomanry. While unrepentant rebels affirmed the right to secede and inveighed against "black Republicans," Andrews found a freedmen's "convention" in North Carolina appealing. The freed slaves wanted to "live soberly and honestly, work faithfully and industriously, save money and buy a few acres of land . . . and educate themselves and their children." Compared to the former secessionists, the freedmen "presented their claims with more dignity" and deserved to have a voice in the new state government. The stated aims of the freemen to "buy a few acres of land" and "live soberly and honestly" seemed to be in lockstep with the Republican ideal of citizenship.[14]

J. T. Trowbridge also traveled south in the summer of 1865 to write a book about conditions in the region. Even in West Virginia, Trowbridge was amazed at the continued strength of rebel sentiment. "The war-feeling here is like a burning bush with a wet blanket wrapped around it," he observed. "[L]ooked at from the outside, the fire seems quenched. But just peep under the blanket, and there it is, all alive, and eating, eating in." After moving into northern Virginia, Trowbridge found the rebel sentiment stronger. Disunion—"the serpent of a barbarous despotism"—still threatened the republic. Slavery, Trowbridge believed, caused disunion and barbaric behavior. The burning of Richmond, "like [the] assassination of Lincoln, like the systematic murder of Union prisoners at Andersonville and elsewhere, —like these and countless other barbarous acts which have branded the Rebel cause with infamy, —this too was inspired by the spirit of slavery, and performed in the interest of slavery. That spirit, destructive of liberty and law . . . was the father of the rebellion." Trowbridge believed that empowering former slaves and white Unionists would extinguish the smoldering embers of secession. In place of secessionists, he wrote, "we may for some years hope to see a very different class of men . . . before kept aloof from political life, men new to the Congressional arena, and therefore more susceptible to the regenerating influence of national ideas and institutions." Black people were "far better prepared to have a hand in making the laws by which they are to be governed, than the whites are to make those laws for them."[15]

Connecting wise land use with loyalty to the Union, visitors to the South offered suggestions on how to improve farming, hoping to impose a northern ideal of agriculture on the region. Similar to Frederick Law Olmsted and the soldiers cited in chapter 3, they believed that slavery had exhausted the soil. Redistributing large plantations to yeomen farmers—black and white—and diversifying crop production would bring agricultural prosperity to the region and encourage loyal sentiments. J. T. Trowbridge believed that slavery had poisoned the land. Trowbridge had a "bright young colored girl" guide his party "to the spot where John Brown's gallows stood": "She led us into the wilderness of weeds . . . the country all around us lay utterly desolate, without enclosures, and without cultivation." Even the bountiful Shenandoah valley, if it "had not been the best part of Virginia . . . would long ago have been spoiled by the ruinous system of agriculture in use here." The decrepit built environment also seemed to reflect the South's low level of civilization. "[W]orse roads are not often seen in a civilized country," Trowbridge wrote of Manassas Junction, Virginia. "It makes me mad to see people drive over and around these bad places . . . and never think of mending 'em! A little work with a shovel would save no end of lost time, and wear and tear, and broken wagons; but it's never done." He concluded: "In travelling through the South one sees many plantations ruined for some years to come by improper cultivation."[16]

Virginia seemed to epitomize everything that was wrong agriculturally with the former "great Slave Empire." At Richmond, Trowbridge "passed amid the same desolate scenes which I had everywhere observed since I set foot upon the soil of Virginia, —old fields and undergrowths, with signs of human life so feeble and so few, that one began to wonder where the country population of the Old Dominion was to be found." Trowbridge was amazed "at the petty and shiftless system of farming [he] witnessed around the city." He continued with a direct comparison between the farms of the North and the South. "All the region between Fredericksburg and Richmond," Trowbridge wrote, "seems not only uninhabited now, but always to have been so, —at least to the eye familiar with New England farms and villages . . . large and fertile Virginia, with eight times the area of Massachusetts, scarcely, equals in population that barren little State." The end result, he concluded, was "that where Southern State pride sees prosperous settlements, the travelling Yankee discovers little more than uncultivated wastes." Near Chancellorsville, Trowbridge reported one conversation with a white southern Unionist describing agriculture under slavery. "This is mighty good land," the man told him, "clay bottom; holds manure jest like a chany bowl does water. But the rich ones jest scratched over a little on't with their slave labor, and let the rest go." The man continued: "What was the result? Young men would go off to the West, if they was enterpris'n and leave them that wa'n't enterpris'n hyer to home. Then as the old heads died off, the farms would run down."[17]

That Unionist, Trowbridge alleged, knew the solution to Virginia's agricultural problems. "The way it generally is," the man described, "a few own too much and the rest own noth'n'. I know hundreds of thousands of acres of land put to no use, which, if it was cut up into little farms, would make the country look thrifty." Already, Trowbridge celebrated, "Northern men and northern methods are coming into [the Shenandoah] Valley as sure as water runs down-hill. It is the greatest corn, wheat, and grass country in the world." Near Richmond, he noted that the Freedmen's Bureau was supporting small farmers, helping transform Virginia agriculture. "To the small farmers about the city" the bureau issued "ploughs, spades, shovels, and other much needed implements—for the war had beaten pitchforks into bayonets." Trowbridge met a man from New Jersey who was introducing free labor and multicrop agriculture. The farmer commented, "I found the land worn out, like nearly all the land in the country. The way Virginia folks have spoilt their farms . . . first, if there was timber, they burnt it off and put a good coat of ashes on the soil. Then they raised tobacco three or four years. Then corn, till the soil got run out and they couldn't raise anything. Then they went to putting on guano; which was like giving rum to an exhausted man; it just stimulated the soil till all the strength that was left was burnt out." Now, Trowbridge proudly noted, under new management, the farm "looked like an oasis in the desert." The built environment could change as well. Harper's Ferry, he observed, "redeemed from slavery and opened to Northern enterprise, should become a beautiful and busy town."[18]

Trowbridge commented directly on the ideal form of land use when visiting eastern Tennessee. He stayed with a white family that had "five hundred acres of land." Yet, since only a father and son "did the work" and the family "never owned negroes," they only had "thirty six [acres] under cultivation." Owning a smaller amount of land, Trowbridge seemed to imply, was more reasonable for individual families. The northerner proceeded to lecture the two men on "not having kept up their cleared fields by proper cultivation, and preserved their forests." In particular, he suggested that they use the "natural manures" accumulating on the farm as fertilizer. This advice came straight from the "agricultural permanence" literature popular in the North starting in the 1820s. Yet, when Trowbridge made his suggestions about manures, the men responded: "We just throw them [the manures] out, and let them get trampled and washed away. We can't haul out and spread." Trowbridge continued: "In vain I remonstrated against this system of farming: Mr. — replied that he was brought up to it, and could not learn another." North Carolina was different. Upon arrival in the state, Trowbridge found that "the natural features of the country improved; the appearance of its farms improved still more. North Carolina farmers used manures, and work with their own hands. They treat the soil more generously than their South Carolina neighbors, and it repays them." Connecting land use and small farming to Union support, Trowbridge concluded: "[T]he small farmers of North Carolina are a plain, old-fashioned, upright, ignorant class of men. . . . Yet, many of these are men of a strong sense as any in the State . . . and they were generally Union men."[19]

Freed blacks offered the best hope for transforming plantation lands from ruin to plenty, proving that they could be sturdy yeomen and citizens. Trowbridge encountered one village near the James River that "was surrounded by freedmen's farms occupying the abandoned plantations of recent Rebels. The crops looked well, though the soil was said to be poor. Indeed, this was by far the thriftiest portion of Virginia I had seen." Even though the farmhouses "were very generally built of split boards . . . there was an air of neatness and comfort about them." At Petersburg, Trowbridge saw "evidences of reviving agriculture . . . a good crop of corn had been raised and some five and thirty negro men and women were beginning the harvest. There was no white man about the place; but they told me they were working on their own account." As a matter of policy, Trowbridge argued, the federal government should promote black homesteads. He quoted the assistant commissioner of the Freedmen's Bureau in Mississippi, who said: "There is no more industrious class of people anywhere than the freedmen who have little homesteads of their own. The colonies under my charge, working lands assigned them by the government, have raised this year ten thousand bales of cotton, besides corn and vegetables for their subsistence until another harvest." At Jefferson Davis's former plantation in Mississippi, Trowbridge witnessed the ideal landscape. "The signal success of the colony," he wrote, "indicates the future of free labor in the South and the eventual division of the large plantations into homesteads to be sold or rented to small farmers. This system suits the freedmen better than any other; and under it he is industrious, prosperous, and happy."[20]

With land, African Americans could become citizens. While in Virginia, Trowbridge celebrated that "mothers and daughters of the first families of Virginia sat serene and uncomplaining in the atmosphere of mothers and daughters of the despised race, late their slaves or their neighbors,' but now citizens like themselves." Black land ownership would also allow the federal government to eventually end its occupation. In Louisiana, he wrote, "the fact that the freedmen had no independent homes, but lived in negro-quarters at the will of the owner, placed him under great disadvantages, which the presence of the Bureau was necessary to counteract." Trowbridge wrote that former slaves seemed to support the Radical Republican's agenda. A man living in Richmond, he reported, "rather expected that the lands of their Rebel masters would be given them, insisting that they ought to have some reward for all their years of unrequited toil." At Hampton, Virginia, Trowbridge conveyed that "the height of the freedmen's ambition was to have little homes of their own . . . and to work for themselves. And who could blame this simple, strong instinct, since it was not only pointing them the way of their own prosperity, but serving also the needs of the country." Freedom and citizenship came from land ownership. "In order to be altogether free," Trowbridge wrote, "and to enjoy the fruits of their freedom, they [freed slaves] must have homes of their own."[21]

Sidney Andrews also commented on the exhausted fields of the plantation South. Where small farms predominated, Andrews found prosperity and beauty. He commented that "western North Carolina is suggestive of Pennsylvania . . . it abounds in small farms rather than in large plantations; and corn, not cotton, is the principal product. There are apple orchards and many peach-trees, some fences, and occasionally a comfortable and pleasantly situated farm house." Milledgeville, Georgia, however, was decidedly unappetizing. "Its private residences," Andrews sneered, "are neither large nor pretty, and the general aspect of the town is dirty, slovenly, and shiftless. It has a filthy river on the east, and lowland piney woods on the south, west, and north." Charleston, South Carolina, was similar: "A city of ruins, of desolation, of vacant houses, of widowed women, of rotting wharves, of deserted warehouses, of wild-weed gardens, of miles of grass-grown streets, of acres of pitiful and voiceful barrenness—that, is Charleston."[22]

Andrews believed that the built environment of the South and the bad manners of its inhabitants provided proof of the region's barbarism. Arriving in South Carolina in September 1865, Andrews had heard "a great deal about the superior civilization of the South." When he arrived at his hotel, the true "quality of this boasted Southern civilization" became apparent. Andrews, noting the "rickety centre table, a sort of writing-desk, the wreck of a piano," and a "horribly filthy" table-spread, claimed that such an establishment "could not receive a week's support in any community of any State from Maine to the Rocky Mountains." He sighed, noting the South's failure to modernize on northern standards. "Yet here it lives on and on, year after year, a witness for Southern civilization. Let us call things by their right names, —then shall we say *Southern barbarism*." As for education, Andrews commented that the "average Southern head doesn't show near as much intellectual force and vigor as the average Northern head; and the beauty of the South is solely in the faces of its young women—half of it at least in the faces of its mulatto and quadroon girls." Many poor whites, he continued, "must be simply called vagabonds. They are generally without fixed home and without definite occupation. They are always thinly clad, their habitations are mere hovels, they are entirely uneducated, and many of them are hardly above beasts in their habits."[23]

The only hope for the region was promoting small farms and convincing the people to practice better agriculture. How southern white families now survived, after "the propping hands of the negroes [had been] taken away," was "a mystery" to Andrews. Similar to Trowbridge, Andrews made the claim that former slaves would make better farmers than "poor whites." While in Goldsboro, North Carolina, in October 1865, he wrote: "I am certain there can be no lower class of people than the North Carolina 'clay eaters,'—this being the local name for the poor whites. . . . They are lazy and thriftless, mostly choose to live by begging or pilfering, and are more unreliable as farm hands than the worst of the negroes."[24]

John Richard Dennett was explicit in his indictment of southern agriculture and his suggestions for improvement. He observed that many men in Virginia "owned five and six thousand acres of land." If only these "half-cleared tracts [could] be broken up into small farms," the "soil would yield a product fourfold greater than now." Dennett believed that "an intelligent and industrious yeomanry composed of colored Virginians" could become the new leaders of society. Near Lynchburg, Virginia, there was ample opportunity for agricultural plenty, but slaveholders had failed to take advantage of the resources. "The soil seemed fertile," Dennett noted; "there was an abundance of timber, the apple trees and the late peach trees were laden with fruit, and all the crops appeared to be thriving well. Indian corn was everywhere, and I saw occasional patches of cotton, tobacco, and broom-corn growing near the houses[;] . . . but a small portion of the land is under cultivation." One man reckoned that "Massachusetts was ahead of Virginia because more emigrants came there and there were more small farms." North Carolina appeared even worse off. The houses there were "seldom more than a log hut; in the brown expanse of cleared land many of the pines have been girdled, and hundreds of the lofty stems, bleached white, are standing and leaning at every angle." Dennett met a farmer in Fayetteville who was astonished to hear that farms in Minnesota and Ohio could produce "sixty bushels [an acre] of wheat." Similar to J. T. Trowbridge, Dennett offered testimony from former slaves expressing their desire for small farms. A man named Lewis from Baton Rouge, Louisiana, told Dennett on February 27, 1866, that "land was a great thing for a man, and made him free and his own man."[25]

South Carolina and Georgia were equally decrepit, as Dennett described near Kingstree, South Carolina: "The surface is very flat and traversed by many sluggish streams; pine barrens alternate with swamps, and by far the larger portion of the country is covered with forests." Dennett explained that wealthy planters owning large tracts of land created this ugly landscape. "The clearing of the small farmer is rarely seen," he observed. "[T]he fields of the great plantations spread wide on either hand till their bounding lines of woods appear as irregular black walls." Dennett continued: "The valleys of the creeks and rivers are possessed by the rich planters, [while] the poor whites, whose local designation is 'backwoods people,'" live in "dwellings . . . seldom to be seen from the public thoroughfares." The Boston native summarized his views of the southern environment while traveling from Macon to Columbus in Georgia. The journey, he wrote, had "little to interest one who has previously travelled for any considerable distance in the South. All along the road is the familiar scene of their desolate-looking forest."[26]

Dennett also witnessed firsthand the controversy over land claims at Port Royal, South Carolina. The area had been under Union control since the spring of 1862, and the northern Freedmen's Aid Commission had begun to teach former slaves how to farm the area. When Dennett arrived in November 1865, however, a number of the plots were reverting back to control by white planters pardoned by Andrew Johnson. While under slavery, "the cleared land [was] much more than half, fenceless, bushy, and unkempt . . . uncultivated." Dennett believed that the black families, under tutelage from the commission, had made the land blossom. Unfortunately, the freedmen lost control and had to negotiate contracts with their former masters. When Dennett rode through Connecticut on his way back to Boston, he contrasted "the carefully cultivated farms, and all the other evidences of intelligence and industrious thrift, with the dreary region I had just left, thinly peopled, full of uncleared forests and undrained swamps and sandy levels, the wretched railways and worse roads, the slovenly plantations with their mean houses."[27]

Schools provided the solutions to these problems, having the potential to create an agrarian republic out of the former slave society. Sidney Andrews urged northerners "to bring here the conveniences and comforts of our Northern civilization, no less than the Northern idea of right and wrong, justice and injustice, humanity and inhumanity." Such was the "work ready for the hand of every New England man and woman." These emigrants must teach whites "what the negro's rights are, and the negro must be taught to wait patiently and wisely for the full recognition of those rights in his own old home." Andrews proclaimed: "Give them [former slaves] education, and all other good things must come in its train—give them that, and the shackling name 'freedom' will vanish like a ghost of the night, as it is, and they will stand before the world in their own right as freemen." Indeed, he believed, "the real question at issue in the South is not, 'What shall be done with the negro?' But 'What shall be done with the white?'" What truly troubled the journalist was that whites appeared to be uninterested in education. In South Carolina, he noted, "the ignorance of the great body of the whites is a fact that will astonish any observer conversant with the middle classes of the North. Travel where you will, and that sure indication of modern civilization, the school-house, is not to be found." Black people, in turn, "all seem[ed] anxious to read—many of them appearing to have a notion that thereby will come honor and business." Andrews hoped "the time would soon come when school-houses would be as numerous in Georgia as in Massachusetts."[28]

Trowbridge also believed that the solution was education—particularly for black people, which also would be a means to punish former slave owners. He could "fancy no finer stroke of poetical justice than the conversion of the seats on which the legislatures of the great slave empire [sat] ... into seats and desks for little negro children learning to read." In fact, in the South, "the prospect for white common schools ... [was] discouraging," while "the prospect is better for the education of freedmen." The federal government, Trowbridge alleged, had a responsibility to protect freedmen's schools from violence. He reported that "teachers were threatened and insulted, and school-houses broken into or burned. The better class of citizens—many of whom see the necessity of educating the negro now that he is free—while they have nothing to do with these acts of barbarism, are powerless to prevent them."[29]

The private letters of influential Radicals who visited the South were perhaps even more important than the accounts by Dennett, Andrews, and Trowbridge in determining Congressional Reconstruction policy. Salmon Chase, appointed chief justice of the U.S. Supreme Court after his stint as treasury secretary, visited Hilton Head, South Carolina, in May 1865. Chase reported that black people wanted the vote. "They attach a very great importance to the right of voting," he explained to President Andrew Johnson, "more perhaps than to any other except that of personal liberty." Chase observed at a political meeting in Charleston: "The audience seemed quite as intelligent as a similar gathering in the North. The colored citizens of Charleston are more intelligent than elsewhere." Citizenship, Chase implied, was connected to the environment in which the former slaves lived and worked. With the exception of a reference to "government employment," Chase's description of the ideal community at Hilton Head seemed to parallel George Julian's hopes for Yosemite. As Chase described, "there is a populous colored village on this Island, named Mitchell after General Mitchell. The number of inhabitants is about three thousand. They have a church, a minister, & schools. A few cultivate the soil in large & small parcels, most are in government employment; but all are doing well."[30]

Chase also discovered that freed slaves were organizing "Union Leagues" throughout the South. This was a positive development, according to the chief justice. "These associations embrace all the most intelligent," he explained. While these loyal men calmly asserted their rights, Chase argued that southern whites were recalcitrant. "They declare," he alleged, "themselves satisfied that the Union must be restored & that Slavery, as a personal relation, must cease: but earnestly urge that some mode of coercing labor must be adopted in lieu of personal slavery." Chase continued: "It is curious to observe how little they seem to realize that any change in personal or political relations has been wrought by the war." Given this situation, Chase suggested that Johnson switch his policy. The governments of the South should be "thoroughly loyal" and "promote the welfare of black as of white citizens." To protect these governments, Chase recommended "making each State a Department & assigning to the command of each Department a General."[31]

Unsatisfied with Chase's recommendations, Andrew Johnson delegated German Republican Carl Schurz as special presidential envoy to the South. Like the journalists, Schurz believed that rampant violence and disorder threatened reunion. In Atlanta, he reported, "freedmen were attacked and maltreated by whites without the least provocation, almost every day. During my sojourn there, one negro was stabbed dead, and three were poisoned, one of whom died." Schurz found a similar scene in Montgomery, Alabama: "Unless the severest punishments known to the laws will be visited upon white men killing negroes[,] the Southern States will soon be a vast slaughter pen for the black race." Schurz found it "absolutely indispensable" that "the country should be garrisoned with troops as thickly as possible." The possibility for another rebellion existed, Schurz argued: "Outrages committed upon Union people and Negroes and the overriding of the spirit of the Emancipation Proclamation may, perhaps, technically not be called 'insurrectionary movements' but in point of fact they are nothing else. It is a continuation of the war, not against armed defenders of the Government, but against its unarmed friends." Carl Schurz shared Trowbridge's sentiments about education, explaining to Andrew Johnson that a "large force of teachers should be sent to the interior of this State [South Carolina] to commence their operations as soon as the crops are in." Schurz was horrified at white opposition to education, recalling: "Unless under the immediate protection of Federal troops, the negro schoolhouses were set on fire and the teachers driven away."[32]

Not all people shared the views of Chase, Schurz, Trowbridge, Dennett, and Andrews. The president received letters urging a different course of action. Henry M. Watterson, Andrew Johnson's longtime friend and a Kentuckian, toured the South in the summer of 1865. Watterson found no opposition to the federal government in the former Confederacy. "Further resistance," he wrote to Johnson, "is regarded as utterly hopeless and foolish. . . . Thousands have reached the conclusion that for the white man at least Emancipation is the true policy." Watterson did not favor black suffrage, writing his preference for a "white man's government" with "free white citizens controlling this country." Watterson advised that Johnson challenge the Radical wing of the Republican Party—defined as the part that believed in black suffrage: "It is clear to my mind that you are to have a war with the friends of Chase, who is evidently a candidate for the next Presidency, and expects to be elected on the issue of negro suffrage. . . . [Y]ou will whip them to death. . . . [T]hese agitators constitute one wing of the concern that brought on the late terrible war. The Southern wing has already been crushed, and the victory will never be complete till the Northern wing is put *hors de combat.*" Watterson, to put the matter lightly, had no interest in the Republican citizenship program for freed slaves.[33]

Johnson continued his Reconstruction policy and began open confrontation with Republicans who favored black suffrage, land redistribution, and punishing former rebels. Carl Schurz, near the end of his life, contemplated why Johnson decided on this course of action. Perhaps Johnson, "the plebeian, who, before the war had been treated with undisguised contempt by the slave-holding aristocracy, could not withstand the subtle flattery of the same aristocracy when they flocked around him as humble supplicants." Maybe, Schurz continued, Johnson believed white assertions that "the only element of trouble in the South consisted in a lot of fanatical abolitionists who excited the negroes with all sorts of dangerous notions." More plausible, Johnson *never* was concerned about black slaves. "After the outbreak of the secession movement," Schurz surmised, "he peremptorily relegated the slavery question to the background in spite of its evident importance in the Civil War."[34]

In 1866 Republicans began open conflict with Johnson on reconstructing southern society. For the Radicals, land redistribution was critical to this effort. In February, Congress passed a bill extending the life of the Freedmen's Bureau. The primary goal was to prevent slavery from returning in the South, where it would again menace the Union. "Wherein," the bill stated, "in consequence of any State or local law, ordinance, police, or other regulation, custom, or prejudice, any of the civil rights or immunities belonging to white persons . . . are refused or denied to negroes, mulattoes, freedmen, refugees, or any other persons, on account of race, color, or previous condition of slavery . . . it is to be the duty of the president of the United States, through the Commissioner [of the Freedmen's Bureau], to extend military protection and jurisdiction over all cases." Since slavery caused the Civil War, Samuel Pomeroy claimed, preventing its reestablishment was crucial. "Everything ought to be required for safety," Pomeroy explained, "but nothing for revenge, nothing by way of punishment. . . . I believe the sentiment of the country is, that we ought now to provide such securities for the future that another rebellion will be impossible in a thousand years." The extension bill also authorized the bureau to build schools for freed people in the South, following the recommendations by Schurz, Dennett, and Andrews that education was necessary for the creation of a black yeomanry. While the bill set aside 3 million acres of public land for black homesteads, Congress rejected a proposition by Thaddeus Stevens to add the "forfeited estates of the enemy" to the land available for freedmen.[35]

Radicals achieved more success with George Julian's Southern Homestead Act, which passed the House on February 8, 1866. Julian believed that the "laws regulating the ownership and disposition of landed property not only affect the well being but frequently the destiny of a people." He continued: "The system of primogeniture and entail adopted by the Southern States of our Union favored the policy of great estates, and the ruinous system of landlordism and slavery which finally laid waste to the fairest and most fertile section of the Republic and threatened its life; while the New England States, in adopting a different system, laid the foundations of their prosperity in the soil itself." Slavery and large estates produced agricultural "waste" and deprived the "most fertile section of the Republic" of its bounty. New England, where families inhabited small plots of land for many generations, enjoyed prosperity and equality. Julian's bill extended "the homestead law of 1862" over the five public-land states that had been part of the Confederacy: Arkansas, Alabama, Florida, Louisiana, and Mississippi. Homesteads, Julian concluded, "are imperatively demanded by the poor whites and the poor blacks of the South who have heretofore constituted the background of the institution of slavery."[36]

Maine congressman John H. Rice believed that the homestead measure would strengthen the Union, improve cultivation, and promote civilization. The antebellum South, Rice asserted, had "fundamental difficulties . . . difficulties growing out of the abnormal condition of those States before they went into rebellion—one of which was the immense land monopolies which had grown up there for the support of slavery and oppression. . . . It is impossible for us to give liberty, protection, and justice to the people of those States, unless we secure them in their homes and in their homesteads." Rice urged freedmen, "under the protection of this law, laboring in your own fields, living in your own houses, intrenched in your own castles, instructing your children in your own schools, and worshipping God in your own churches, you can demand and extort from your enemies justice and equality of civil rights before the laws." Granting small farms to freedmen ensured "liberty and independence," while land monopolies guaranteed that "the masses of the people will be oppressed, ignorant and miserable." Land redistribution, Rice concluded, was a "labor which needs to be done everywhere, in the North as well as in the South, in the East and the West; and most abundantly in the monarchies and oligarchies of the Old World." Julian's Southern Homestead Act went into effect on June 21, 1866.[37]

On February 24, 1868, the House voted 126 to 47 to impeach Andrew Johnson, who had blocked many Congressional Reconstruction laws. Radicals, including George Julian and Thaddeus Stevens, wrote the charges, eight of which dealt with Johnson's attempt to remove Secretary of War Edwin M. Stanton without Congress's approval. One charge accused the president of exciting "the odium and resentment of all the good people of the United States against Congress and the laws by it duly and constitutionally elected." George Julian recalled that "the popular feeling against the president was now rapidly nearing its climax and becoming a sort of frenzy. Andrew Johnson . . . was devil-bent upon the ruin of his country; and his trial connected itself with all the memories of the war, and involved the nation in a new and final struggle for its life." The Senate trial began on March 4, 1868, and continued for eleven weeks. Johnson was acquitted by one vote. Justin Morrill, now a senator, commented: "Our martial heroes triumphed and utterly vanquished rebellion in the field. . . . [N]ow, shall a civilian—not having miraculous virtues certainly—command, galvanize and nurse the monster again to life?"[38]

Republican defeats in the 1867 elections were one of the reasons that the Senate failed to gain the majority necessary for impeachment. The defeats also stalled efforts at land redistribution by making enough senators wary of following the Radicals. In Ohio, Minnesota, and Kansas—all reliably Republican states—the party attempted to enfranchise northern blacks. Despite 80 percent of the Republican electorate favoring the proposals, voters in each state rejected the ballot measures. Democrats, using race-baiting propaganda, won control of the Ohio legislature and made gains in several other northern states. The public would support radical measures if they believed these policies safeguarded the Union; voters did not favor the measures if the Republicans portrayed suffrage and land redistribution as purely egalitarian. In California, Democrat gubernatorial candidate Henry Haight won election, indicting the Republicans for seeking "indiscriminate suffrage regardless of race, color, or qualification." Democrats also won control of the California state legislature. As Utahan Brigham Young observed, "The question of extending suffrage to the negro is a vexed one, and is likely to provoke a great amount of feeling throughout the nation." Samuel Pomeroy concluded: "The canvas upon the question of 'Impartial Suffrage' is becoming interesting & earnest. . . . [T]he late elections in Penn. & Ohio. have damaged our friends, and they are now fearful of the result. The campaign in Kansas has not been well managed. . . . Republicans who are merely politicians are weakening."[39]

Despite ominous signs of northern impatience with Reconstruction, southern Republican Parties grew in power in 1868 and 1869. Among black and white Republicans in the South, school construction received top priority. African American Republican John Roy Lynch, recalling his own experience "reading books and newspapers and listening to the recitations in the white schools" as a slave, argued that the Republican governments should provide equal education for all. The Freedmen's Bureau, working with northern philanthropic organizations and local politicians like Lynch, succeeded in establishing nearly 3,000 schools throughout the South by 1869. Teachers reported widespread enthusiasm for the schools. An educator in Florida relayed how one elderly freedwoman, "just beginning to spell, seems as if she could not think of any thing but her book, says she spells her lesson all the evening, then she dreams about it, and wakes up thinking about it." John Eaton, superintendent of freedmen and later head of the government's Bureau of Education, recalled: "Upon the whole the most important and probably most permanent result of the military effort to secure justice and well-being to the Negro was the establishment of a rudimentary but well articulated school system." Unlike Indian families, African Americans tended to embrace the government's efforts to promote schooling.[40]

Southern Republicans also called for land redistribution and drastic change in plantation agriculture. In Alabama, the "Loyal League"—a grassroots alliance between black leaders and Republicans—called for large plantations to be broken up into small farms. Leader Albert Griffin argued that cotton farms were "destined soon to be cut up into small farms, to be controlled by their owners and sons." The result would be that a "laboring, self-reliant and intelligent population will multiply all over the country." Another predicted that black citizens would "have an opportunity to secure a homestead, and the latent wealth of the state will be brought to the surface and distributed among the people." Many of these league members, historian Michael W. Fitzgerald explains, "wanted to settle on their own in the woods, and raise corn, potatoes, wheat, cabbage—anything but cotton." This desire seemed to mirror the Republican ideal of land use perfectly; freed people would become citizens by farming multiple crops on small plots of land.[41]

As 1870 approached, land redistribution seemed less of a possibility. Absent redistribution, Republicans asserted that suffrage was the only sure way to guarantee black safety, and thus the South's loyalty, without maintaining a lengthy federal presence in the region. General John A. Rawlins, a close friend of Ulysses S. Grant, argued that the vote "was the only sure protection to person and property. It gives one a voice in government, secures to him respect, and insures him the equal benefit of the laws." California Republican and Central Pacific Railroad president Leland A. Stanford wrote to Cornelius Cole: "This cry against the ignorance of the negroes and their consequent inability to vote for the best interests of the country has with me not the least weight. The poorer and more ignorant a man is, the more consequence that he should have the power to protect himself." Black congressman John Lynch realized that for northern voters, African American suffrage served primarily as a means to destroy "the power and influence of the Southern aristocracy" responsible for secession, not as an egalitarian measure welcoming an oppressed minority into American democracy. Both Stanford and Cole, after all, opposed any effort to extend citizenship rights to Chinese immigrants in California. Nevertheless, Congress passed the Fifteenth Amendment in early 1869 declaring that states could not deny the right to vote based on color, race, or previous condition of servitude. Julian, ever the Radical, had originally tried for more. On December 8, 1868, he offered a proposed amendment stating that "all citizens of the United States, whether native or naturalized shall enjoy this right [suffrage] equally, without any distinction or discrimination whatever founded on race, color, or sex." The more-limited version became part of the U.S. Constitution on March 30, 1870.[42]

Between the beginning of Congressional Reconstruction in 1866 and the addition of the Fifteenth Amendment to the U.S. Constitution in 1870, Congress also formulated new policies for the western United States. The establishment of Yellowstone National Park, made possible by a strengthened federal government, was discussed in the previous chapter. Republicans proffered remarkably similar solutions to the alleged problems of both African Americans and Native Americans. Both groups, they believed, needed to become small farmers and build settled communities, schools, and "civilization." Just as in Reconstruction policy for the South, new ways of dealing with Native Americans faced violent opposition from white westerners in favor of genocide. Nevertheless, there was a critical difference between racist white attitudes in the South and those in the West. Southern whites—and northern financiers who invested in southern agriculture—believed the region needed black people as poor laborers in order to revive cotton, tobacco, and sugar production. Black landownership and voting rights seemed to stand in the way of this goal. White people in the West came to support federal efforts to force Indians on farms. When the federal government compelled Indians to stop their nomadic lifestyle and switch to farming, Indian landholdings would, by necessity, diminish dramatically. Whites would quickly move onto land formally possessed by Indians. With the defeat of the Nez Perce tribe in 1877, nearly all the tribes of the West had been forced to become small farmers.

Republicans began discussing a new Indian policy in Congress in 1863 after an uprising of Sioux in Minnesota. Minnesota Republican William Windom termed the 1862 incident "the most terrible and destructive Indian outbreaks ever known on this continent, for which these guilty tribes should be held strictly accountable." Windom demanded that Congress cut off annual annuities to the tribe and give them to "victims" of the attack. Unlike previous debates, some congressmen suggested that whites— not the Sioux—were to blame for the conflict. "Many of the Indians were dissatisfied with their lands," Republican Samuel Clement Fessenden of Maine alleged. "They complained that they had been deprived of their hunting grounds and the means of subsistence." Fessenden read a plea by religious reformer Henry B. Whipple urging the government to curb these abuses. "Four years ago," Whipple described, "the Sioux sold the Government about eight hundred thousand acres of land, being a part of their reservation. The plea for this sale was the need of more funds to aid them in civilization." Unfortunately, the government did not live up to its bargain, prompting the uprising. "The Indians waited at the agencies two months," he explained, "dissatisfied, turbulent, mad, hungry, and then came the outbreak." Fessenden suggested that the government should instruct Indians "in the cultivation of the soil" and the "arts of civilization" so that "they can become independent."[43]

Fessenden did not invent the idea that the government should "civilize" Indians by forcing them to become farmers. Thomas Jefferson, for instance, believed that Indians needed to be "civilized" in order to survive in America. Accepting "civilization" meant giving up a hunting-and-gathering lifestyle and becoming the yeomen farmers that the third president idealized. As the historian Francis Prucha explains, "Jefferson strongly urged the Indians to accept the white man's ways. And for this he had a single formula. The hunter state must be exchanged for an agricultural state; the haphazard life dependent upon the chase must give way to a secure and comfortable existence marked by industry and thrift; private property must replace communal ownership. . . . [T]he central point was conversion to farming." Later, between 1816 and 1822, Superintendent of Indian Trade Thomas L. McKenney wanted to push tribes toward agriculture, private property, and Christianity. Indians who accepted the government program, however, had no guarantees that they would be able to remain on their land. In 1830 President Andrew Jackson approved the removal of "civilized" Cherokee Indians from lands desired by whites in Georgia. The government also did not hesitate to undertake military action against Indians who refused removal. Between 1835 and 1842, the U.S. Army fought the Seminoles in Florida, forcing almost 3,000 of them to relocate to Indian Territory (modern-day Oklahoma).[44]

During the Civil War, as evidenced by Fessenden's arguments, religious reformers and political Radicals became horrified at the deadly Indian conflict in the West. Besides the 1862 Sioux uprising in Minnesota, Colorado militia and units of the First Colorado Cavalry attacked a group of peaceful Cheyenne and Arapaho Indians in November 1864. The Cheyenne chief, Black Kettle, raised an American flag and then a white flag to indicate the tribes' peaceful intentions, but the soldiers continued the attack. What followed, in the words of one Philadelphia newspaper, "was an indiscriminate, wholesale murder of men, women and children, accompanied by the disfigurement of dead bodies of both sexes, in every revolting and sickening form and manner." The paper continued: "Unborn babes were torn from the wombs of dying mothers, and scalped; children of the most tender ages were butchered; soldiers adorned their hats with portions of the bodies of both males and females, and the flag and uniform of the United States were disgraced by acts of fiendish barbarity." Even the *Freedom's Champion* of Atchison, Kansas, which normally had "no friendship for the Indians," denounced the Sand Creek Massacre as "cowardly, brutal butchery."[45]

Congress debated the appropriate government response to the incident in early 1865. Iowa Republican James Harlan believed that actions by state governments and military officers had negated the benevolent intentions of the federal government. "We have been appropriating millions of money each year for the purpose of educating and instructing the Indian tribes on our border and in the plains; but that policy is being reversed," he explained. Harlan lamented that frontier states were "now engaged in the extermination of the Indians." Democrat James W. Nesmith of Oregon responded: "You cannot civilize the Indian . . . but I have succeeded sometimes in civilizing them with powder and ball." Democrat John Conness of California, the sponsor of the Yosemite Park bill, was one of the few westerners to express shame "over the miserable and cruel and cowardly murders perpetrated . . . against these poor defenseless creatures." Congress responded by creating the Doolittle Committee on March 3, 1865. The committee, chaired by Wisconsin Republican James R. Doolittle, sought to determine "the causes of the deterioration of the Indians, the best forms of land tenure, the effects of schools and missions, the use of annuities, and whether the Indian office should be transferred to the War Department."[46]

As the committee deliberated, visitors to the trans-Mississippi West recorded impressions that were remarkably similar to the views of the journalists and politicians who traveled south during early Reconstruction. As in the South, visitors viewed land use as one of the primary influences on society. Small farms, practicing "improved" agriculture, allowed for community formation and eliminated the need for further expansion. Settled communities permitted the rise of schools and civilization. Equitable land distribution created the conditions for loyalty to the Union. Most telling, the ideological foundations for Indian policy in the West and Radical Reconstruction policy in the South proved extraordinarily similar. As with their goals for freed slaves, Republicans believed that Indians needed to become small farmers and receive education. As educated yeomen, Native Americans would become "civilized" with white cultural values and replace tribal affiliations with loyalty to the United States. The difference was that unlike African Americans in the South, many Indians had no desire to become small farmers. Toohoolhoolzote, a Nez Perce chief, asserted in 1877 that "any arrangement that would surrender homeland and lead to farming, cutting into and profaning the Earth Mother, 'wasn't true law at all.'"[47]

One of the most prominent commentators on the West was Albert D. Richardson of the *New York Tribune*. Richardson traveled throughout the region between 1850 and 1866, recording his observations in a massive book entitled *Beyond the Mississippi*. Dismissing any natural constraints on small cultivation in the arid West, Albert Richardson promoted the theory that "rain follows the plow." If farmers moved west to cultivate small farms, they would surely find success. "There is a curious logical connection," he maintained, "between civilization and rain. . . . [T]hirty years ago, Missourians living on the opposite bank of the river thought the soil of Kansas good for nothing on account of its rainless climate. Since the young State was settled, it has suffered only twice from dry seasons." Railroads, Richardson envisioned, would carry farmers' produce to ports for export around the world. "California thrives in her manifold industries," he explained. "[T]he State is exporting eight millions of bushels of wheat annually—a large portion of it to China." For other areas to take advantage of this lucrative trade, Richardson suggested, "our deserts must be reclaimed [and] a Northern and a Southern railway must be opened from the Mississippi to the Pacific." Richardson's ideal West was a society of small farmers connected to a global market by railroads.[48]

For Richardson, railroads also encouraged western loyalty to the Union. In Olympia, Oregon (now Washington), Richardson "saw many eyes grow wet at mention of our martyred President [Abraham Lincoln], and heard every voice thrill in cheers for our redeemed republic." Such a reaction made his heart swell "with pride and hope for the swarming, potential America of the future." Richardson exclaimed: "May its name be omnipotent to the weary and troubled of every zone! May its flag betoken to the nations, Stability and Progress, Liberty and Law, Opportunity for the lowliest, and Justice pure and exact upon all men." In California, the disunion sentiment exhibited during the war dissipated with the near completion of the transcontinental railroad. Richardson argued that the railroad "will strengthen us politically. There is infinite pathos in hearing everybody on the Pacific coast, from children to gray-haired men, speak of the East as 'home.' Still, at the outset of the great rebellion, a large party favored a Pacific republic." He admonished the nation to "do away with isolation; cut through the mountains!" and surely such sentiments would disappear.[49]

Small farms ensured progress and loyalty to the Union. Richardson contrasted the hunting-and-gathering lifestyle of some Californian Indian tribes with the promised benefits of a farming society. "The aboriginal Californians lived upon worms and grasshoppers, and were [the] most wretched and degraded of all barbarians," he sneered. But with the growth of the white population of the state, "the next generation ought to see here the best average society in the Union, and therefore in the world." Further railroad construction would transform the entire West into a mecca for farmers. "We need them [railroads] to develop vast mining and farming regions now lying idle," Richardson explained; "to end, once and for all, the Indian troubles; and to enable us to command that vast commerce of the East for which all the nations are striving." The aim was environmental transformation: "Thousands upon thousands of miles of sage-brush and grease-wood, dwarf-cedar and cactus, sand and alkali, from British Columbia to northern Mexico and from western Kansas to the Sierra Nevadas, will yield barley oats and fruit."[50]

Richardson was conflicted about Indians, writing: "The Indian is cruel, bloodthirsty, and treacherous; but he often behaves quite as well as the Pale-Face." He came to the conclusion that schools should be established for both Indians and white settlers to transform them into small farmers. "In western Arkansas," Richardson wrote, "schools are very rare, and many children grow up incredibly ignorant. At the time of my visit[,] several of the State legislators were unable to write their own names." In contrast to "their white Arkansas neighbors, the Choctaws appropriated money freely for the education of their children. At ten large mission boarding schools six hundred pupils were studying." The result of these efforts, Richardson argued, was that the Choctaw children "were intelligent and in average capacity equaled white children." Comanches, however, by "never tilling the soil," were "insensible alike to the comforts and wants of civilization, daring, treacherous, and bloodthirsty."[51]

The "ideal" Indian, Richardson believed, was one who farmed a small plot of land, spoke English, and embraced white American culture. For instance, Governor Walker, the leader of the Choctaw Nation, was "educated in Kentucky, intelligent and agreeable; nearly as white as myself, and with no betrayal of Indian origin in speech or features. . . . [H]is farm of one hundred acres was all inclosed and under high cultivation." Before turning to farming and embracing education, the Choctaws were "cruel and barbarous." Now, they were "governing themselves, educating their children, protecting life and property far better than adjacent Arkansas and Texas, and rapidly assuming the habits of enlightened men." The experience led him to believe that Indians could be civilized if the government sponsored education programs and convinced them to start farming. The environment in Indian Territory seemed well suited for such aims. "Adapted to every product from cotton to Indian corn," Richardson wrote, "it is the most beautiful farming country under our flag."[52]

Samuel K. Bowles, editor of the influential *Springfield Republican*, traveled with Schuyler Colfax, speaker of the House of Representatives, on a trip west in the summer of 1865. Bowles recorded countless observations on the degree of civilization in the West. The region, he believed, could achieve greatness now that the Union had won the Civil War and could impose its vision of an agrarian society. "This Republic, saved, reunited, bound together as never before," Bowles proclaimed, "expands under such personal passage and footstep tread; how magnificent its domain; how far-reaching and uprising its material, moral and political possibilities and promises." For the United States to realize these alleged benefits, the army needed to eliminate the "threat" that Indian tribes posed to white settlers. Bowles, like Richardson, recommended that Native Americans be placed on reservations and taught how to farm. "The government is ready to assist in their [Indian's] support," he elaborated, "to grant them reservations, to give them food and make them presents; but it must and will, with sharp hand, enforce their respect to travel, their respect to lives and property, and their respect to trade." If Indians did not agree to such a plan, Bowles said that a "strong military force" should "wholly exterminat[e] them." In fact, he argued, "if the policy of extermination is the only possible one, the sooner it is adopted, and carried out, the better."[53]

Bowles also commented on existent land-use practices in the West. Just as the observers of the South recommended, he argued that the government should distribute land to yeomen farmers to ensure agricultural productivity, a republican society, and the absence of oligarchs. Bowles noted that in the Willamette valley of Oregon, "much of the farming is unwisely done; the farms are generally too large, the original locations being mostly of six hundred and forty acres each." These large, inefficient farms existed because the "agricultural population are largely Missourians, Kentuckians, and Tennesseans"—former slave owners who did not follow New England methods of farming. Small farms could make use of the "fertility of soil and variety of surface and production." Schuyler Colfax, Bowles's confidant, argued that the Homestead Act produced agricultural wealth and social prosperity. In a speech at Virginia City, Nevada, Colfax stated: "You will find a policy which is the truest and wisest that a great country could adopt in order to have its people tilling the soil, becoming producers of national wealth, adding to our agricultural resources, calling our people away from the crowded cities to make them tillers of the soil of the Republic. . . . That policy is to give them an estate at a nominal price, throwing open our public lands to them, that they may become owners of the soil of the Republic."[54]

Bowles believed that the United States should promote the growth of New England–style towns, with people living close to each other on small plots of land. In the Rocky Mountains, he found "companionship and society as various and as cultured and as organized as in New England; cities of thousands of inhabitants . . . away up in their narrow valleys." Bowles observed: "All this seems dream-like." Future towns would be "thriving, orderly, peaceable, busy, supporting . . . [a] daily paper, with churches and schools, and all the best materials of government and society that the East can boast of." Even the desert and the barren plains, Bowles believed, could be transformed into lush New England villages through irrigation. "Irrigation," he explained, "will supply agriculture with its lacking; and through and by all these means combining, and worked with the energy and enterprise of the American people, stimulated by the great profits sure to be realized from wise and preserving use of opportunities, the western half of the American nation will fast move forward in civilization."

Northern-style agriculture was the foundation of civilization for Bowles and provided the key to long-term prosperity in the West. Agriculture, he asserted, "hitherto despised" in mining regions, was "asserting its legitimate place as the base of all true and steady prosperity." In fact, Bowles continued, "the uncertainty, the recklessness, the gambling habit which the varied and fickle results of coal mining throw over the whole business and morals and manners of a community . . . are very great obstacles to a real and permanent prosperity, and growth in high civilization."[55]

While farming had the potential to turn California into a sublime garden, mining could destroy the natural beauty of the state. Bowles was horrified by the hydraulic gold-mining practices at the Mariposa mine once run by Frederick Law Olmsted. "Tornado, flood, earthquake and volcano combined," Bowles recorded, "could hardly make greater havoc, spread wider ruin and wreck, than are to be seen everywhere in the path of the larger gold-washing operations." The streams and rivers of the area, "though naturally pure as crystal," were changed to a "thick yellow mud." The mines were "truly a terrible blot upon the face of nature." They had an equally bad effect on farms: "A farmer may have his whole estate turned to a barren waste by a flood of sand and gravel from some hydraulic mining up-stream; more, if a fine orchard or garden stands in the way of the working of a rich gulch or bank, orchard and garden must go." Bowles linked the harm toward nature with a diminished human society. In Mariposa, "villages are decreasing in population, the best people are going away; viciousness of all sorts seems to be increasing." The message was clear: small farms were better for both people and nature.[56]

In contrast to Radical Republicans such as George Julian, Samuel Bowles and Albert Richardson argued that proper land use included not only small farming but nature parks as well. Natural beauty highlighted the greatness of America. The West, Richardson proclaimed, had such "grand natural curiosities and wonders" that "all other countries combined fall far below it." Richardson delighted in a tour of Yosemite given by Frederick Law Olmsted. After the tour, Richardson suggested that the famous El Capitan be renamed "Mount Abraham Lincoln" to honor the beloved president of a victorious Union. Yosemite was "incomparably the most wonderful feature of our continent." Scoffing at "European travelers," Richardson wrote that "there is no spot, the wide world over, of such varied beauty and measureless grandeur." Such beauty could only be preserved in a park. The Yosemite act, Richardson wrote, secured "to the proper national uses, incomparably the largest and grandest park, and the sublimest natural scenery in the whole world."[57]

Samuel Bowles was equally effusive about the natural beauty of the West, proclaiming: "Neither the Atlantic States nor Europe offer so much of the marvelous and the beautiful in Nature; offer such strange and rare effects,—such combinations of novelty, beauty and majesty, —as were spread before us in our Ride Across the Continent." No area anywhere in the world was "so grand, so full of awe, so full of elevation, as the Yosemite Valley!" Bowles envisioned the western Rockies as "Our Switzerland," an area where eastern travelers could gather to witness the "panorama of mountain beauty." The "natural cathedral of sand, stone, and clay" at Church Butte, Wyoming, surpassed "the Milan or the Cologne cathedral, worn with centuries, ill-shapen with irregular decay." Bowles hoped that other areas of natural beauty could be preserved like Yosemite. "This wise cession and dedication by Congress, and proposed improvement by California . . . furnishes an admirable example for other objects of natural curiosity and popular interest all over the Union."[58]

Just as with the South, politicians also received different advice about the West. Democratic senator James Willis Nesmith of Oregon recommended genocide for Native Americans. Responding to criticism of the Sand Creek Massacre, Nesmith argued: "You must remember that the people of Colorado have been engaged in a war of extermination not provoked by themselves but brought on by the Indians." Explaining that he had witnessed their "degraded, thieving, murdering, plundering" instincts, Nesmith "thought it would be well if the whole race could be exterminated." Even Radical Samuel Pomeroy presented a petition from his constituents demanding "that the mild, conciliatory, and even magnanimous conduct of our Government toward these savages, not being understood or appreciated by them, but only construed to be weakness and cowardice, should now be followed by the most vigorous and decisive measures until these hostile tribes are effectively punished for their crimes."[59]

At the time of the establishment of the Doolittle Committee in March 1865, Republican politicians already had several new ideas about Indian policy. James R. Doolittle himself praised the "civilized" tribes of Indian Territory as models for future groups. The Cherokees, Creeks, Seminoles, Choctaws, and Chickasaws owned land "in fee simple" and "had advanced to such a degree of civilization that they were capable of self-government." Doolittle hoped that other tribes could be "induced, to go and join their fortunes with the Indians in this Territory, and better their condition and advance in civilization." Ohio Republican John Sherman recommended arrangements with Indian tribes "by which we give them help upon their farms, send women to teach their children; send schoolmasters and blacksmiths and Indians." Sherman, however, also urged that the government stop treating tribes as independent nations. "To send a party of people to negotiate and treat with Indians," he explained, "is the most ridiculous farce that can be transacted in our Government. It is the most shameless prostitution not only of the money of the Government but of the name, and credit and fame of the Government." Sherman added: "I have no objection to gathering them into reservations; but the idea of treating them as independent nations ought to have been abandoned years ago." Doolittle and Sherman were motivated by more than a desire to "civilize" Indians and convert their villages to model agrarian communities; both also realized that forcing tribes onto small plots of land would open up space for white farmers.[60]

Doolittle reported his findings on March 16, 1866, just as Congress began feuding with President Johnson over the Civil Rights Act and the Freedmen's Bureau. Similar to Reconstruction policy for the South, Doolittle recommended greater federal oversight for the West. He proposed "that there shall be established five inspection districts of Indian affairs" in the West, encompassing California, Nevada, Arizona, Oregon, Washington, Idaho, Colorado, Utah, New Mexico, Kansas, Indian Territory, and the Dakotas." Inspectors, who were to come from "the Quakers, Baptists, Presbyterians, Episcopalians and other religious bodies," would look "into the condition of [Indian] farms and schools . . . hear their complaints . . . ascertain whether all the stipulations of treaties are kept, and whether all moneys, goods, and supplies are faithfully and justly applied and distributed." Doolittle explained his preference for overseers with religious affiliation. "There is a great desire," he argued, "on the part of the whole people of the United States to look into the condition of these Indians, in reference to their schools, and in reference to their religious instruction." With such a policy enacted, Doolittle concluded, the government could end atrocities and stop fighting Indians. "There is but one way to deal with these Indians on the plains," he surmised; "you must feed them or fight them. There is not much honor to be won by the Army or by the Government in fighting with these Indians."[61]

Before the beginning of the Grant administration, Congress adopted several new measures to curb violence. On June 20, 1867, following Senator Doolittle's recommendations, Congress created the U.S. Indian Peace Commission. The commission aimed to settle all Indian tribes on reservations. If the tribes refused, Congress authorized the secretary of war to forcibly remove them. Thus, one of the ironies of the "Peace Commission" was that despite its stated goal to bring peace to the West, if Indians refused to become yeoman farmers, the army would "forcibly" place them on reservations. Once the Indians were on reservations, the commission recommended, "agriculture and domestic manufactures should be introduced as rapidly as possible; schools to teach the children English; courts and other institutions of government; farmers and mechanics sent to instruct the Indians; and missionary and benevolent societies invited." Nevertheless, when Grant took office in March 1869, Plains Indians and white settlers seemed destined for conflict. The year before, conflict with the Cheyenne had broken out along the Washita River in Indian Territory.[62]

As Grant biographer Jean Edward Smith notes, "Rather than fight, [Grant] chose to make peace with the Plains Indians." Elected by a heavy majority against Democratic opponents Horatio Seymour and Francis Preston Blair, Grant stated in his inaugural address that "the proper treatment of the original occupants of this land—the Indians—is one deserving of careful study." He continued: "I will favor any course toward them which tends to their civilization and ultimate citizenship." Grant began a new course in Indian affairs dubbed the "Peace Policy." Similar to the congressional antecedents, the policy aimed to place Native Americans on reservations, where Indians could be kept from contact with white settlers and learn agriculture. Grant also called upon religious organizations to provide "competent, upright, faithful, moral, and religious" agents to aid in "educating" the Indian population and distributing goods free from corruption. Finally, government would fund churches and schools so that tribes could better appreciate "the comforts and benefits of a Christian civilization and thus be prepared ultimately to assume the duties and privileges of citizenship." In sum, the Peace Policy ended the treaty system that senators such as John Sherman had criticized and transformed Indians into "wards of the Government."[63]

The experiences of three men—General John Eaton, General Oliver Otis (O. O.) Howard, and Captain Richard Henry Pratt—show how Republicans applied the same ideals about land use to both African Americans and Indians during Reconstruction. According to Republicans, the West and the South had different land-use problems. In the West, Republicans believed, Native Americans had ignored farming possibilities by relying on hunting and gathering and were consequently living a "barbaric" lifestyle. In the South, slave plantations monopolized and exhausted the soil, allowing the rise of oligarchs threatening to the Union. Though each situation was unique, Republicans espoused the same solution for both: a proliferation of small farms. If Native Americans became small farmers, they could rise in the ranks of "civilization," and the West would experience a boom in agricultural production. If freed slaves became small farmers, they could change both nature and politics in the South; the region would no longer be led by the aristocratic "chivalry" responsible for secession, and exhausted land would blossom under new farming methods.

Eaton was in charge of the Freedmen's Bureau in the valley of the Mississippi district. Later, he became head of the Bureau of Education in the Grant administration. Beginning work in 1865, Eaton wrote that the "systems of education and industry devised for the Negro . . . completely demonstrated the ideal of free labor and of ultimately equal rights and opportunities for all." Eaton helped former slaves establish small farming communities at Davis Bend, Mississippi (Jefferson Davis's former plantation), and President's Island in Tennessee. To help "civilize" former slaves, Eaton recommended "churches and philanthropic associations for the schooling of contrabands in camps and barracks." The general believed that Grant's "attitude toward the Indian" was "closely concerned with the fate of the freemen." Just as with the freedmen, Eaton recommended placing "several of the Indian reservations in the hands" of religious organizations and favoring a course "which tends to [the Indians'] civilization and ultimate citizenship." Grant, Eaton argued, should follow this course of action despite the fact that "the average American . . . associated him [the Indian] with blood-curdling massacres."[64]

O. O. Howard served as the head of the Freedmen's Bureau in 1865, where he aggressively promoted land redistribution and education for freed slaves. In a June 14, 1865, letter to his subordinates, Howard explained his aims for the bureau. The employees were to "do all that behooves the Government in answering the question—'What shall we do with the Negro?'" The answer was clear: the freedmen should become citizens of the republic. In order to become citizens, he wrote, white "teachers, ministers, farmers and superintendents" needed to educate freed slaves in duties of American citizenship. To promote a black yeomanry, Howard frequently wrote to his close friend, Senator Samuel Pomeroy of Kansas, and urged him to pass an act redistributing land. Though the plan failed due to President Johnson's opposition, Pomeroy called for each ex-Confederate planter to give ten acres of land to every African American family living on the property at the time of the Emancipation Proclamation. In exchange, the planter would receive a pardon from the government. In defending the plan, Pomeroy labeled it a "Southern Homestead Act." "I need not argue to you," he alleged, "the advantage of a *Homestead* to the family and to the laborer."[65]

Howard's goals for land redistribution in the South never achieved fruition. The former abolitionist, however, continued such efforts in the West after his tenure at the Freedmen's Bureau ended. Howard arrived at Fort Vancouver—near present-day Portland, Oregon—in September 1874 as the new commander of the Department of the Columbia. By 1876, violence threatened to break out between the Nez Perce tribe and whites intruding on their territory in the Wallowa valley, a remote region in north-eastern Oregon. Howard's solution for white and Indian conflict in the West paralleled his proscription for freed slaves in the South: Indians needed to become small farmers on reservations. In May of 1877, during negotiations with the Nez Perce, Howard dismissed the Nez Perce claim to a hunting and gathering lifestyle as a "flourish of words." He stated: "Twenty times over I hear that the earth is your mother. . . . I want to hear it no more."[66]

Captain Richard Pratt served as a lieutenant with the Eleventh Indiana Cavalry during the Civil War. Unlike many volunteers, he applied to be-come an officer in the Regular Army after Appomattox. Pratt achieved a commission with the Tenth U.S. Cavalry, a unit made up of black enlisted men and white officers. In service on the frontier, Pratt became familiar with both Cherokee Indians and black soldiers. Cherokees, he wrote, "had manly bearing and fine physiques. Their intelligence, civilization, and common sense was a revelation, because I had concluded that as an army officer I was there to deal with atrocious aborigines." About the enlisted men, Pratt wrote: "Our Negro troopers grew in our estimate by their ready obedience and faithful performance of duty." After the passage of the Four-teenth and Fifteenth Amendments, Pratt had a discussion with a fellow officer as to the new "duties" the amendments mandated. "It seemed plain that under this amendment the Negro could not be relegated in army ser-vice to the Negro units of enlisted men solely," he recalled, "and the Indian could not continue to be imprisoned on separate tribal reservations. The rights of citizenship included fraternity and equal privilege for develop-ment." In the aftermath of the Civil War, Pratt viewed both freed slaves and Indians as potential citizens. But in order to be citizens, both groups had to adopt Anglo-American land-use practices and culture.[67]

While in army service near Fort Leavenworth in 1867, Pratt became concerned that instead of granting "equal privilege for development," the army sought to destroy Indians. General William T. Sherman wrote to Pratt's headquarters: "It is better the Indian race be obliterated." Pratt thus came to believe that "the white man's depravities and criminality were a greater menace to civilization than the Indians they maligned." Texans, he claimed, demanded federal protection "in order to secure the removal of

Federal troops from Reconstruction duties." The captain began arguing that Indians should be civilized through being taught how to farm. In Indian Territory, Pratt wrote in a letter to a newspaper, "the soil is fertile, farms are ready cleared . . . and every disposition of climate and country seems calculated to favor their primitive mode of life and for gradually bringing them to civilization." For Pratt, "civilization" meant giving up a hunting-and-gathering lifestyle and tilling fertile soil on a small farm. After fighting Cheyenne Indians in 1868, Pratt endorsed a policy promoted by his commanding general, William Babcock Hazen. Hazen's plan "was to build a house for each band chief at some favorable point along a creek or river, and break up, fence and plant corn and other products on a considerable acreage, put a farmer in charge of each band to show them how to raise crops to live on, and thus encourage them to quit their roving habits."[68]

After several Indian tribes surrendered to Pratt's unit in 1874, he urged tribal leaders that "their only safe course was to quit being tribal Indians, go out and live among us as individual men, adopt our language, [and] our industries." E. D. Townsend, an adjutant general in the Grant administration, ordered Pratt to take charge of Indian prisoners selected for imprisonment and reeducation at Fort Marion in St. Augustine, Florida. Pratt began his tenure at Fort Marion with an assault on Indian culture. He forced prisoners to cut their hair and "wear the clothing of the white man." To break down tribal affiliations, he ordered members from different groups to "guard" each other at night. Pratt also instructed the prisoners how to make a living in a free labor economy. He reported to Philip Sheridan—his new superior—that "the prisoners have made from $3,000 to $4,000 since they came, polishing sea beans, selling drawing books, bows and arrows, canes, etc." Furthermore, he invited one "Miss Mather . . . a friend of Miss Harriet Beecher Stowe" and an experienced teacher of freed slaves, to "educate" the prisoners. Stowe herself commended the prison for its civilizing effects. She wrote that the Indians "were looked upon in their transit with the mingled fear and curiosity with which one regards dangerous wild beasts. Gloomy, scowling, dressed in wild and savage habiliments." After Pratt's efforts, Stowe "found now no savages," observing during a visit: "The bell soon rang for school hours, and hurrying from all quarters came more dark men in the United States uniform, neat, compact, trim, with well-brushed boots and nicely kept clothing, and books in their hands."[69]

Despite Ulysses S. Grant replacing Andrew Johnson in 1868, the Republican Party faced stiff challenges to its Reconstruction policy in the West and the South between 1870 and 1876. First, the land-reform programs in the South, most notably Julian's Southern Homestead Act, failed to achieve the desired results. Second, a wave of violence broke out that threatened the viability of the southern Republican governments and the implementation of the Fourteenth and Fifteenth Amendments. Third, after 1873 the Republicans failed to broaden their electoral coalition beyond former slaves and diehard Unionists in the South. In the West, corruption and ongoing violence threatened the Peace Policy. Tribes who acquiesced, either by desire or compulsion, to the "civilization" program complained of poor agricultural training and funding shortages. Other tribes, such as the powerful Sioux of the northern Plains and the Nez Perce of the Northwest, refused to move onto reservations and fought hard to maintain their way of life. By 1874, however, the U.S. government was moving away from Reconstruction in the South while stepping up efforts in the West. Republicans gave up on transforming southern land-use practices, allowing the emergence of sharecropping and Jim Crow, while continuing to claim that Indians should become small farmers living in settled communities.

As a result of the Fourteenth and Fifteenth Amendments, as well as the Congressional Reconstruction acts, Republicans seized control of every former Confederate state except Virginia. These governments tried to build schools and railroads to create jobs and a new economy. Many subsidized railroad construction by giving loans of state bonds to companies. Together, the projects led to increased levels of taxation and government debt—which is unsurprising considering the relative lack of schools and railroads that existed before the war. Between 1868 and 1872, most southern railroads had been rebuilt, 3,300 miles of track were added, and public school systems were created. The taxes and debt incurred by these projects lent fodder to critics of Republican rule. As former slave John Roy Lynch, who served as a Republican congressman from Mississippi, recalled: "A new public school system was, for the first time, to be put in operation. . . . Money had to be raised for these purposes in addition to what was necessary to meet the current demands. There were only two ways in which the money could be raised—to borrow it or raise it by taxation."[70]

Efforts at land redistribution, the linchpin of the Radical program for changing southern agriculture and society, largely failed. Andrew Johnson had stalled much of the early efforts by pardoning former Confederates and restoring their property rights. Congress had been unwilling to entertain further confiscation and redistribution laws, especially after the Radical Republicans suffered defeats in the 1867 elections. In July 1868, believing that the Fourteenth Amendment would guarantee black rights, Congress ended the Freedmen's Bureau, ordering that bureau agents withdraw from the South by January 1, 1869. The one policy that the Radicals succeeded in passing—George W. Julian's 1866 southern homestead bill—failed to achieve the desired results.[71]

Julian, in formulating the plan, observed that nearly 47,700,000 acres of public land remained in former Confederate States. Unfortunately, yellow pine trees and cypress covered much of this land, making it unsuitable for farming. Freedmen's Bureau assistant commissioner Major General Wager Swayne reported that in Alabama, most of the public domain, "while extremely valuable for the manufacture of Rosin Turpentine and Lumber," was of no use to black people without capital and the proper tools. Swayne believed that freedmen preferred to buy an existing plot of improved farmland rather than risk planting on marginal soil. In Mississippi, Brevet Brigadier General Alvan C. Gillem reported that most of the public land was "either sandy pine barren or swamp, totally unfit for agricultural purposes."[72]

Moreover, violence and intimidation prevented many blacks from even applying. In Arkansas, Major General E. O. C. Ord wrote that freedmen "were being defrauded in various ways by the white population: refusal of pay for work done, threats, beatings, even murder." Florida provided the only marginal success. In that state, 419 ex-slave families settled on the public domain in 1868. Even these families, however, experienced hardship. One observer wrote: "Sprinkled along Mosquito Lagoon for about ten miles, over one thousand freedmen had been quickly reduced to a savage's existence. They lacked shelter, food, and other means to sustain life." The failure of redistribution undercut prospects for black political power in the South. As the black intellectual W. E. B. Du Bois later noted, land redistribution "could have rebuilt the economic foundations of Southern society, confiscated and redistributed wealth, and built a real democracy of industry for the masses of men."[73]

Violence threatened Republican policy in the South and the West. Violence, in fact, proved to be the indispensible element in derailing southern Reconstruction. Former Confederate general Nathan Bedford Forrest established the Ku Klux Klan in Tennessee during the summer of 1868, warning: "I intend to kill radicals. . . . [T]here is not a radical in this town [Memphis, Tennessee] but is a marked man, and if trouble should break out, none of them would be left alive." In Jackson County, Florida, over 150 people died in paramilitary violence. The death toll included black political leaders and a Jewish Republican named Samuel Fleischman. Prior to the

1868 presidential election, Republicans succeeded in registering more than 9,300 black voters in twenty-two Georgia counties. Yet, Ulysses S. Grant received only eighty-seven votes in these counties. Charles Sumner recognized what was happening: "Others may be cool and indifferent; but I have warred with Slavery too long, in all its different forms, not to be aroused when this old enemy shows its head under an *alias*. Once it was Slavery; now it is Caste."[74]

A group of "Col'd Citizens" from Tuscaloosa, Alabama, pleaded to President Grant in 1871 for help. The men reported that "the Clique Known as the K.Ks [Ku Klux] Visited the House of our most guieless [*sic*] Col'd Citizens and Shot him dead after which they Rob'd his house of about $200 in money and carried off his Gun and pistol.... [W]e hope as our Lives, Liberty, and Property are in Eminent Perill [*sic*] that you . . . Do something." John A. Minnis, a U.S. attorney residing in Montgomery, Alabama, recognized the intent of the violence: to reestablish white Democratic authority. "I have examined two white men," he reported to Grant, "who had belonged to these 'Klans.' One said its objects were to put down the d___d *Radicals* and *negroes*, using their language, another speaking of a different 'Klan' said it was to keep the Radicals from voting the negroes. It has never come to my knowledge that any Democrat has been maltreated or even threatened."[75]

Likewise, in April 1871, white settlers massacred Apaches who had surrendered to the U.S. Army at Camp Grant in Arizona Territory for transfer to a reservation. One C. A. Luke, from Prescott, Arizona, defended the slaughter and attacked the government's Peace Policy. He implored Grant: "In the name of this suffering people, to give no heed to pretending peace Commissioners, for peace with the Indians in this Country is altogether impossible, until they have [been] thoroughly wiped [out]." Samuel F. Tappan, a supporter of the Peace Policy, warned: "Unless [Grant's] wise and humane Indian Policy is made permanent and powerful by incorporation into the law of the land and a simple form of government for the Indian, it must sooner or later prove their destruction, and the recent fate of the apaches at Camp Grant, Arizonia [*sic*], falls upon the remnants of the race."[76]

Between 1870 and 1874, Grant and the Republican Congress responded aggressively to the violence. A *New York Herald* reporter quoted the president as stating, "My policy is peace. When I said, 'Let us have peace,' I meant it. I want peace on the Plains as everywhere else." In April 1871, Congress passed the Ku Klux Klan Act, bringing civil rights crimes under the jurisdiction of federal law. The act also allowed military intervention and the suspension of habeas corpus by the president. Grant had aggressively lobbied for the bill and did not hesitate to declare nine counties of the South Carolina upcountry in a "condition of lawlessness" in October 1871. Federal soldiers entered the area, making numerous arrests of Klansmen. For a time, the administration was successful. Violence ceased by the summer of 1872, and the ensuing presidential election of that year, in the words of historian James McPherson, "was the fairest and most democratic presidential election in the South until 1968." Grant also defended the Peace Policy. In a message to Congress, he asked: "Can not the Indian be made a useful and productive member of society? If the effort is made in good faith, we will stand better before the civilized nations of the earth and our own consciences for having made it." In his second inaugural address, Grant declared: "I entertain the confident hope that the policy now pursued will in a few years bring all the Indians upon reservations, where they will live in houses, and have school-houses and churches, and will be pursuing peaceful and self-sustaining avocations."[77]

While Grant won the election of 1872, that contest and the ensuing economic depression of 1873 foretold the demise of Reconstruction in the South. Many of the Radical Republicans, including George W. Julian and Carl Schurz, broke with the president in the early 1870s, forming a new "Liberal Republican" party allied with Democrats. This party nominated former Republican stalwart Horace Greeley for the 1872 election. Greeley, the antislavery editor of the *New York Tribune* and an aggressive defender of Yosemite, recommended that after receiving their new rights, former slaves needed to "root, hog, or die." Even the Radical George Julian wrote: "The final ratification of the Fifteenth Constitutional Amendment, which was declared in force on the thirteenth of March, 1870, perfectly consummated the mission of the Republican party.... [W]hat the country needed was not a stricter enforcement of party discipline[,] not military methods and the fostering of sectional hate, but oblivion of the past." The departure of idealists previously devoted to political and civic equality for black Americans deprived the Republican Party of much of its energy and commitment to enforcing the Fourteenth and Fifteenth Amendments. The Liberal Republicans' stance also meant that during the election of 1876, when both Democrats and Republicans campaigned for white votes, Democrats vehemently opposed Reconstruction while Republicans were loath to continue it.[78]

Identifying the reasons for the Radicals' abandonment still mystifies historians, but several claims can be made. First, many Radicals were angered by Grant's attempt to annex the island of Santo Domingo—the modern nations of Haiti and the Dominican Republic. Second, idealistic Republicans became angry with the "machine" politicians who were gaining increasing control of the party. B. Gratz Brown, a liberal Republican from Missouri, complained that the "ordinary party machinery" was "overborne . . . by official control and dependent . . . upon the direction of those who have shown such grievous incapacity." Third, and perhaps most important, some Republicans worried that increased federal power threatened long-standing American traditions of federalism. For example, Salmon P. Chase had used a states' rights argument against the Fugitive Slave Law during the 1850s, arguing for the "right of the states to protect the liberty of their citizens against other citizens claiming rights under federal authority." As the historian Andrew Slap concludes, "Reconstruction required uses of federal power that they [Republicans] admitted could be seen as tyrannical. While they ironically supported military rule to safeguard republican government, by the late 1860s, they also increasingly feared that wartime changes in the North threatened that very system."[79]

Despite the withdrawal of prominent Radicals such as Julian and Schurz, the 1872 election showcased Reconstruction's continuing power. The Klan had been broken; Grant and the Republicans carried most of the South and the traditionally Republican North. Yet, the triumph proved to be a double-edged sword for southern Republicans. Black voters had turned out in huge numbers in 1872 for Republicans, while nearly all whites had supported Democrats. The support led southern blacks to demand Senate and congressional positions. Blanche K. Bruce, a former slave and later a schoolteacher from Mississippi, became the first African American to serve a full term in the Senate. More than ever, however, southern Democrats could promote white supremacy and tar Republicans as an alien force. John Roy Lynch bitterly recalled the effectiveness of the charge of "Negro domination": "To constitute 'Negro domination' it does not necessarily follow that Negroes must be elected to office, but that in all elections in which white men may be divided, if the Negro vote should be sufficiently decisive in determining the result, the white man or men . . . elected . . . would represent 'Negro domination.'" Lynch claimed—with perhaps a little exaggeration—that prior to the widespread use of this label, a "Southern white man could become a Republican without being socially ostracized." Now, many were turning to the Democratic Party.[80]

The panic of 1873, caused by the failure of prominent banking company Jay Cooke and Company, led to an economic collapse that threatened southern Reconstruction. Numerous businesses failed. Within a year, half of the nation's iron foundries suspended production. Within three years, over half of the country's railroads had defaulted on their loans. Track construction ceased. As historian Eric Foner points out, "The sixty-five months following the Panic of 1873 remains the longest period of uninterrupted economic contraction in American history." After the failure of many railroad lines, southern Republican governments were left with little money, having underwritten many of the operations with state bonds. Moreover, as with most elections in American history, voters in a time of recession turned against the party in power in 1874 and 1875. In the South, with whites turning out in huge numbers for the Democrats, Republicans lost control of every state except for Florida, Louisiana, Mississippi, and South Carolina, where blacks comprised a majority of the population. On the national level, Democrats won control of the House of Representatives and gained ten seats in the Senate.[81]

In the states with black majorities, Democrats and white militias resorted to violence to overcome opposition. Democrats in John Roy Lynch's state started the "Mississippi Plan" to gather all whites into the Democratic Party and intimidate black voters. One Democratic newspaper carried the slogan, "Carry the election peacefully if we can, forcibly if we must." The difference between 1874 and a few years earlier, when similar violence threatened Republican rule, was that the government was unwilling to intervene. To be fair, the issue was not simply a lack of will; the Supreme Court 's *Slaughterhouse* decision decreed that the Fourteenth Amendment did not interfere with state control of citizenship. Yosemite defender Stephen J. Field, dissenting from the decision, argued that if the court interpreted the amendment in this fashion, "it was a vain and idle enactment, which accomplished nothing and most unnecessarily excited Congress and the people on its passage." *U.S. v. Cruikshank* (1876) overturned several convictions the government had obtained using the Ku Klux Klan Act, arguing that the federal government could only prohibit state and not individual violations of civil rights.[82]

Northern Republican leadership, deprived of its Radical element by retirement, death, and the Liberal Republican revolt, also believed that the continuing commitment to Reconstruction could lead to electoral defeat. John Roy Lynch observed that during the 1874 elections, "nearly all Democratic clubs in the state [Mississippi] were converted into armed military companies. Funds with which to purchase arms were believed to have been contributed by the national Democratic organization. Nearly every Republican meeting was attended by one or more of those clubs or companies, the members of which were distinguished by red shirts indicative of blood." At first, Lynch thought of fighting back, since "some of the colored Republicans had been Union soldiers." Yet, "seventy-five percent" of the white population "were not only tried and experienced soldiers, but they were fully armed and equipped for the work before them." When black militia mobilized in Louisiana in 1873, an attack by white paramilitaries left seventy of them dead.[83]

Lynch and Mississippi's white Republican governor, Aldebert Ames, decided to plea for federal intervention. Lynch met with Republican congressional leader James G. Blaine to urge the influential representative to support the federal elections bill, a measure granting protection to black voters. "If that bill had become a law," Blaine responded, "the defeat of the Republican party throughout the country would have been a foregone conclusion. . . . I could not have carried my own state, Maine, if that bill passed." Governor Ames's request for federal soldiers from the Grant administration was also denied. Before the request came in, "a committee of prominent Republicans from Ohio called on" the president and "informed him in a most emphatic way that if the requisition of Governor Ames were honored, the Democrats would not only carry Mississippi, which would be lost to Republicans in any event, but the Democratic success in Ohio would . . . be an assured fact." Weary of economic depression, tired of military efforts, and with the goal of reunion secured, many northern voters gave up on southern Reconstruction.[84]

Grant called on Congress one last time in January 1875 to suspend habeas corpus and declare martial law to combat the Ku Klux Klan and other white paramilitary organizations. Congress refused. Rutherford B. Hayes ended the last protections for Republican regimes in South Carolina, Florida, and Louisiana after his election to the presidency in 1876. Southern Democrats had threatened to prevent Hayes's inauguration after the close contest with Democrat Samuel Tilden if the president-elect continued to support southern Republicans. The outcome of Reconstruction in the South, however, was already a foregone conclusion before the election. Ulysses S. Grant sadly noted: "Looking back, over the whole policy of reconstruction, it seems to me that the wisest thing would have been to have continued for some time the military rule. . . . [M]ilitary rule would have been just to all: the negro who wanted freedom, the white man who wanted protection, the Northern man who wanted Union."[85]

While Reconstruction came to an end in the South, the Greater Reconstruction continued in the West, culminating in Henry Laurens Dawes's General Allotment Act of 1887. The federal government, despite repeated failures, continued to try to convert Indians into yeomen farmers. As historian David Rich Lewis explains, "The physical realities of reservations and the environmental changes resulting from consolidation and directed subsistence change became major obstacles in the creation of self-sufficient agrarian communities." In the dry West, Indians had poor access to water, which was often diverted to white farms before it reached reservations. Government-appointed agricultural advisors also refused to recognize viable Indian farming methods—such as controlled burning—as legitimate practices. Moreover, these advisors were often political appointees, ill equipped to teach farming techniques. Finally, confined on reservations, tribes lacked the access to credit and markets needed for success. Nippawa, a Native American residing in Lyons County, Kansas, relayed these problems to President Grant in June 1871. The farming advisor, Nippawa complained, "takes no interest in learning our boys to farm." He continued: "We have never had land enough broken to raise enough to last us one year. . . . [E]vry thing we get we have to get it from the trader and pay his prices." Nippawa concluded: "Wee, wish to farm but wee have not the means to farm." While some Indian families achieved success with grazing, efforts at farming generally failed.[86]

An 1875 travelogue by journalist Edward King shows how northerners like Dawes had abandoned efforts at land allotment and civilization in the South while continuing such plans for Native Americans in the West. During Reconstruction, after the Union had been secured, many Americans came to believe that black people could not be "civilized" and become a part of American society. King described how "the Negro was . . . susceptible of civilization only to a certain degree; devoid of moral consciousness, and usually, of course, ignorant." Yet, King was proud of the "common schools among the Cherokee," believing that "civilization was beginning to do its work." The journalist claimed that civilized Indians began "losing their savage traits" and looked like white men. Indeed, in the West, continuing violence spurred further government efforts to "civilize" Indian tribes. Unlike those in the South, local whites demanded that the army remove Native Americans from their lands, allowing settlers to claim new property.[87]

During the 1870s, the government's reservation policy faced major challenges from continued violent conflict and white pressures for land. Warfare continued on the Plains and in the Northwest despite Grant's desire for peace. For example, in 1873 President Grant ordered Major General Edward Canby to negotiate with the hostile Modoc Indian tribe in Oregon to force the group onto a reservation. The Modocs, led by a fierce warrior nicknamed "Captain Jack," shot Canby when talks broke down. General Sherman, now the chief commander in the U.S. Army, wired to the general of the Pacific division: "You will be fully justified in their extermination." Grant, however, wanted the Modocs punished not "as an act of revenge . . . but as an act of justice as well as protection of peaceful settlers." The president continued to defend the Peace Policy after the Red River War in 1874 and 1875. Grant ordered the captured leaders of the Red River tribes to be sent to Fort Marion, Florida, for "re-education" and "civilization" under Captain Richard Pratt. On February 1, 1876, Secretary of Interior Zachariah Chandler reaffirmed the reservation policy as war began with the powerful Sioux tribe of the northern Plains. He announced that "all Indians not on the reservations were to be considered hostile" and mandated that the army force all tribes onto reservations.[88]

At the surrender of the Nez Perce in October 1877, Generals O. O. Howard and Nelson Miles promised Chief Joseph that the tribe would be allowed to return to their homeland. Instead, as historian Elliott West describes, when word came to General Sherman of the surrender, he ordered that "'all these captured Indians must never be allowed to return to Oregon' but sent forever to Indian Territory where, as happy farmers, they would 'soon be self-supporting.'" Congress waited over six months before providing an appropriation to establish the Nez Perce in the territory. In the meantime, at a prison camp in Kansas, twenty-one men, women, and children died from disease and malnutrition. Upon arrival, the Nez Perce called their designated acreage in Indian Territory "Eeikish Pah," or "The Heat." The land proved ill suited to farming, and disease rates remained high. In 1880 the Nez Perce chief Joseph related to a reporter that since the end of the war, 153 of his people had perished. By 1884, the tribe had moved from being farmers to leasing more than 80 percent of their holdings to ranchers and receiving income from what an agent called "Indian curiosities and trinkets."[89]

During the Hayes administration, many government officials realized that concentrating tribes on reservations did not end violence or create prosperity. Instead, they argued, existing reservations should be divided into 160-acre parcels allotted to individual Indians. Indians could then take up farming, become civilized, and eventually assimilate into white society. Carl Schurz, appointed secretary of the interior by Hayes, wanted to "set the Indians to work as agriculturists or herders, thus to break up their habits of savage life." The government, he recommended, should "educate [Indian] youth of both sexes, so as to introduce to the growing generation civilized ideas, wants and aspirations." Next, Schurz claimed that the government should "allot parcels of land to Indians in severalty and to give them individual title to their farms in fee . . . to foster the pride of individual ownership of property." The ultimate goal was to "treat the Indians like other inhabitants of the United States, under the laws of the land." John Wesley Powell, a one-armed veteran of Shiloh and a western explorer, gave similar recommendations. Since traditional tribal lands represented "everything most sacred to Indian society," Powell claimed, "removal of the Indians [was] the first step to be taken in their civilization." After Indians had been removed, he explained, "individual land tenure would undermine both the clan system and 'traditional modes of inheritance,'" leading to citizenship and assimilation.[90]

The economic motives behind allotment, however, were as strong as or stronger than Powell's and Schurz's ideas. Whites both in and bordering the West believed that if Indians did not develop lands to their full economic potential, the tribes forfeited any claim to them. For this reason, the Greater Reconstruction continued for Indians while stalling in the South. The *New Orleans Times-Picayune* argued that Indians could not "any longer be permitted to usurp for the purposes of barbarism, the fertile lands, the products of mines, the broad valleys and wooded mountain slopes, which organized society regards as magazines of those forces which civilization requires for its maintenance and development." Farmers angry at the lack of arable land available for homesteads demanded that the government open up Indian lands to those who would "use" it. As historian Frederick Hoxie astutely notes, "Reformers could not arouse Congress with simple rhetoric. The goal of total assimilation galvanized support for a new land policy among a wide range of political interests."[91]

The General Allotment Act of 1887 was the culmination of several decades of Republican thought on civilization and proper land use. Written by Henry Laurens Dawes, the idealistic Massachusetts Republican who had defended Yosemite State Park, the General Allotment Act authorized the president to break up Indian reservations and distribute 160 acres of the land to family heads, 80 acres to each person over eighteen, and 40 acres to children under eighteen. The remaining reservation acreage was to be opened to homesteaders. Dawes believed that reducing the size of reservations "would bring the two races closer together and allow American institutions—its schools, its political system, and its expanding economy—to raise up the Indian." During the 1850s, 1860s, and into the 1870s, Republicans believed that the United States should organize its land to favor small farmers. Small farmers, by tilling the soil for multiple generations, promoted civilization. Yeomen also created the social conditions ripe for a republic, preventing "oligarchs" and "aristocrats" from rising to destroy the Union.

Yet, by the 1880s, due to the departure of Radicals like George Julian and white desires for Indian land, the Republican Party stopped favoring small farmers in almost every arena except Indian policy. Even in Indian policy, allotment would fail to create a prosperous Indian yeomanry. White people desiring tribal land gained the most from the bill. Between 1887 and the 1934 Indian Reorganization Act overturning Dawes's law, Indian landholdings shrunk from 138 to 52 million acres. The government opened up 22 million acres to direct white settlement, and 38 million acres went into the public domain. Over time, Indians often lost the land allotted to them, increasing white ownership. In its attempts to turn freed slaves and Indians into prosperous small farmers—the ideal form of land use for white northerners in the mid-nineteenth century—the Greater Reconstruction proved a failure.[92]

CONCLUSION

Retrenchment in the South, Allotment in the West

After the failures of southern Reconstruction, George Washington Julian gave land reform in the West one last chance. Appointed as the surveyor general of New Mexico Territory in July 1885 by Democratic president Grover Cleveland, Julian found what he deemed widespread fraud, speculation, and corruption in the territory's disbursement of public lands. New Mexico was strikingly different than other parts of the United States. The territory was originally part of Spain and then Mexico; the Mexican government had issued about 400,000 acres in communal land grants prior to the U.S. conquest. At the time of Julian's appointment, former Mexicans—"nuevomexicanos"—still lived in the territory and practiced communal farming. The Indiana Radical viewed these long-standing traditions of land use as wasteful, stagnant, and monopolistic. The solution was the same one he had advocated for the South during Reconstruction: "Small land-holdings, thrifty tillage, and compact settlements will supersede great monopolies, slovenly agriculture and industrial stagnation." Julian invalidated communal land grants in the territory in favor of individual allotments, intending to transform New Mexico into a place of independent family farmers.[1]

Julian's efforts failed. One of his first targets was the Las Vegas land grant, a half-million-acre communal land property that the Indianan wanted to reduce to less than 10,000 acres. After Anglo-American residents began erecting fences on the disputed land, local residents of Mexican descent responded by organizing a secret group called the "Gorras Blancas" (White Caps). The faction organized public protests and nighttime fence cuttings. Stephen Wallace Dorsey, a former Republican senator living in New Mexico, warned Julian that even without this organized opposition, small farms were hard to manage in the western deserts. Dorsey argued that the arid region required "a different system of disposal and settlement than the more fertile areas for which the homestead policy had been originally designed." Dorsey was right. Julian's accusations of fraud undermined both fraudulent and legal homestead claims in the territory, and his assault on communal landholdings instigated significant local resistance. New Mexicans successfully convinced the next U.S. president—Benjamin Harrison—to remove the feisty Indianan from his post. Julian muttered that New Mexico would soon "degenerate into barbarism." The Republican Party and America as a whole had moved on from the land-development debates that were at the center of Julian's political experience.[2]

Nevertheless, ideas linking multigeneration land use with civilized communities, free labor, the safety of the Union, and increased agricultural prosperity produced new institutions and sweeping changes in American life. The U.S. Department of Agriculture (USDA) began collecting and distributing seeds several months after its establishment in 1862. The USDA's aim was to improve production by identifying the most productive plant strains and spreading them throughout the nation. In 1865 the USDA distributed 763,231 seed packages. By 1880, the department passed out over a million packages per year. In the early 1870s, the USDA also began experimenting on fruit fungi and diseases. As California geologist William Brewer noted, chemistry and other sciences "revolutionized some of the [mechanical] arts and produced great changes in agriculture." The new department pioneered reductive soil science, determining the soil components that enabled plant growth. While present-day critics of the USDA have lamented this focus, the original intent of the USDA's applied science was to encourage agricultural permanence on small farms. The USDA also experimented with domesticating the American bison and introducing new plant and animal species to the United States.[3]

The Homestead Act was one of the most celebrated laws in U.S. history, but it had a decidedly mixed effect. While thousands of people acquired land titles, speculation and competing land grants to colleges and railroads sealed off access to the most productive plots. Between 1860 and 1900, the number of farm acreage in the United States rose from 407,213,000 to over 838,000,000. Of these acres, 80 million were homesteads. Corporations also exploited the law to acquire land monopolies. Out of the homesteads, a sizable number went into corporate hands. A timber company, for example, could pay several people to file adjacent homestead claims and then purchase the land from each of them. Ironically, one of the law's biggest successes was stimulating immigration by Europeans desirous of land. The law also confronted harsh environmental realities in the West. The arid environment made farming 160-acre plots difficult. Larger farms were generally more productive in the region because of the low yield per acre in comparison to more fertile plots in the East. Despite the aspirations of wartime Radicals, small farming became less and less tenable in the late nineteenth century.[4]

Land-grant colleges grew to their modern size and influence only after 1900. In the first decades after the Civil War, few people enrolled in the schools. The institutions also provided few extension services to their communities. Instead, wealthy young people received their education from private colleges, and middle-class adults frequented the increasingly popular Chautauqua lectures. African American schools were the exception. Alcorn State University in Mississippi became the first black land-grant university in 1871. Hampton University of Virginia became the second a year later. The former abolitionist Frederick Douglass wrote to Justin Morrill in excitement: "I see no great or happy future for my race or for the Republic outside general education and it seems to me that you, dear sir, standing where you do can do no better work for the nation than to press this idea." In 1872 Morrill called for the creation of a permanent trust to provide more funding for land-grant colleges. The Vermonter did not succeed until August 1890, when Congress passed, and President Benjamin Harrison signed, the "Second Morrill Land Grant Act." The act gave states $15,000 a year to maintain their colleges. (The amount later was increased to $25,000.) With the increase in support, land-grant schools thrived. By 2001, 106 land-grant colleges and universities existed in the United States.[5]

The nature parks in Yosemite and Yellowstone are also a legacy of Civil War–era ideas about civilization and union. Park supporters such as Frederick Law Olmsted wanted to demonstrate the continuing viability of republican government by establishing Yosemite State Park during a bloody civil war. These men believed that, unlike European nations, America needed to secure public access to its greatest natural features. Both wishes emanated from the belief that America was the one shining light of liberty in the world. Reflecting ideas that Olmsted developed in the 1850s, park supporters also thought that Yosemite had an important civilizing mission. The government, however, did not establish the park to "preserve" the valley and the Mariposa Big Tree Grove from mankind's destructive influence; Olmsted and the other first managers actually wanted to encourage visitation to these areas. Their goals for the valley contradicted the aims of George W. Julian and James Mason Hutchings, who believed that the government should reserve the land for small farmers. As a result of Hutchings's determined opposition, California did not implement Olmsted's plan for protecting the park. In this failure, however, politicians such as Samuel Pomeroy found reason to put future "natural curiosities" under federal control. Yosemite itself became a national park in October 1890, following the suggestion of the *New York Times* that "national pride," engendered by a national park, "would insure a degree of tasteful attention that has utterly failed to be elicited by State pride."[6]

President Ulysses S. Grant presided over the completion of the first transcontinental railroad on May 10, 1869, at Promontory Point, Utah. The Central Pacific, headed by Leland Stanford, Charles Crocker, Mark Hopkins, and Collis P. Huntington—all founding members of the Republican Party in California—had worked eastward from California. The Union Pacific had been built west from Omaha, Nebraska. Workers, businessmen, and engineers produced four more transcontinental railroads over the next several decades. The railroads led to an explosion of westward migration, the creation of a nationwide market, and the conquest of Native American tribes. "I regard the building of these railroads as the most important event of modern times," wrote General William T. Sherman in 1883, "and believe that they account fully for the peace and good order which now prevail throughout the country, and for the extraordinary prosperity which now prevails in this land." Sherman, referring to the Indian wars, believed that the railroad, "in the great battle of civilization with barbarism . . . has become the *greater* cause" of victory. Both sport and market hunters used railroad lines to devastate the buffalo herds that tribes depended on for survival. Yet, contrary to the framers' intentions for the 1862 Pacific Railroad Act, the transcontinental line *did not* promote the establishment of small farms in the West. Instead, the improved transportation infrastructure allowed for large commercial corn and beef operations.[7]

Ultimately, Republican ideas on the proper relationship between civilization, land use, and society failed to improve the social and economic lives of Indians in the West and black people in the South. Allotment divided families, negated Indian access to valuable mineral reserves and timberland, and failed to produce prosperous farming communities. Despite the hopes for land kindled by Reconstruction, African Americans experienced the rise of sharecropping, impoverishment, lynching, and a renewed commitment by many white Americans to racial supremacy. If these ideas failed, one might ask, why were they important? Moreover, since the North *did* become an industrial powerhouse—with the

Republican Party of the 1880s and 1890s calling for tariff protection, the gold standard, and an unregulated market—what is the explanatory value of the party's earlier agrarian views?[8]

Understanding northerners in the Civil War era as a people with a fundamentally agrarian outlook on life allows historians to make new connections between seemingly different topics. An example from this book is the link between Reconstruction policy in the American South and Indian policy in the West. Historians have often lamented the failure of land redistribution in the postwar South as a "lost moment," a period in history where economic and political equality could have been secured for the freed slaves. Yet, scholars also rightly criticize federal efforts to force Native Americans to give up their tribal identity and become small farmers. What is missing from both stories is the fact that the same fundamental ideology was behind both agendas. Republicans at the time did not see any inconsistency in promoting African American land rights in the South while curtailing Native American freedoms in the West. Both groups, they believed, would become small farmers and, in doing so, adopt white cultural values. Since most northerners lived in rural communities and celebrated the environmental and political benefits of small farming, converting others to their lifestyle seemed natural. Richard Henry Pratt is the perfect example of this impulse.[9]

Furthermore, I suggest that historians rethink employing the industrial revolution as the leitmotif for the nineteenth-century United States. Yes, the United States did become the world's preeminent industrial power. And yes, in the late eighteenth and early nineteenth centuries, a self-sufficient economy of small farms and artisans gave way to a system in which farmers and producers created goods for a distant marketplace. Nevertheless, most Americans continued to live in rural areas. Farmers continued to produce for both themselves and urban markets. What this study shows is that the physical environment—farms—in which ordinary people lived shaped their politics and views on ideal land use. To northerners in the mid-nineteenth century, a future of small farmers extending westward seemed within reach. Even in the 1880s, George Julian clung to this vision during his tenure as territorial governor of New Mexico. The agrarian dream also proved stubbornly resilient in Indian policy because it suited the purposes of white settlers desirous of Indian land.

While scholars and the general public have long been tempted to look at the industrial economy of the late 1800s and early 1900s and find past "causes," this book shows that one cannot understand the complexity and nuance of the Civil War era without understanding the agrarian world that the participants lived in. In 1865 the victorious Republican Party seemed poised to shape America in the image of the farming communities in which many party members had grown up. Instead, after the end of Reconstruction, America entered what Mark Twain called the "Gilded Age." Arguments about how to acquire, manage, and profit from land no longer were near the center of politics, as they had seemed to be in the 1850s and 1860s. The old Republicanism of the Civil War seemed obsolete. In 1873 famous New York diarist George Templeton Strong noted that "Republicanism has grown immoral in its old ages and survived much of its usefulness." The Republican Party of the "Gilded Age" instead shifted to policies that encouraged industrial growth. Knowledge of this later development, however, does not absolve historians from presenting the politics of the Civil War era as it was understood by the men and women who lived in that world.[10]

Notes

ABBREVIATIONS

ADC   Anna E. Dickinson Collection, Manuscript Division, Library of Congress, Washington, D.C.

CFP   Cole Family Papers, Charles E. Young Research Library, Department of Special Collections, University of California, Los Angeles

CG   *Congressional Globe*

DEB   *Daily Evening Bulletin* (San Francisco)

G&JP   Joshua R. Giddings and George Washington Julian Papers, Manuscript Division, Library of Congress, Washington, D.C.

KSHS   Kansas State Historical Society, Lawrence, Kansas

NYDT   *New-York Daily Times*

NYT   *New York Times*

SFB   *San Francisco Bulletin*

INTRODUCTION

1. Wright, *Old South, New South*, 52; Paludan, *A People's Contest*, 170, 173; Bushman, "Markets and Composite Farms in Early America," 351.

2. Paludan, *A People's Contest*, 152, 156.

3. Stoll, *Larding the Lean Earth*, 122; Brady, *War upon the Land*, 17. For earlier discussions of soil differences, see Bagley, *Soil Exhaustion and the Civil War*; and Majewski, *Modernizing a Slave Economy*.

4. For information on the naming of the Republican Party, see Gienapp, *Origins of the Republican Party*, 105.

5. Foner, *Free Soil, Free Labor, Free Men*, 4; Wilentz, *The Rise of American Democracy*, 765; McPherson, *For Cause and Comrades*, 27–28.

6. Richard White, "'Are You an Environmentalist or Do You Work for a Living?,'" in *Uncommon Ground*, ed. Cronon, 172.

7. Rodgers, "Republicanism," 18; Onuf, *Statehood and Union*, 110–11, 113.

8. Lorain, *Nature and Reason Harmonized*, 525. Special thanks must be given to Benjamin Cohen, a former colleague at the University of Virginia, for alerting me to this source. For an extensive discussion of Lorain's work, see Cohen, *Notes from the Ground*, 97.

9. Eric Foner and William Gienapp argue that a commitment to "free labor ideology, grounded in the precepts that free labor was economically and socially superior to slave labor and that the distinctive quality of Northern society was the opportunity it offered wage earners to property-owning independence" united the Republicans (Foner, *Free*

Soil, Free Labor, Free Men, xxxvi). See also Gienapp, Origins of the Republican Party, 353–54; Gienapp, "Who Voted for Lincoln?," in Abraham Lincoln and the American Political Tradition, ed.. Thomas, 70.

10. Gallagher, Confederate War, 72, 98. Historians often miss how the debate over land development changed after 1848, either talking about the salience of Jeffersonian "agrarianism" or the ubiquity of "manifest destiny" throughout the nineteenth century. For one example, see Somkin, Unquiet Eagle, 117.

11. Paludan, A People's Contest, 156.

12. Philip Shaw Paludan argues that the Homestead Act "helped Northerners look away from the problems of an industrializing society" (Paludan, A People's Contest, 167). To a certain extent, this characterization is putting the cart before the horse. I contend that northerners thought they were creating an agricultural society in the West and did not envision the industrialization and urbanization of the later nineteenth century.

13. See Runte, Yosemite, 3.

14. George W. Julian, "The Overshadowing Question," in Speeches on Political Questions, ed. Child, 448; Marx, The Machine in the Garden, 23.

15. Earle, Jacksonian Antislavery, 15; Gallagher, Union War, 152. Two recent books have tried connecting events in the United States West and South during Reconstruction. Heather Cox Richardson focuses on the image of the West in nineteenth-century American politics, arguing that the popular mythology of the region created a belief held nationwide that "success came through hard work and that all Americans were working their way up" (Richardson, West from Appomattox, 5). Elliott West, in The Last Indian War: The Nez Perce Story, seeks the "common thread to emancipation, the Freedmen's Bureau, and federal occupation of the South on the one hand and western railroad surveys, reservations, Indian wars, and Yellowstone National Park" on the other (West, The Last Indian War, 21). I argue that the link northerners saw between land use and social structure provided one of the "common threads."

16. Susan-Mary Grant and Phillip Shaw Paludan contend that investigating the thoughts and beliefs of representative individuals or "thinkers" gives shape to otherwise abstract discussions of ideology and attitudes in the North during the Civil War era. See Grant, North over South, 11; and Paludan, A Covenant with Death, xii.

CHAPTER 1

1. Seward, "Freedom in the New Territories," in The Senate, 1789–1989: Classic Speeches, ed. Byrd, 308.

2. Foner, Free Soil, Free Labor, Free Men, xiv; Berwanger, The Frontier against Slavery, xii; Freehling, The Road to Disunion, vol. 1, 306; Morrison, Slavery and the American West, 278.

3. For a description of Jefferson's views on Missouri, see Freehling, The Road to Disunion, vol. 1, 119–22, 144.

4. Seward, "Freedom in the New Territories," 300, 311. There was also a gender dimension to the debate over slavery's expansion. Some northerners believed slavery was "incongruous to northern family ideals," pointing to the sexual exploitation of slave

women as harmful both to black and white families. See Pierson, *Free Hearts and Free Homes*, 18.

5. Seward, "Freedom in the New Territories," 299, 309.

6. Ibid., 299–300. One historian has persuasively argued that Seward was *more* concerned about an East-West split than a North-South severing. See Wilson, *Space, Time, and Freedom*, 219.

7. Peterson, *The Jefferson Image*, 167; Seward, "Freedom in the New Territories," 311.

8. Onuf, *Statehood and Union*, 110; Wood, *Creation of the American Republic*, 52, 55, 56; Wilson, *Space, Time, and Freedom*, 4, 12; McCoy, *The Elusive Republic*, 75, 10.

9. Onuf, *Jefferson's Empire*, 143.

10. Gates, *History of Public Land Law*, 219; Robbins, *Our Landed Heritage*, 7–8; White, *"It's Your Misfortune and None of My Own,"* 138; Hyman, *American Singularity*, 25; Onuf, *Statehood and Union*, 21.

11. Hyman, *American Singularity*, 20–21, 24; Onuf, *Jefferson's Empire*, 113; Onuf, *Statehood and Union*, 109–10, 113; Cohen, *Notes from the Ground*, 28.

12. Robbins, *Our Landed Heritage*, 17–18; Ellis, *American Sphinx*, 137.

13. Appleby, *Capitalism and a New Social Order*, 99; Onuf, *Jefferson's Empire*, 55–56; White, *"It's Your Misfortune and None of My Own,"* 63.

14. Ellis, *American Sphinx*, 84; Onuf, *Jefferson's Empire*, 5, 19–20; Wallace, *Jefferson and the Indians*, 95; Appleby, *Thomas Jefferson*, 107.

15. White, *"It's Your Misfortune and None of My Own,"* 74; Onuf, *Jefferson's Empire*, 45; Watson, *Liberty and Power*, 9.

16. *Annals of Congress*, 15th Cong., 2nd sess., February 1819, 1178; *Annals of Congress*, 15th Cong., 2nd sess., February, 1819, 1206.

17. R. King to J. A. King and C. King, February 20, 1820, in King, *Life and Correspondence of Rufus King*, 6:279; Stoll, *Larding the Lean Earth*, 70; Lorain, *Nature and Reason Harmonized*, x, 525; Onuf, *Statehood and Union*, 126, 130; Rothman, *Slave Country*, 116. Lorain was also morally opposed to slavery, writing: "[I]t cannot . . . be readily imagined, that I would wish to see slavery existing in any part of my native country, where the rights of man have been so highly and justly appreciated" (Lorain, *Nature and Reason Harmonized*, 525).

18. Ellis, *American Sphinx*, 84–85; D. Corry to R. King, February 7, 1820, in King, *Life and Correspondence of Rufus King*, 6:268; King, *Substance of Two Speeches*, 35; B. P. Chase to R. King, November 28, 1820, in King, *Life and Correspondence of Rufus King*, 6:363.

19. Stoll, *Larding the Lean Earth*, 125, 129; *Annals of Congress*, 15th Cong., 2nd sess., February 1819, 1210, 1205.

20. J. A. King to Tompkins, March 27, 1820, in King, *Life and Correspondence of Rufus King*, 6:322; Cohen, *Notes from the Ground*, 97.

21. Howe, *What Hath God Wrought*, 149, 62; Wilson, *Space, Time, and Freedom*, 23

22. See Forbes, *Missouri Compromise*, 5; and Holt, *Rise and Fall of the American Whig Party*, 4.

23. Gates, *History of Public Land Law*, 219, 224–26; White, *"It's Your Misfortune and None of My Own,"* 139.

24. Holt, *Rise and Fall of the American Whig Party*, 2; Morrison, *Slavery and the American West*, 16, 19; Feller, *Public Lands in Jacksonian Politics*, xii; Wilson, *Space, Time, and Freedom*, 4, 30

25. Wilentz, *Rise of American Democracy*, 443; Robbins, *Our Landed Heritage*, 74, 89, 91; Gates, *History of Public Land Law*, 234–35, 237–39; Feller, *Public Lands in Jacksonian Politics*, 194–95; Robbins, *Our Landed Heritage*, 105, 111; Holt, *Rise and Fall of the American Whig Party*, 168–69.

26. Nash, *Wilderness and the American Mind*, 47, 56; Cohen, *Notes from the Ground*, 106; Evans, "Storm over Niagara," 8.

27. Carr, *Wilderness by Design*, 12–14, 16–18.

28. Nash, *Wilderness and the American Mind*, 72–73; Runte, *National Parks*, 11; Jefferson, *Notes on the State of Virginia*, 22; Catlin, *North American Indians*, 261–62.

29. Holt, *Rise and Fall of the American Whig Party*, 91–92, 95, 107, 168.

30. Joshua R. Giddings, "Annexation of Texas, Delivered in Committee on the Whole House on the State of the Union, January 22, 1845," in *Speeches in Congress*, ed. Giddings, 134; Freehling, *The Road to Disunion*, vol. 1, 356, 424, 353.

31. Holt, *Rise and Fall of the American Whig Party*, 178–80, 199. See also White, *"It's Your Misfortune and None of My Own,"* 76.

32. "James Knox Polk Inaugural Address," March 4, 1845, in *U.S. Presidential Inaugural Addresses*, 87; Dusinberre, *Slavemaster President*, 135; Julian, *Political Recollections*, 46.

33. Holt, *Rise and Fall of the American Whig Party*, 250–51; Earle, *Jacksonian Antislavery*, 136; David Wilmot, "Slavery in the Territories, Speech of Mr. David Wilmot of Pennsylvania, in the House of Representatives," in *Appendix to the Congressional Globe*, 30th Cong,, 1st sess., August 3, 1848, 1077.

34. "Restriction of Slavery—Mr. Wilmot," *Appendix to the Congressional Globe*, H., 29th Cong., 2nd sess., 315, 317–18.

35. Ibid., 318.

36. "The Wilmot Proviso; Speech of Mr. B. R. Wood, of New York, in the House of Representatives, February 10, 1847," *Appendix to the Congressional Globe*, 29th Cong., 2nd sess., 344–45; "Extract from an Address," *The Liberator*, December 3, 1847. See also Varon, *Disunion!*, 187–88.

37. *CG*, 31st Cong., 1st sess., February 2, 1850, 257.

38. "The California Constitution—The Elections for Congress—Prosperity and Destiny of the New State," *Weekly Herald*, December 14, 1849, 1; "New Mexico," *Emancipator and Republican*, 2.

39. Holt, *Rise and Fall of the American Whig Party*, 333–34, 338; Julian, *Political Recollections*, 56–58.

40. Julian, *Political Recollections*, 57; Holt, *Rise and Fall of the American Whig Party*, 339

41. George W. Julian, "Public Lands," *CG*, H., 31st Cong., 2nd sess., 136; *CG*, 31st Cong., 1st sess., August 12, 1850, 1561.

42. Carey, *The Olive Branch*, 266.

43. Carey, *Principles of Political Economy; Part the First*, xii, 340–41; Carey, *Principles of Political Economy; Part the Second*, 20.

44. Carey, *Principles of Political Economy; Part the Second*, 11–12; Carey, *Principles of Political Economy; Part the Fourth*, 95; Carey, *Principles of Political Economy; Part the Second*, 18–19; Carey, *Principles of Political Economy; Part the Fourth*, 102.

45. Carey, *Principles of Political Economy; Part the First*, 341; Carey, *Principles of Political Economy; Part the Second*, 17–18; Carey, *Principles of Political Economy: Part the Fourth*, 102.

46. Henry Carey, "The Slave Question," *Scioto Gazette* (Chillicothe, Ohio), January 17, 1849, 1.

47. "Money and Business," *Boston Daily Atlas*, March 29, 1851, 1; "Henry C. Carey, Esq.," *North American and United States Gazette*, November 17, 1851, 1; "The Plow, the Loom, and the Anvil," *Vermont Chronicle*, April 27, 1852, vol. 17, 66; "Speech of Hon. J. Meacham, of Vermont," *Vermont Watchman and State Journal*, June 24, 1852, 1; "Political Matters," *Milwaukee Daily Sentinel*, June 12, 1852, 1; Justin S. Morrill to Horace Greeley, January 15, 1870, in Parker, *Life and Public Services*, 238; Richardson, *The Greatest Nation of the Earth*, 164.

48. Parker, *Life and Public Services*, 48–50; Morrill, *Wanderings and Scribblings*, n.p.

49. Lyman Beecher, "Land Monopoly," *Boston Investigator*, February 13, 1850, 1; Beecher, *Plain and Pleasant*, 39–40.

50. Tuttle H. Audas, "To the Planters of the Cotton Growing States," *The Mississippian*, January 12, 1849, 1; Ruffin, *Essays and Notes on Agriculture*, 276–77.

51. Mr. Geo. W. Julian of Indiana, "The Slavery Question," *CG*, H., 31st Cong., 1st sess., May 15, 1850, 578; Hon. Geo. W. Julian, "The Public Lands," *CG*, H., 31st, Cong., 2nd sess., January 29, 1851, 136; Thaddeus Stevens, "Speech of Feb. 20, 1850," in Julian, *Political Recollections*, 110.

52. Julian, "Slavery Question," *CG*, 573; Julian, "Public Lands," *CG*, 135–36; Julian, "Slavery Question," *CG*, 579.

53. Stoll, *Larding the Lean Earth*, 69; Charles Sumner, "Justice to the Land States and Policy of Roads, Speeches in the Senate of the United States on the Iowa Railroad Bill, 27th Jan., 17th Feb., and 16th March, 1852," in *Recent Speeches and Addresses*, 16; Julian, "Slavery Question," *CG*, 579.

54. Julian, "Public Lands," *CG*, 135–36.

55. Julian, *Political Recollections*, 104; *CG*, 31st Cong., 2nd sess., February 28, 1851, 752; *CG*, 31st Cong., 1st sess., January 30, 1850, 263; "Free Labor—Slave Labor—Mr. Clay," *Georgia Telegraph*, January 14, 1851, 2.

56. Cole, *Memoirs of Cornelius Cole*, 97, 92, 96; George Swain to William Swain, December 7, 1849, in Holliday, *The World Rushed In*, 340; George Swain to William Swain, January 5, 1850, in ibid., 342; George Swain to William Swain, February 9, 1850, in ibid., 346; William Swain to George Swain, April 1850, in ibid., 367.

57. Holt, *Rise and Fall of the American Whig Party*, 368, 374, 381, 384; Julian, *Political Recollections*, 97.

58. Holt, *Rise and Fall of the American Whig Party*, 553–54; Joshua R. Giddings to George W. Julian, February 21, 1852, no. 180, vol. 2, G&JP; Charles Sumner, "Acceptance of the Office of Senator of the United States, Letter to the Legislature of Massachusetts, 14th May, 1851," in *Recent Speeches and Addresses*, 4; Charles Sumner,

"Freedom National; Slavery Sectional, Speech in the Senate of the United States, 26th August 1852, on His Motion to Repeal the Fugitive Slave Bill," in *Recent Speeches and Addresses*, 80; T. H. Stevens to Hon. G. W. Julian, October 16, 1852, no. 22, vol. 2, G&JP.

CHAPTER 2

1. O'Connor, *Lords of the Loom*, 165; Paludan, *A People's Contest*, 151.

2. Lause, *Young America*, 3, 5, 72.

3. Grant, *North over South*, 37.

4. Gienapp, *Origins of the Republican Party*, 89.

5. Holt, *Rise and Fall of the American Whig Party*, 599; Gienapp, *Origins of the Republican Party*, 18, 25, 27, 33.

6. Gienapp, *Origins of the Republican Party*, 54, 66; William H. Seward, "The True Basis of American Independence; An Address before the American Institute, New York," October 29, 1853, in Baker, *The Works of William H. Seward*, vol. 4, 146; Geo. W. Julian to Committee of Invitation, Centerville, Indiana, April 29, 1853, no. 234, vol. 2, G&JP.

7. Gienapp, *Origins of the Republican Party*, 70; Huston, *Stephen A. Douglas*, 45.

8. Gienapp, *Origins of the Republican Party*, 72; S. P. Chase, Charles Sumner, J. R. Giddings, Edward Wade, Gerrit Smith, and Alex. De Witt, "Appeal of the Independent Democrats in Congress to the People of the United States. Shall Slavery be Permitted in Nebraska," in *CG*, 33rd Cong., 1st sess., January 30, 1854, 282.

9. Paludan, *A People's Contest*, 154; Morris, *How to Get a Farm*, 15–16.

10. Gienapp, *Origins of the Republican Party*, 75, 105–6; J. R. Giddings to Dear Boy [Son], February 12, 1854, no. 252, vol. 2, G&JP; "Mass Convention of the Freemen of Wisconsin," *Daily State Journal* (Madison, Wis.), July 14, 1854, 1.

11. Langsdorf, "S. C. Pomeroy," *Kansas Historical Quarterly*, 231; Gienapp, *Origins of the Republican Party*, 169; S. C. Pomeroy to Sir [Edward Everett Hale], July 27, 1854, #624, folder 3, box 1, New England Emigrant Aid Company Collection, KSHS; New England Emigrant Aid Company, *Charter, Officers, and Objects of the Company*, 1855, Port Vault K 235 N42c 1855, KSHS.

12. Oertel, *Bleeding Borders*, 42; S. C. Pomeroy to J. M. S. Williams, September 17, 1855, #624, folder 6, box 1, New England Emigrant Aid Company, KSHS.

13. Holt, *The Fate of Their Country*, 112, 115; Gienapp, *Origins of the Republican Party*, 184; C. Clay to Dear Sir [George W. Julian], September 1, 1854, no. 270, vol. 2, G&JP; Cole, *Memoirs of Cornelius Cole*, 96–97, 84, 113–15; Cornelius Cole to Hon. E. D. Morgan, Sacramento, Cal., May 3, 1856, no. 217, folder 1, box 1, CFP.

14. Justin S. Morrill to S. Smith, August 29, 1854, in Parker, *Life and Public Services*, 60; Parker, *Life and Public Services*, 68.

15. Stowe, *Uncle Tom's Cabin*, 373, 326, 25; Geo. W. Julian to Committee of Invitation, Centerville, Indiana, April 29, 1853, no. 234, vol. 2, G&JP.

16. Frederick Law Olmsted, "Appeal to the Citizens of Staten Island, By the Board of Managers of the Richmond County Agricultural Society" (New York, December 1849), in *The Papers of Frederick Law Olmsted*, vol. 1, ed. Beveridge and McLaughlin, 334;

Charles E. Beveridge and Charles Capen McLaughlin, "Introduction," in *The Papers of Frederick Law Olmsted*, vol. 2, ed. Beveridge and McLaughlin, 7.

17. Charles E. Beveridge and Charles Capen McLaughlin, "Introduction," in *The Papers of Frederick Law Olmsted*, vol. 2, ed. Beveridge and McLaughlin, 5; Frederick Law Olmsted, "The People's Park at Birkenhead, near Liverpool by W., Staten Island, New York," May 1851, in *The Papers of Frederick Law Olmsted; Writings on Public Parks, Parkways, and Park Systems*, 71, 74; Roper, *FLO*, 69; Olmsted, *Walks and Talks*, 62, 106; Frederick Law Olmsted to Frederick Kingsbury, Tosomock, October 17, 1852, in *The Papers of Frederick Law Olmsted*, vol. 2, ed. Beveridge and McLaughlin, 83.

18. Grant, *North over South*, 12; Yeoman, "The South: Letters on Productions, Industry and Resources of the Slave States, Number One," *New York Daily Times*, February 16, 1853, in *The Papers of Frederick Law Olmsted*, vol. 2, ed. Beveridge and McLaughlin, 86–87; Yeoman, "The South, Letters on the Productions, Industry, and Resources of the Slave States, Number Seven," *New York Daily Times*, March 17, 1853, in *The Papers of Frederick Law Olmsted*, vol. 2, ed. Beveridge and McLaughlin, 104.

19. Yeoman, "The South, Letters on the Productions, Industry, and Resources of the Slave States, Number Eleven," *NYDT*, April 13, 1853, in *The Papers of Frederick Law Olmsted*, vol. 2, ed. Beveridge and McLaughlin, 136–38, 133; Yeoman, "The South, Letters on the Productions, Industry, and Resources of the Slave States, Number Fourteen," *NYDT*, April 28, 1853, in *The Papers of Frederick Law Olmsted*, vol. 2, ed. Beveridge and McLaughlin, 151.

20. Yeoman, "The South, Letters on the Productions, Industry, and Resources of the Slave States, Number Thirty-Four," *NYDT*, August 19, 1853, in *The Papers of Frederick Law Olmsted*, vol. 2, ed. Beveridge and McLaughlin, 200; Fred. to Charles Loring Brace, Cumberland River, December 1, 1853, in *The Papers of Frederick Law Olmsted*, vol. 2, ed. Beveridge and McLaughlin, 233.

21. Yeoman, "The South, Letters on the Productions, Industry, and Resources of the Slave States, Number Twenty-Seven," *NYDT*, June 30, 1853, in *The Papers of Frederick Law Olmsted*, vol. 2, ed. Beveridge and McLaughlin, 180.

22. Yeoman, "A Tour in the Southwest, Number Ten, San Antonia de Bexar," April 1854, *NYDT*, May 18, 1854, in *The Papers of Frederick Law Olmsted*, vol. 2, ed. Beveridge and McLaughlin, 293; Yeoman, "A Tour in the Southwest: Number Twelve," Texas, April 1854, *NYDT*, June 3, 1854, in *The Papers of Frederick Law Olmsted*, vol. 2, ed. Beveridge and McLaughlin, 300–301.

23. Fred. Law Olmsted to James B. Abbott, September 17, 1855, in *The Papers of Frederick Law Olmsted*, vol. 2, ed. Beveridge and McLaughlin, 365; O. [Frederick Law Olmsted] to James B. Abbott, October 4, 1855, in *The Papers of Frederick Law Olmsted*, vol. 2, ed. Beveridge and McLaughlin, 368; Frederick Law Olmsted, "Appeal for Funds for the San Antonio Zeitung," October 1854, in *The Papers of Frederick Law Olmsted*, vol. 2, ed. Beveridge and McLaughlin, 315, 317; Frederick Law Olmsted, "A Few Dollars Wanted to Help the Cause of Future Freedom in Texas," ca. October 1854, in *The Papers of Frederick Law Olmsted*, vol. 2, ed. Beveridge and McLaughlin, 319.

24. Hiram Hill to Dear Brother, December 7, 1855, #382, folder 4, box 1, Hiram Hill Collection, KSHS; Bradford R. Wood, "Office of the N.Y. State Kansas Committee, no. 4442 Broadway, Albany," April 18, 1856, Port Vault 325 N421Ln 1856, KSHS; Kansas

Central Committee of Iowa, "To the Friends of Free Kansas," July 4, 1856, Port Vault K 325 K133t 1856, KSHS; William Y. Roberts and S. C. Pomeroy to C. K. Holliday, Esq., June 24, 1856, #386, folder 3, #386, Cyrus Kurtz Holliday Collection, KSHS; Oertel, *Bleeding Borders*, 45.

25. Julian, *Political Recollections*, 147, 150; Gienapp, *Origins of the Republican Party*, 258; Lause, *Young America*, 114.

26. Charles Sumner, "The Crime against Kansas. The Apologies for the Crime. The True Remedy, Speech in the Senate of the United States, 19th and 20th May, 1856, on Mr. Douglas's Report on Affairs in Kansas," in *Recent Speeches and Addresses*, 614, 619, 621, 646, 597.

27. "The Brutal Attack upon Senator Sumner," *Farmer's Cabinet*, May 29, 1856, 2; Justin Smith Morrill to My Dear Wife, May 22, 1856, in Parker, *Life and Public Services*, 75; J. R. Giddings to Dear Daughter, May 28, 1856, no. 352, vol. 2, G&JP; "Great Mass Meeting, in Faneuil Hall, the Outrage on a Massachusetts Senator Rebuked by Men of all Political Parties," *Boston Daily Atlas*, May 26, 1856, 1; "The Assault upon Mr. Sumner," *Boston Daily Atlas*, May 24, 1856, 2. For an explanation of "restrained manhood," see Greenberg, *Manifest Manhood*, 11.

28. "Affairs in Kansas," *Farmer's Cabinet*, May 29, 1856, 2; Freehling, *The Road to Disunion*, vol. 2, 79; Mr. Dunn to Mr. T. W. Higginson, October 23, 1856, #380, folder 2, box 1, Thomas W. Higginson Collection, KSHS; Charles E. Dewey to Thaddeus Hyatt, South Potawatomie Creek, December 24, 1856, #401, folder 3, box 2, Thaddeus Hyatt Collection, KSHS.

29. "Republican National Convention: The Platform and Resolutions," *Weekly Herald*, June 21, 1856, 4; Greeley, *Proceedings of the First Three Republican National Conventions*, 70, 68, 72. Hornblower had been one of the "Young Americans," a faction in the Democratic Party that, according to historian Yonatan Eyal, favored "the Whig line of thinking . . . economic growth, and American Nationalism." Young Americans also believed fervently in republican government, sympathizing with the European rebels "who hungered for republics of their own" (Eyal, *The Young American Movement*, 2, 5–6).

30. Greeley, *Proceedings of the First Three Republican National Conventions*, 72, 74, 80, 76, 78.

31. McClellan, *A History of the Colonial and Republican Governments of the United States of America*, 180–81; "Resolutions adopted at Philadelphia, 17th of June, 1856," in Upham, *Life, Explorations and Public Services of John C. Fremont*, 356–57.

32. Greeley, *Proceedings of the First Three Republican National Conventions*, 81; "The Republican Nominee," *Dayton Gazette*, in *Ohio State Journal*, July 2, 1856, 1; "Fremont in the Field," *New York Mirror*, in *Ohio State Journal*, July 2, 1856, 1; "Col. J. C. Fremont Nominated," *Steubenville Herald*, in *Ohio State Journal*, July 2, 1856, 1.

33. J. C. Fremont, "Acceptance of the Philadelphia Nomination, New York, July, 8, 1856," in Upham, *Life, Explorations and Public Services of John C. Fremont*, 364–65; E. D. Morgan to C. Cole, Esq., September 4th, 1856, no. 217, folder 6, box 2, CFP.

34. J. Collamer, G. A. Grow, Sml. Galloway, Mason W. Tappen, Schuyler Colfax, and A. H. Cragin, *Border Ruffian Code*, 7, i, 5, 7–8.

35. Upham, *Life, Explorations and Public Services of John C. Fremont*, 114.

36. Olmsted, *A Journey in the Seaboard Slave States*, 64–65, 89.

37. Ibid., 382, 479, 87, 297; Brady, *War upon the Land*, 17.

38. C. C. Andrews, "Letter XI. The True Pioneer, Crow Wing, October, 1856," in Andrews, *Minnesota and Dacotah*, 114, 124, 134.

39. Holt, *Political Crisis of the 1850s*, 198–99; Wm. Kinsley to Geo. W. Julian, September 24, 1856, no. 281, vol. 2, G&JP; Frederick Law Olmsted to Dear Friend, December 29, 1856, in Olmsted, *A Journey through Texas*, xxviii.

40. Freehling, *Road to Disunion*, vol. 2, 109, 117, 119; Varon, *Disunion!*, 298.

41. William Goodwell to Hon. Geo. W. Julian, Office of American Abolition Society, June 18, 1857, no. 400, vol. 2, G&JP; Julian, *Political Recollections*, 159, 170; Cole, *Memoirs of Cornelius Cole*, 96–97; Scrapbook of Cornelius Cole, 1858, #217, box 26, CFP.

42. S. P. Chase to Julian, May 8, 1857, no. 399, vol. 2, G&JP. David Brown's *Southern Outcast: Hinton Rowan Helper and the Impending Crisis of the South* is the most recent investigation of Helper's life and philosophy. Brown explains that Helper had "yeoman values and faith in Jeffersonian agrarianism" (Brown, *Southern Outcast*, 18).

43. Brown, *Southern Outcast*, 271, 83, 72; Freehling, *Road to Disunion*, vol. 2, 242; Helper, *Impending Crisis*, 56–57, 67.

44. Helper, *Impending Crisis*, 76–77, 129.

45. Ibid., 43, 60, 113, 25.

46. Ibid., 26, 116.

47. Ibid., 113, 121, 112.

48. Freehling, *Road to Disunion*, vol. 2, 242–45; Brown, *Southern Outcast*, 128, 182.

49. Wolfe, *Impending Crisis Dissected*, 8–9; D. Worth to Hon. Geo. W. Julian, February 6, 1860, Greensboro, N.C., no. 488, vol. 2, G&JP; D. Worth to G. W. Julian, Esq., May 1860, no. 500, vol. 2, G&JP.

50. Freehling, *Road to Disunion*, vol. 2, 247, 265–66.

51. Wolfe, *Impending Crisis Dissected*, 70; Robert M. Toombs to Alexander H. Stephens, February 10, 1860, in Freehling, *Road to Disunion*, vol. 2, 266; Wolfe, *Impending Crisis Dissected*, 7.

52. Mr. [Edwin D.] Morgan, "Opening Address," in Greeley, *Proceedings of the First Three Republican National Conventions*, 83; Hon. David Wilmot, "The Chairman's Inaugural," in ibid., 86.

53. Greeley, *Proceedings of the First Three Republican National Conventions*, 104, 118–19.

54. Ibid., 139–40.

55. "The Platform as Amended and Adopted," in ibid., 131–32; J. R. Giddings to Julian, May 25, 1860, no. 502, vol. 2, G&JP.

56. Cornelius Cole, Letter to Gwin, published in the *San Francisco Daily Times*, March 11, 1859, folder 1, box 1, CFP; "Republican Mass Meeting, Speeches of Harvey S. Brown and William H. Weeks," *Evening Bulletin* (San Francisco), August 24, 1860, 3; Cornelius Cole to His Excellency, E. D. Morgan, Governor of New York, June 18, 1859, folder 1, box 1, CFP; "REPUBLICAN DEMONSTRATION! IMMENSE MASS MEETING! Col. Baker's Address at the American Theatre," *SFB*, October 27, 1860, 3.

57. George W. Julian, "Indiana Politics, Delivered at Raysville, July 4, 1857," in *Speeches on Political Questions*, ed. Child, 127–28; Caleb B. Smith to Hon. Geo. Julian,

February 13, 1859, no. 466, vol. 2, G&JP; Julian, *Political Recollections*, 159, 170; S. P. Chase to Hon. G. W. Julian, April 9[?], 1860, no. 494, vol. 2, G&JP.

58. Olmsted, *A Journey through Texas*, xiii, xviii, xiv.

59. Ibid., 62, 140, xvii.

60. C. Robinson, "Letter to Hon. Henry Wilson," *The Liberator*, March 9, 1860, 40; Theodore Parker, "Theodore Parker on Rome, Slavery, Wine, and the Cotton Crop," *The New York Herald*, April 7, 1860, 5; Edward Bates, "Letter from Judge Bates," *Milwaukee Daily Sentinel*, October 9, 1860, 1.

61. Huston, *Stephen A. Douglas*, 160, 162; McPherson, *Ordeal by Fire*, 121–25; Freehling, *Road to Disunion*, vol. 2, 338.

62. *Charleston Mercury*, November 1, 1859, in Freehling, *Road to Disunion*, vol. 2, 372; ibid., 422; Foner, *Free Soil, Free Labor, Free Men*, 315.

63. M. Brisbane to Hon. George W. Julian, January 21, 186, no. 547, vol. 2, G&JP; Caleb B. Smith to Hon. Geo. W. Julian, January 2, 1861, no. 535, vol. 2, G&JP; H. Wilson to Hon. Geo. W. Julian, Senate Chamber, January 19, 1861, no. 544, vol. 2, G&JP; Justin S. Morrill to Wife, December 7, 1860, in Parker, *Life and Public Services*, 119.

64. S. P. Chase to Dear Friend [George W. Julian], December 15, 1860, no. 531, vol. 2, G&JP; Crofts, *Reluctant Confederates*, 202–5.

65. George W. Julian to Friend [Joshua R. Giddings], December 11, 1860, no. 527, vol. 2, G&JP; Giddings to Julian, February 22, 1861, no. 549, vol. 2, G&JP; Grant, *North over South*, 131.

CHAPTER 3

1. Freehling, *Road to Disunion*, vol. 2, 521–22; Lankford, *Cry Havoc!*, 82–83; Varon, *Disunion!*, 292.

2. Quiner, *Military History of Wisconsin*, 64; O'Connor, *Lords of the Loom*, 167

3. Gallagher, *Union War*, 34.

4. Tyrrell, *True Gardens of the Gods*, 3.

5. Richards, *California Gold Rush*, 111, 116, 129; Cornelius Cole, "Address to Court in Robt. Sandy, and Carter; Aff. for Certiorari," p. 1 [1852], folder 2, box 27, CFP.

6. Richards, *California Gold Rush*, 207, 219, 5, 28; Hittell, *A History of the City of San Francisco*, 305–9; O'Meara, *Broderick and Gwin*, 226; Cornelius Cole to Mr. W. H. Seward, September 19, 1859, folder 1, box 1, CFP.

7. Richards, *California Gold Rush*, 215–16; Melendy and Gilbert, *Governors of California*, 85, 87; Richards, *California Gold Rush*, 36–37; Cornelius Cole to "Dear Judge" [Steven J.] Field, June 1, 1858, folder 1, box 1, CFP.

8. Melendy and Gilbert, *Governors of California*, 88; Richards, *California Gold Rush*, 226, 229; Cornelius Cole, "Our Tendency, 1860," p. 1 [1860], folder 1, box 27, CFP.

9. Brewer, *Up and Down California*, 45; "Letter from New York: Speculations on Pacific Coast Secession—The Wily Ones, Gwin and Lane," *SFB*, April 18, 1861, 1; "The Proposed Dismemberment of California," *DEB*, April 25, 1861, 2.

10. Richards, *California Gold Rush*, 231; Simonds, *King in California*, 51–54; Melendy and Gilbert, *Governors of California*, 107.

11. "Governor Nye's Address," in *Transactions of the California State Agricultural Society during the Year 1861*, 164; Tyrrell, *True Gardens of the Gods*, 39; Rose, *Henry George*, 19; George, *Our Land and Land Policy*, viii.

12. King, *The Death of Mr. Webster*, 8; King, "Discourse, Delivered in Boston, before the Ancient and Honorable Artillery Company, on the Occasion of Their Two Hundred and Thirteenth Anniversary, June 2nd, 1851," in King, *Patriotism and Other Papers*, 50–51, 54.

13. Frothingham, *Tribute to Thomas Starr King*, 194, 197; Edwin P. Whipple, "Memoir," in *Christianity and Humanity*, ed. Whipple, xxxviii–xliii; Simonds, *King in California*, 56, 63–64.

14. Simonds, *King in California*, 62; Cole, "Our Tendency, 1860," 1; Brewer, *Up and Down California*, 88, 119–20.

15. Simonds, *King in California*, 60; Thomas Starr King, "Thoughts and Things," in *Patriotism and Other Papers*, 175; Cornelius Cole, "Two Schools of Politics," p. 1, undated speech, folder 1, box 27, CFP.

16. King, "The Supreme-Court Decision, and Our Duties," in *Christianity and Humanity*, ed. Whipple, 236; Cole, "Parties and Pacific Railroad," p. 2, undated speech, folder 2, box 27, CFP.

17. "Address of Governor Stanford at the Opening of the Tenth Annual Fair of the State Agricultural Society," in *Transactions of the California State Agricultural Society during the Year 1863*, 44, 49.

18. "Annual Address of T. Starr King," in *Transactions of the California State Agricultural Society during the Year 1863*, 66–67.

19. Cornelius Cole, "Speech on Pacific Railroad," p. 2, undated speech, folder 1, box 27, Writings of Cornelius Cole, 1850–1857, CFP.

20. Cole, "Parties and Pacific Railroad," 2.

21. Richards, *California Gold Rush*, 229; "Legislative Proceedings," *DEB*, April 19, 1861, 3; "The Rev. T. Starr King Tonight," *DEB*, April 19, 1861, 3; "The Rev. Thos Starr King on the Battle of Lexington," *DEB*, April 20, 1861, 3; Frothingham, *Tribute to Thomas Starr King*, 200; "Thomas Starr King as U.S. Senator for California," *DEB*, September 2, 1862, 2. King had no desire to become a senator, writing: "[T]here is some talk of making me senator; but I would swim to Australia before taking a political post" (Frothingham, *Tribute to Thomas Starr King*, 203).

22. "The Presidential Campaign," *DEB*, June 3, 1864, 2.

23. Paludan, *A People's Contest*, 153; White, *Railroaded*, 456.

24. Huston, *Stephen A. Douglas*, 100–101; Jefferson Davis, "Speech in U.S. Senate, December 14, 1858," in *Jefferson Davis: The Essential Writings*, ed. Cooper, 157. For an explanation of Davis's ideal route, see Davis, "Speech in Mississippi City, Mississippi, October 2, 1857," in ibid., 134–35; and *CG*, 36th Cong., 1st sess., May 29, 1860, 2444, 2448.

25. *CG*, 36th Cong., 2nd sess., January 5, 1861, 250–51.

26. Ibid., 253–55, 61.

27. *CG*, 36th Cong., 2nd sess., January 9, 1861, 293; *CG*, 36th Cong., 2nd sess., January 15, 1861, 383, 387.

28. *CG*, 37th Cong., 2nd sess., April 8, 1862, 1580, 1707.

29. *CG*, 37th Cong., 2nd sess., April 17, 1862, 1701; *CG*, 37th Cong., 2nd sess., June 12, 1862, 2677.

30. *CG*, 37th Cong., 2nd sess., April 17, 1862, 1703, 1707; *CG*, 37th Cong., 2nd sess., May 5, 1862, 1948; *CG*, 37th Cong., 2nd sess., June 19, 1862, 2807.

31. Gienapp, *Lincoln and Civil War America*, 110–13; Grimsley, *Hard Hand of War*, 123; McPherson, *Tried by War*, 59; Grimsley, *Hard Hand of War*, 70; *CG*, 37th Cong., 2nd sess., April 18, 1862, 1726; *CG*, 37th Cong., 2nd sess., April 17, 1862, 1709.

32. *CG*, 37th Cong., 2nd sess., May 6, 1862, 1971; *CG*, 37th Cong., 2nd sess., June 20, 1862, 2832; Dodge, *How We Built the Union Pacific Railway*, 10; *CG*, 37th Cong., 2nd sess., June 12, 1862, 2676. The Central Pacific Railroad would later pay money to Cornelius Cole in exchange for political support of the road. See White, *Railroaded*, 117.

33. Ross, *Democracy's College*, 14, 11, 24; Kett, *Pursuit of Knowledge under Difficulties*, 136.

34. *CG*, 35th Cong., 1st sess., December 15, 1857, 32; Cross, *Justin Smith Morrill*, 13, 35; Gates, *Agriculture and the Civil War*, 255; Ross, *Democracy's College*, 35; Cross, *Justin Smith Morrill*, 72.

35. *CG*, 35th Cong., 1st sess., April 20, 1858, 1692; Phillips, "Antebellum Agricultural Reform," 801.

36. *CG*, 35th Cong., 1st sess., April 20, 1858, 1692–93; *CG*, 35th Cong., 2nd sess., February 1, 1859, 723.

37. *CG*, 35th Cong., 1st sess., April 20, 1858, 1692–95; quoted in Phillips, "Antebellum Agricultural Reform," 821; *CG*, 35th Cong., 2nd sess., February 1, 1859, 720.

38. Cross, *Justin Smith Morrill*, 12–13; Stoll, *Larding the Lean Earth*, 24, 201; Carr, *Wilderness by Design*, 16–17; Parker, *Life and Public Services*, 223. See Marsh, *Man and Nature*.

39. *CG*, 35th Cong., 1st sess., April 20, 1858, 1694, 1697; Parker, *Life and Public Services*, 262.

40. Kett, *Pursuit of Knowledge under Difficulties*, 135, 138; Bronson Murray, "Memorial of the Fourth Industrial Convention of the State of Illinois," in Powell, *The Movement for Industrial Education*, 407–8.

41. "Governor's Message," *Weekly Wisconsin Patriot*, January 16, 1858, 2; "Governor's Message," *Weekly Wisconsin Patriot*, January 15, 1859, 3.

42. *CG*, 35th Cong., 2nd sess., February 1, 1859, 718; James Buchanan, "President's Veto Message," *Daily Ohio Statesman*, March 2, 1859, 1; "The President's Veto Message," *Daily Confederation*, March 3, 1859, 2.

43. Ross, *Democracy's College*, 61; Simon, "Politics of the Morrill Act," 108; Richardson, *The Greatest Nation of the Earth*, 156; Justin Smith Morrill to President Atherton, Pennsylvania State College, February 5, 1894, in Parker, *Life and Public Services*, 227.

44. "Lecture on Agricultural Chemistry," *The Plough, the Loom, and the Anvil*, vol. 2, 74; *CG*, 36th Cong., 1st sess., April 27, 1860, 1874; Dupree, *Science in the Federal Government*, 149; Phillips, "Antebellum Agricultural Reform," 799.

45. *CG*, 36th Cong., 1st sess., April 27, 1860, 1874–76.

46. "Correspondence of the Baltimore Sun," *The Sun*, January 30, 1861, 4; "Pennsylvania Horticultural Society," *Philadelphia Inquirer*, February 20, 1861, 2; "U.S.

Agricultural Society," *The Sun*, January 11, 1861, 2; F. E. F., "The Advantage of Agricultural over Mercantile Pursuits," *Pittsfield Sun*, November 7, 1861, 4.

47. *CG*, 37th Cong., 2nd sess., February 17, 1862, 855–56; Dupree, *Science in the Federal Government*, 149.

48. *CG*, 37th Cong., 2nd sess., February 17, 1862, 857; "The Agricultural Department," *Philadelphia Inquirer*, April 16, 1862, 2; *CG*, 37th Cong., 2nd sess., April 17, 1862, 1691.

49. Young, "Congress Looks West," in *The Frontier in American Development*, ed. Ellis, 381–82; Feller, *Public Lands in Jacksonian Politics*, 194.

50. *CG*, 36th Cong., 1st sess., March 19, 1860, 1223, 1539, 1299.

51. Ibid., 1551, 1635, 1555–56.

52. Ibid., 1510–11, 1295.

53. Ibid., 1630–31, 1652.

54. "The Homestead Bill," *Freedom's Champion* (Atchison, Kansas), March 24, 1860, 3; "The 'Homestead Bill': The Abolition 'Free Labor' Philosophy Illustrated," *Weekly Georgia Telegraph*, March 24, 1860, 1.

55. "Veto of the Homestead Bill," *The Constitution* (Washington, D.C.), June 23, 1860, 2; Julian, *Political Recollections*, 216. For an explanation of Buchanan's veto, see Baker, *James Buchanan*, 117–18.

56. *CG*, 37th Cong., 2nd sess., December 4, 1861, 14; *CG*, 37th Cong., 2nd sess., December 18, 1861, 136; *CG*, 37th Cong., 2nd sess., February 21, 1862, 910.

57. *CG*, 37th Cong., 2nd sess., February 28, 1862, 1031.

58. *CG*, 37th Cong., 2nd sess., December 18, 1861, 136; Hon. G. W. Julian, "Confiscation and Liberation," May 23, 1862, *CG*, 37th Cong., 2nd sess., 185; Julian, *Political Recollections*, 220; *CG*, 37th Cong., 2nd sess., February 28, 1862, 1034.

59. *CG*, 37th Cong., 2nd sess., May 5, 186, 1938–39.

60. Ibid., 1937–40.

61. *CG*, 37th Cong., 2nd sess., February 28, 1862, 1034; "Resolutions on National Affairs," *Farmer's Cabinet*, July 24, 1862, 2; Foner, *Free Soil, Free Labor, Free Men*, 29.

62. Bogue, "Senators, Sectionalism, and the 'Western' Measures of the Republican Party," in *Frontier in American Development*, ed. Ellis, 45; J. N. Pierpont to Hon. Geo. W. Julian, March 22, 1864, no. 824, vol. 5, G&JP; L. Maria Child to Mr. Julian, March 27, 1864, no. 818, vol. 5, G&JP; Wilson, *The Death of Slavery*, 10.

63. Wilson, *Lincoln's Sword*, 223. Peter Luebke, a graduate student at the University of Virginia, discovered the value of the regimental histories cited in this chapter. Those written between 1863 and 1866 provide a tremendous amount of information about what Union soldiers thought about the Civil War. See Luebke, "'To Transmit and Perpetuate the Fruits of This Victory': Union Regimental Histories, 1865–1866."

64. "A Colored Man" [untitled broadside], New Orleans, La., September 1865, in Berlin, Fields, Miller, Reidy, and Rowland, *Free at Last*, 456; Spotswood Rice to Kittey Diggs, September 3, 1864, in Berlin, Fields, Miller, Reidy, and Rowland, *Free at Last*, 481–82; Glatthaar, *Forged in Battle*, 79, 246.

65. Manning, *What This Cruel War Was Over*, 12; Gallagher, *Union War*, 6.

66. Driggs, *Opening of the Mississippi*, 58, 100, 51.

67. James T. Miller to Brother, September 7, 1864, in *Bound to Be a Soldier*, ed. Mannis and Wilson, 109–10; James T. Miller to Dear Mother, October 11, 1863, in ibid.,

122; H. S. Huidekoper and R. L. Ashhurst, "Resolution of the Soldiers of the 150th Pennsylvania Volunteers," March 11, 1863, in *Loyalist's Ammunition*, 7.

68. Williams, *Life in Camp*, 114, 27, 115.

69. Eddy, *History of the Sixtieth Regiment New York State Volunteers*, 200, 209

70. Myers, *A Daily Journal of the 192 Reg't Penn'a Volunteers*, 17, 63.

71. Ibid., 134, 154, 156–57

72. Hart, *History of the Fortieth Illinois Inf.*, 21, 19, 103, 105, 101, 122–23.

73. Kinnear, *History of the Eighty-Sixth Regiment*, 135–36, 95–96.

74. "X" to the *Buffalo Courier*, July 22, 1862, in Mills, *Chronicles of the Twenty-First Regiment New York State Volunteers*, 202; Bould Soger to the *Express*, May 23, 1862, in ibid., 174. 176; ibid., 256.

75. Gage, *From Vicksburg to Raleigh*, 274–75.

76. Tourgée, *The Story of a Thousand*, 31, 17, 72.

77. Henry T. Jones to My Dear L., Baton Rouge, La., February 21, 1863, in Jones, *Life with the Forty-Ninth Massachusetts*, 138; Henry T. Jones to My Dear L, Hinsdale, Mass., September 8, 1862, in ibid., 15; Henry T. Jones to My Dear L., Baton Rouge, La., February 21, 1863, in ibid., 138; Henry T. Jones to My Dear L., Camp Banks, Baton Rouge, La., March 13, 1863, in ibid., 162.

78. Paludan, *A People's Contest*, 381; Morris, *How to Get a Farm*, 16.

CHAPTER 4

1. *CG*, 38th Cong., 1st sess., May 17, 1864, 2300.

2. Abraham Lincoln, "Message to Congress, December 1, 1862," in *This Fiery Trial*, ed. Gienapp, 150; Brewer, *Up and Down California*, 88. As Jen A. Huntley describes, nineteenth-century Americans "valued Yosemite as *scenery*: a highly visual, even pictorial approach to the landscape that apprehended it almost exactly as a three-dimensional work of art, a spectacle" (Huntley, *Making of Yosemite*, 7).

3. Foner, *Free Soil, Free Labor, Free Men*, 4; Mr. Geo. W. Julian of Indiana, "The Slavery Question," in *CG*, 31st Cong., 1st sess., May 14, 1850, 573; Hon. Geo. W. Julian, "The Public Lands," in *CG*, 31st Cong., 2nd sess., January 29, 1851, 136; *CG*, 40th Cong., 2nd sess., June 3, 1868, 2816.

4. Larry M. Dilsaver and William C. Tweed argue that "there was no state government to put in charge of the lands [of Yellowstone]. Congress responded by creating a 'national' park" (Dilsaver and Tweed, *Challenge of the Big Trees*, 63). Louis C. Cramton asserts, "In 1872 this region [Yellowstone] was a part of the public domain of the United States within certain of its Territories and, therefore, the question of turning it over to a State for administration was not at that time directly an issue" (Cramton, *Early History of Yellowstone*, 1). Paul Schullery, the foremost historian of the park, argues: "Because it [Yellowstone] had been established as a federal reservation in 1872, prior to the statehood of any of these territories, the park eventually would have many advantages in its self-management; most later parks, created in existing states, have had to reconcile their needs with state laws" (Schullery, *Searching for Yellowstone*, 33). Jen A. Huntley does make the apt comparison that "both Yosemite and later Yellowstone were set aside to preserve 'scenery,' not nature or the environment," but she

does not differentiate between Yellowstone's creation as a federal park and Yosemite's founding as a state park (Huntley, *Making of Yosemite*, 132–33).

5. Runte, *Yosemite*, 3; Sachs, *The Humboldt Current*, 209; Huntley, *Making of Yosemite*, 2; Brady, *War upon the Land*, 140. Huntley and Carr do not discuss in depth the national controversy over Yosemite's establishment or connect the controversy to the creation of Yellowstone National Park.

6. Jefferson, *Notes on the State of Virginia*, 22; Catlin, *Manners, Customs, and Condition*, 261–62; Nash, *Wilderness and the American Mind*, 101. Catlin was one of the most popular explorers among Radical Republicans, who viewed him as an "exemplary antislavery activist" (Sachs, *The Humboldt Current*, 92).

7. Russell, *One Hundred Years in Yosemite*, 48; Sanborn, *Yosemite*, 78–80; Bunnell, "*California As I Saw It*," 298, 304; *Mariposa Gazette*, August 9, 1855, 1. The "Mariposa Battalion" ended up capturing several hundred people of the Yosemite (Miwok) and Chowchilla (Yokut) tribes in Yosemite valley. The prisoners became forced laborers. See Huntley, *Making of Yosemite*, 56–57.

8. Matthews, *Golden State in the Civil War*, 139; King, *The White Hills*, 103–4.

9. *SFB*, June 15, 1859, 4; Hutchings, *In the Heart of the Sierras*, 130, 135–37. For other accounts of Yosemite in California newspapers, see "Yosemite Falls and Valley," *Daily Democratic State Journal*, December 16, 1853, 3; *San Joaquin Republican*, June 20, 1857, 4; "Panorama of Yosemite Falls and Valley," *DEB*, May 18, 1857; "Advertisements," *SFB*, December 17, 1858, 1; James Denman, "The Sublime and Beautiful of California—No. 1, the Big Tree Grove," *SFB*, June 15, 1857; James Denman, "The Sublime and Beautiful of California—No. 6, First Two Days in the Yosemite Valley," *SFB*, July 8, 1857, 1; "Narrative of a Trip to Yo-Semite," *SFB*, June 2, 1860, 1; and A Lady Correspondent, "The Valley of Yosemite," *SFB*, July 18, 1863, 1.

10. Winks, *Frederick Billings*, 278, 275, 277. Frederic Church's landscape art was very popular during the Civil War. In the spring of 1861, Church exhibited a painting entitled *The North*, featuring imposing icebergs and the wrecked remains of a ship. Profits from the exhibition went to an organization supporting the families of Union soldiers (Sachs, *The Humboldt Current*, 179).

11. Huntley-Smith, "Publishing the 'Sealed Book,'" 213. Historian Robert Righter asserts: "It was, no doubt, Olmsted who led a group of Californians 'of fortune, of taste and of refinement' to Senator John Conness's office in early 1864 to ask that he introduce a bill granting custodianship of Yosemite Valley to the state of California" (Righter, *The Battle over Hetch Hetchy*, 22).

12. Charles McLaughlin and Charles E. Beveridge, "Introduction," in *The Papers of Frederick Law Olmsted*, vol. 4, ed. McLaughlin and Beveridge, 42; Fred. to Charles Loring Brace, December 1, 1853, in *The Papers of Frederick Law Olmsted*, vol. 2, ed. McLaughlin and Beveridge, 234–35. See also Roper, *FLO*, 87–93.

13. Roper, *FLO*, 126, 128; Carr, *Wilderness by Design*, 19–21.

14. "A Bogus Greeley on Yosemite," *SFB*, September 3, 1859, 3; "Greeley among the Big Trees," *Farmers' Cabinet*, October 5, 1859, 1.

15. Israel Ward Raymond to Hon. John Conness, February 20, 1864, in Huth, "Yosemite: The Story of an Idea," 67. Advertisements printed by I. W. Raymond appeared in the *New York Herald* and the *San Francisco Bulletin*. See *New York Herald*, May 18, 1856;

New York Herald, June 14, 1857, 7; "Extra California Steamer, at Reduced Rates," *New York Herald*, March 29, 1858, 7; "Arrival of the 'Golden Age,'" *SFB*, May 14, 1860, 3; and *SFB*, December 3, 1864, 6; Somerville, *The Aspinwall Empire*, 76–77. Conness began his career as a Democrat but joined the Republican-led Union Party after secession.

16. Winks, *Frederick Billings*, 282; Roper, *FLO*, 239; Huth, "Yosemite: The Story of an Idea," 68; Sachs, *The Humboldt Current*, 209. John Sears suspects that Thomas Starr King and Horace Greeley became involved as well. See Sears, *Sacred Places*, 128.

17. Huntley, *Making of Yosemite*, 116; Anderson, "Carleton E. Watkins," 33–34; Frederick Law Olmsted, "Preliminary Report upon the Yosemite and Big Tree Grove," in *The Papers of Frederick Law Olmsted*, vol. 5, ed. Ranney, Rauluk, and Hoffman, 488–89; "Fine Arts," *NYT*, December 12, 1862, 2.

18. *CG*, 38th Cong., 1st sess., May 17, 1864, 2300–301.

19. *CG*, 40th Cong., 2nd sess., June 3, 1868, 2816. George W. Julian served as chairman of the Committee on Public Lands from 1863 to 1870.

20. Hutchings, *In the Heart of the Sierras*, 149–51. The 1864 statue and Governor Frederick F. Low's proclamation accepting it are replicated here. For the original text of the bill, see Sanger, *The Statutes at Large, and Treaties of the United States of America, Passed at the First Session of the Thirty-Eighth Congress*, 325; Roper, *FLO*, 260–61.

21. Frederick Law Olmsted, "Preliminary Report upon the Yosemite and Big Tree Grove," 488–89.

22. Ibid., 504–5, 502.

23. Ibid., 503, 505–6.

24. Roper, *FLO*, 287; Victoria Post Ranney, Gerald J. Rauluk, and Carolyn F. Hoffman, "Introduction," in *The Papers of Frederick Law Olmsted*, vol. 5, ed. Ranney, Rauluk, and Hoffman, 35; Frederick Law Olmsted to John Olmsted August 25, 1865, in *The Papers of Frederick Law Olmsted*, vol. 5, ed. Ranney, Rauluk, and Hoffman, 435–36; Bowles, *Across the Continent*, 231; "An Overland Journey; the Wonderful Yo Semite Valley," *Chicago Tribune*, September 13, 1865, 3; "The Yosemite Valley," *New Hampshire Sentinel*, August 12, 1869.

25. "The Big Trees of California, from the N.Y. Tribune," *Pittsfield (Mass.) Sun*, November 30, 1865, 1.

26. Ranney, Rauluk, and Hoffman, "Introduction," 23; Roper, *FLO*, 287; Victoria Post Ranney, Gerald J. Rauluk, and Carolyn F. Hoffman, "Biographical Information of William Ashburner," in *The Papers of Frederick Law Olmsted*, vol. 5, ed. Ranney, Rauluk, and Hoffman, 201; Olmsted, "Governmental Preservation of National Scenery," 62.

27. Hutchings, *In the Heart of the Sierras*, 151–53; Frederick Law Olmsted, "Preliminary Report upon the Yosemite and Big Tree Grove," 508.

28. Irvin, *Biennial Report of the Commissioners*, 7–8; Hutchings, *In the Heart of the Sierras*, 153–54.

29. Foner, *Free Soil, Free Labor, Free Men*, 280; George W. Julian, "Homesteads for Soldiers on the Lands of Rebels," speech in the House of Representatives, March 18, 1864, in *Speeches on Political Questions*, ed. Child, 214–15. Jen A. Huntley agrees that Hutchings's agitation hampered the commissioners' ability to control development. See Huntley, *Making of Yosemite*, 125.

30. Hutchings, *In the Heart of the Sierras*, 153–54; Huntley-Smith, "Publishing the 'Sealed Book,'" 5; Irvin, *Biennial Report of the Commissioners*, 10; "Letter from Sacramento, from Our Own Correspondent, the Yosemite Valley Claims," *SFB*, January 16, 1868, 1.

31. Irvin, *Biennial Report of the Commissioners*, 9; Davis, *History of Political Conventions*, 267; Kuykendall, "History of the Yosemite Region," 21; Hutchings, *In the Heart of the Sierras*, 154; *CG*, 40th Cong., 2nd sess., June 3, 1868, 2816; *U.S. Congressional Serial Set*, "Bills and Resolutions, House of Representatives, 40th Cong., 2nd sess., H.R. 1118," 1868; "Letter from Sacramento," *SFB*, January 16, 1868, 1. The Democrats won the governorship and a majority in the California legislature, running in opposition to Radical Reconstruction, which they argued would lead to Chinese enfranchisement. See Benedict, *The Impeachment and Trial of Andrew Johnson*, 69.

32. Supreme Court of California, *Frederick F. Low v. J. M. Hutchings*, no. 2, 723, July Term 1871.

33. "The Yosemite Grant Again," *SFB*, January 17, 1868, 2; *CG*, June 3, 1868, 40th Cong., 2nd sess., 2816.

34. Frederick Law Olmsted, "The Great American Park of the Yo Semite," *New York Evening Post*, June 18, 1868, 2; "The Great American Park of the Yo Semite," *Weekly Wisconsin Patriot*, July 2, 1868; Victoria Post Ranney, Gerald J. Rauluk, and Carolyn F. Hoffman, "Introduction," in *The Papers of Frederick Law Olmsted*, vol. 5, ed. Ranney, Rauluk, and Hoffman, 466.

35. *CG*, 40th Cong., 2nd sess., June 5, 1868, 2860; "Minor Topics," *NYT*, June 23, 1868, 4.

36. "The Yosemite in Congress," *New York Daily Tribune*, June 24, 1868.

37. "The Yosemite Job," *SFB*, February 12, 1868, 2; "The Yosemite Valley Job," July 16, 1868, *Flake's Bulletin*, 8; "The Yosemite Claim," *SFB*, July 2, 1869, 2; "The Yosemite Valley Claim," *SFB*, January 13, 1870; *CG*, 41st Cong., 2nd sess., January 18, 1870, 549; *CG*, 41st Cong., 2nd sess., April 8, 1870, 2515; Davis, *History of Political Conventions*, 300. Republicans selected Cole as senator before losing control of the state legislature in September 1867. Cole served in office from March 4, 1867, to March 3, 1873.

38. George W. Julian, "The Overshadowing Question," in *Speeches on Political Questions*, ed. Child, 448; "The Yosemite Valley Claim," *Chicago Tribune*, January 7, 1870, 2; "Eastern View of the Yosemite Question," *SFB*, February 8, 1870, 2.

39. Hutchings, *In the Heart of the Sierras*, 157; James Mason Hutchings, "Communications: The Yosemite Valley, to the Editor of the New York Times," *NYT*, February 18, 1870, 2; Julian, "The Overshadowing Question," 448; "The Yosemite Valley Claim," *Chicago Tribune*, January 7, 1870, 2. Jen A. Huntley Smith found that Hutchings gave lectures decrying "the destruction of forests in and around Yosemite and the Big Trees," but the invalidation of his land claims left Hutchings feeling "marginalized by . . . new ideas about landscape and environment" (Huntley-Smith, "Publishing the 'Sealed Book,'" 239, 208).

40. *CG*, 41st Cong., 2nd sess., July 2, 1870, 5130–31.

41. Ibid., 5131; Benedict, *Preserving the Constitution*, xii; George W. Julian, "The Yosemite Valley and the Right of Preemption," *CG*, June 3, 1870, 41st Cong., 2nd sess., 5134.

42. Hutchings, *In the Heart of the Sierras*, 158; "Yosemite in Congress," *NYT*, 4; *CG*, 41st Cong., 2nd sess., June 3, 1870, 4043; *NYT*, July 3, 1870, 4.

43. Supreme Court of California, *Frederick F. Low v. J. M. Hutchings*, 1871; Julian, "Overshadowing Question," in *Speeches on Political Questions*, ed. Child, 449; Hutchings, *In the Heart of the Sierras*, 161.

44. Swisher, *History of the Supreme Court of the United States*, 807; Supreme Court of the United States, *Yosemite Valley Case*, January 6, 1873. In 1850 California had passed the Possessory Act, authorizing settlers to "occupy up to 160 acres and empower[ing] them to take legal action against persons interfering with or injuring such land or possession." In a number of decisions between 1859 and 1861, Field invalidated the legislation. See McCurdy, "Stephen J. Field and Public Land Law Development in California," 246, 250.

45. Swisher, *History of the Supreme Court of the United States*, 809; Supreme Court of the United States, *Yosemite Valley Case*, January 6, 1873; Huntley, *Making of Yosemite*, 131.

46. Bowles, *Across the Continent*, 231; Huth, "Yosemite: The Story of an Idea," 69; "Yosemite in Congress," *New York Daily Tribune*, June 24, 1868.

47. Bensel, *Yankee Leviathan*, 114, 182, 225; McPherson, *Ordeal By Fire*, 516–17; Foner, *Short History*, 10, 195.

48. Irvin, *Biennial Report of the Commissioners*, 9.

49. Ibid., 10; Huntley, *Making of Yosemite*, 164–65.

50. "Condition of California," *NYT*, June 20, 1871, 1; *CG*, 41st Cong., 2nd sess., July 2, 1870, 5129; John Muir, quoted in Sanborn, *Yosemite*, 229. Muir and Hutchings also came to distrust each other after Muir developed a "close" relationship with Hutchings's wife, Elvira. See Huntley, *Making of Yosemite*, 142; and Worster, *A Passion for Nature*, 177, 179.

51. Hutchings, *In the Heart of the Sierras*, 130; Russell, *One Hundred Years in Yosemite*, 98, 103, 108; Grace Greenwood, "Notes of Travel: Eight Days in the Yosemite," *NYT*, July 29, 1872.

52. "The Impending Doom of Yosemite," *NYT*, February 14, 1872, 4; "Yosemite," *SFB*, May 30, 1871, 2; Winks, *Frederick Billings*, 285–86.

53. "A Wonderful Region," *SFB*, October 31, 1870, 2; Winks, *Frederick Billings*, 285; Schullery, *Searching for Yellowstone*, 59.

54. Cramton, *Early History of Yellowstone*, 25; Schullery, *Searching for Yellowstone*, 59–60.

55. *CG*, 42nd Cong., 2nd sess., January 23, 1872, 520; "Asking for His Rights," *Helena Daily Herald*, February 8, 1872, 3.

56. *CG*, 42nd Cong., 2nd sess., January 30, 1872, 697.

57. *CG*, 42nd Cong., 2nd sess., February 27, 1872, 1243–44; *CG*, 42nd Cong., 2nd sess., March 5, 1872, 1416.

58. "The Impending Doom of Yosemite," *NYT*, February 14, 1872, 4.

CHAPTER 5

1. West, *The Last Indian War*, xix, xxi.

2. Foner, *Reconstruction*, 49. For examples of historians making claims that Lincoln formed Reconstruction policy based on his "racist" beliefs, see Escott, *"What Shall We Do with the Negro?"*; and Bennett, *Forced into Glory*.

3. George Julian, "The Cause and Cure of Our National Troubles," January 12, 1862, in *Radical Republicans and Reconstruction*, ed. Hyman, 42–43; Charles Sumner, "Senate Speech on Reconstruction," July 7, 1862, in *Radical Republicans and Reconstruction*, ed. Hyman, 104.

4. Foner, *Reconstruction*, 61–62; "The Wade-Davis Manifesto," August 5, 1864, in *Radical Republicans and Reconstruction*, ed. Hyman, 144–45.

5. S. C. Pomeroy to Miss. A. E. Dickinson, April 22, 1864, reel 11, ADC; S. C. Pomeroy to Anna E. Dickinson, June 4, 1864, reel 11, ADC; S. C. Pomeroy [*Pomeroy Circular*] (Washington, D.C.: [1864]), 1; Pomeroy, *Platform and Party of the Future*, 5.

6. Pomeroy, *Platform and Party of the Future*, 6–8.

7. Bancroft and Dunning, *Reminiscences of Carl Schurz*, 222; Foner, *Reconstruction*, 66; *American Annual Cyclopaedia and Register of Important Events of the Year 1865*, 207, 210–11.

8. Foner, *Reconstruction*, 68; Gienapp, *Lincoln and Civil War America*, 198; Belz, *Abraham Lincoln, Constitutionalism, and Equal Rights*, 138; *American Annual Cyclopaedia and Register of Important Events of the Year 1865*, 295; *CG*, 38th Cong., 2nd sess., February 21, 1865, 961.

9. *CG*, 38th Cong., 2nd sess., February 22, 1865, 988; L. Maria Child to Mr. Julian, April 8, 1865, no. 861, vol. 5, G&JP.

10. Bancroft and Dunning, *Reminiscences of Carl Schurz*, 150; Julian, *Political Recollections*, 243; Foner, *Reconstruction*, 183–84; Bancroft and Dunning, *Reminiscences of Carl Schurz*, 150–53.

11. Boney, *A Union Soldier in the Land of the Vanquished*, 11, 49, 66–67, 49–50.

12. Dennett, *The South As It Is*, vi–vii, 41, 45, 68, 145–6, 149, 154, 156.

13. Andrews, *South since the War*, 27–28, 40–41.

14. Ibid., 60, 86–87, 126, 131, 224.

15. Trowbridge, *The South*, 71, 87, 150, 197, 590.

16. Ibid., 46, 63, 73, 70, 84, 482.

17. Ibid., 143, 180, 143, 116.

18. Ibid., 116, 70, 165, 180, 68.

19. Ibid., 308–9, 311, 578, 581. Historian Steven Stoll explains that proper use of manure "became fundamental to rural reform . . . farmers capable of making manure and applying it to fields in an intensive system plowed half or a third as many acres as the typical farmer and enjoyed a cascade of benefits" (Stoll, *Larding the Lean Earth*, 36).

20. Trowbridge, *The South*, 220, 212, 362, 384.

21. Ibid., 69, 409, 78, 151, 222, 533.

22. Andrews, *South since the War*, 109, 289, 1.

23. Ibid., 17, 21, 40, 177.

24. Ibid., 180–81, 177.

25. Dennett, *The South As It Is*, 16–17, 88, 90, 169, 342.

26. Ibid., 187, 277–78 .

27. Ibid., 201, 342, 357.

28. Andrews, *South since the War*, 4, 21, 159, 224, 227, 235.

29. Trowbridge, *The South*, 183, 228.

30. S. P. Chase to the President [Andrew Johnson], Hilton Head, May 17, 1865, in *Advice after Appomattox*, ed. Simpson, Grant, and Muldowny, 27.

31. S. P. Chase to President Johnson, May 21, 1865, in ibid., 34–35; S. P. Chase to the president [Andrew Johnson], May 23, 1865, in ibid., 37.

32. Carl Schurz to His Excellency Andrew Johnson, August 13, 1865, in ibid., 90; Carl Schurz to His Excellency Andrew Johnson, August 21, 1865, in ibid., 103; Carl Schurz to His Excellency Andrew Johnson, August 29, 1865, in ibid., 106. Carl Schurz to His Excellency Andrew Johnson, September 4, 1865, in ibid., 121; Carl Schurz to His Excellency Andrew Johnson, September 23, 1865, 147; Carl Schurz to His Excellency Andrew Johnson, July 28, 1865, in Ibid., 84–85; Bancroft and Dunning, *Reminiscences of Carl Schurz*, 188–89.

33. H. M. Watterson to His Excellency Andrew Johnson, June 7, 1865, in *Advice after Appomattox*, ed. Simpson, Grant, and Muldowny, 44, 40; H. M. Watterson to His Excellency Andrew Johnson, June 20, 1865, in ibid., 50; H. M. Watterson to His Excellency Andrew Johnson, July 8, 1865, in ibid., 57.

34. Bancroft and Dunning, *Reminiscences of Carl Schurz*, 203.

35. *CG*, 39th Cong., 1st sess., January 12, 1866, 209; *CG*, 39th Cong., 1st sess., January 20, 1866, 337; McPherson, *Ordeal by Fire*, 515; Foner, *Reconstruction*, 244–45.

36. Julian, *Political Recollections*, 296; *CG*, 39th Cong., 1st sess., February 7, 1866, 715–16.

37. *CG*, 39th Cong., 1st sess., February 7, 1866, 716–17.

38. McPherson, *Ordeal by Fire*, 531; Julian, *Political Recollections*, 314; Cross, *Justin Smith Morrill*, 117.

39. McPherson, *Ordeal by Fire*, 529; Berwanger, *West and Reconstruction*, 173–74, 127; Samuel Pomeroy to Mss. Anna Dickinson, October 16, 1867, reel 11, ADC.

40. Franklin, *Reminiscences of an Active Life*, x, 70; Foner, *Short History*, 65–66, 43; Eaton and Mason, *Grant, Lincoln, and the Freedmen*, xvii, xxii, 192.

41. Fitzgerald, *Union League Movement in the Deep South*, 160–61.

42. John A. Rawlins, "General Grant's Views in Harmony with Congress; Speech, Galena, Illinois, June 21, 1867," in *Radical Republicans and Reconstruction*, ed. Hyman, 392; Leland Stanford to Hon. C. Cole, February 9, 1867, in Cole, *Memoirs of Cornelius Cole*, 259; Franklin, *Reminiscences of an Active Life*, 138; Julian, *Political Recollections*, 324.

43. *CG*, 37th Cong., 3rd sess., January 4, 1863, 192–93. For a description of the 1862 Sioux uprising, see Richardson, *West from Appomattox*, 36.

44. Wallace, *Jefferson and the Indians*, 95, 248; Prucha, *The Great Father*, 50, 55, 75, 85.

45. "General McCook on the Sand Creek Massacre," *Philadelphia Inquirer*, August 19, 1865, 3; "Sand Creek Again," *Freedom's Champion*, November 23, 1865, 1.

46. *CG*, 38th Cong., 2nd sess., January 13, 1865, 250–52; Prucha, *The Great Father*, 154; West, *The Last Indian War*, 100.

47. West, *The Last Indian War*, 118.

48. Richardson, *Beyond the Mississippi*, 79, 579. John Wesley Powell exploded the myth that "rain follows the plow" in his 1878 *Report on the Lands of the Arid Region of the United States*. See Sachs, *The Humboldt Current*, 255.

49. Richardson, *Beyond the Mississippi*, 414, 460.

50. Ibid., 444, 606, 368.

51. Ibid., 367, 217, 222, 230.

52. Ibid., 219, 224.

53. Bowles, *Across the Continent*, 6, 1, 69, 11.

54. Ibid., 179-80, 64; Schuyler Colfax, "The Mines and Their Taxation," speech at Virginia City, Nevada, June 26, 1865, in ibid., 409-10.

55. Ibid., 31, 34, 41, 172, 197.

56. Ibid., 302, 307-10.

57. Richardson, *Beyond the Mississippi*, i, 420, 426, 429, 435.

58. Bowles, *Across the Continent*, viii, 31, 77, 231.

59. *CG*, 38th Cong., 2nd sess., January 13, 1865, 251; *CG*, 39th Cong., 1st sess., December 6, 1865, 12.

60. *CG*, 38th Cong., 2nd sess., February 23, 165, 1023; *CG*, 38th Cong., 2nd sess., March 1, 1865, 1230, 1233.

61. *CG*, 39th Cong., 1st sess., March 16, 1866, 1485; *CG*, 39th Cong., 1st sess., April 18, 1866, 2011.

62. Prucha, *The Great Father*, 155-56; West, *The Last Indian War*, 101-2.

63. Smith, *Grant*, 520; "President Grant's Inaugural Address," *Idaho Tri-Weekly Statesman*, March 11, 1869, 2; Waugh, *U.S. Grant*, 133; Prucha; *The Great Father*, 153, 164.

64. Eaton and Mason, *Grant, Lincoln, and the Freedmen*, 205-6, 274-75, 277.

65. McFeeley, *Yankee Stepfather*, 84-85, 133.

66. West, *The Last Indian War*, 108, 117-18.

67. Pratt, *Battlefield and Classroom*, xviii, 5, 7.

68. W. T. Sherman to Headquarters Mil. Div. of the Missouri, June 25, 1867, in ibid., 16; ibid., 42, 53; Dickory [R. H. Pratt] to Editor, December 6, 1867, in ibid., 20; ibid., 36.

69. Ibid., 100, 114, 118; R. H. Pratt to Gen. P. H. Sheridan, May 25, 1876, in ibid., 153; Harriet Beecher Stowe, "The Indians at St. Augustine," *Christian Union*, August 18, 1877, 1. Elliott West points out that for former abolitionists like Stowe, "the slaves' plight was linked to that of Indians" (West, *The Last Indian War*, 102).

70. Donald, Baker, and Holt, *Civil War and Reconstruction*, 580, 591; Foner, *Short History*, 168; Franklin, *Reminiscences of an Active Life*, 125.

71. Gates, "Federal Land Policy in the South," 304.

72. Hoffnagle, "The Southern Homestead Act," 616-17, 619.

73. Ibid., 621-22, 624, 627-28; Du Bois, *Black Reconstruction in America*, 476.

74. McPherson, *Ordeal by Fire*, 543-44; Foner, *Short History*, 186; Charles Sumner, "Speech, February, 1869," in *Radical Republicans and Reconstruction*, ed. Hyman, 488.

75. G. T. F. Boulding to Ulysses S. Grant, May 2, 1871, in *Papers of Ulysses S. Grant*, vol. 22, ed. Simon, 13-14; John A. Minnis to Ulysses S. Grant, December 12, 1872, in ibid., 19.

76. C. A. Luke to Ulysses S. Grant, August 22, 1871, in ibid., 76-77; Samuel F. Tappan to Ulysses S. Grant, May 25, 1871, in ibid., 78.

77. *New York Herald*, June 8, 1871, in ibid., 78; Smith, *Grant*, 546-47; Foner, *Short History*, 195-97; Donald, Baker, and Holt, *Civil War and Reconstruction*, 597; McPherson, *Ordeal by Fire*, 567; Smith, *Grant*, 523, 529.

78. Julian, *Political Recollections*, 330-31; Richardson, *The Death of Reconstruction*, 96; Holt, *By One Vote*, xiii.

79. L. Maria Child to Mr. Julian, January 31, 1872, no. 905, vol. 5, G&JP; B. Gratz Brown to Hon. Geo. W. Julian, February 28, 1872, no. 912, vol. 6, G&JP; Michael Les Benedict, "Salmon P. Chase and Constitutional Politics," in Benedict, *Preserving the Constitution*, 136; Slap, *Doom of Reconstruction*, xii.

80. Donald, Baker, and Holt, *Civil War and Reconstruction*, 600; Franklin, *Reminiscences of an Active Life*, 133, 147.

81. Foner, *Reconstruction*, 512–13; Donald, Baker, and Holt, *Civil War and Reconstruction*, 600; McPherson, *Ordeal by Fire*, 594.

82. Foner, *Short History*, 224–25; McPherson, *Ordeal by Fire*, 594.

83. Franklin, *Reminiscences of an Active Life*, 166–67.

84. Ibid., 161.

85. Holt, *By One Vote*, 240; Smith, *Grant*, 571.

86. Lewis, *Neither Wolf nor Dog*, 170–71; Nippawa and Three Others to Ulysses S. Grant, June 19, 1871, in *Papers of Ulysses S. Grant*, vol. 22, ed. Simon, 379–80.

87. King, *The Great South*, 33, 91, 210.

88. Smith, *Grant*, 535; Prucha, *The Great Father*, 171.

89. West, *The Last Indian War*, 293, 299, 301–2.

90. Prucha, *The Great Father*, 194–95; Hoxie, *A Final Promise*, 24.

91. Hoxie, *A Final Promise*, 14, 44.

92. McDonnell, *Dispossession of the American Indian*, 2; Hoxie, *A Final Promise*, 50; McDonnell, *Dispossession of the American Indian*, 10.

CONCLUSION

1. Taylor-Montoya, "Under the Same Glorious Flag," 15, 150; Williams, "George W. Julian and Land Reform in New Mexico," 80; Taylor-Montoya, "Under the Same Glorious Flag," 150.

2. Taylor-Montoya, "Under the Same Glorious Flag," 16; Williams, "George W. Julian and Land Reform in New Mexico," 80–81, 83–84.

3. Wiest, *Agricultural Organization*, 70, 191, 142; Gates, *Agriculture and the Civil War*, 304. See Pollan, *The Omnivore's Dilemma*, 146, for a criticism of the USDA.

4. Shannon, *Farmer's Last Frontier*, 51, 57; Paludan, *A People's Contest*, 162.

5. Kett, *Pursuit of Knowledge under Difficulties*, 141; Cross, *Justin Smith Morrill*, 85–86.

6. George G. Mackenzie, "Needs of the Yosemite: Natural Beauty Destroyed by Bad Management," *NYT*, February 23, 1890, 10.

7. Waugh, *U.S. Grant*, 130; Athearn, *William Tecumseh Sherman*, 344; Cronon, *Nature's Metropolis*, 216 , 214.

8. Bensel, *Political Economy of American Industrialization*, 11.

9. Gallagher, *Union War*, 152–53; McDonnell, *Dispossession of the American Indian*, 120.

10. Bushman, "Markets and Composite Farms in Early America," 351; Brooks D. Simpson, "The Reforging of a Republican Majority," in *Birth of the Grand Old Party*, ed. Engs and Miller, 159; Bensel, *Political Economy of American Industrialization*, xvii.

Bibliography

MANUSCRIPT COLLECTIONS

Lawrence, Kans.
    Kansas State Historical Society
        Thomas W. Higginson Collection
        Hiram Hill Collection
        Cyrus Kurtz Holliday Collection
        Thaddeus Hyatt Collection
        New England Emigrant Aid Company Collection
Los Angeles, Calif.
    Charles E. Young Research Library, Department of Special Collections,
        University of California, Los Angeles
        Cole Family Papers
Washington, D.C.
    Manuscript Division, Library of Congress
        Anna E. Dickinson Collection
        Joshua R. Giddings and George Washington Julian Papers

GOVERNMENT DOCUMENTS

Annals of Congress
Appendix to the Congressional Globe
Congressional Globe
Seward, William H. "Freedom in the New Territories." March 11, 1850. In *The Senate, 1789–1989: Classic Speeches, 1830–1993*, edited by Robert C. Byrd. Washington, D.C.: Government Printing Office, 1994.

NEWSPAPERS

Boston Daily Atlas
Boston Investigator
Christian Union
The Constitution (Washington, D.C.)
Daily Confederation
Daily Democratic State Journal
Daily Evening Bulletin (San Francisco)
Daily Ohio Statesman
Daily State Journal (Madison, Wis.)
Dayton Gazette
Emancipator and Republican
Evening Bulletin (San Francisco)
Farmer's Cabinet
Flake's Bulletin (Texas)
Freedom's Champion (Atchison, Kans.)
Georgia Telegraph (Macon, Ga.)
Helena Daily Herald
Idaho Tri-Weekly Statesman

The Liberator
Mariposa Gazette
Milwaukee Daily Sentinel
The Mississippian
North American and United States Gazette
The North Star
New-York Daily Times
New York Daily Tribune
New York Evening Post
New York Herald
New York Mirror
New York Times

Ohio State Journal
Philadelphia Inquirer
Pittsfield (Mass.) Sun
San Francisco Bulletin
Scioto Gazette (Chillicothe, Ohio)
Steubenville Herald
The Sun (Baltimore)
Vermont Chronicle
Vermont Watchman and State Journal
Weekly Georgia Telegraph
Weekly Herald (New York)
Weekly Wisconsin Patriot

PRINTED PRIMARY SOURCES

Books

The American Annual Cyclopaedia and Register of Important Events of the Year
    1865, Embracing Political, Civil, Military, and Social Affairs; Public Documents;
    Biography, Statistics, Commerce, Finance, Literature, Science, Agriculture, and
    Mechanical Industry. New York: D. Appleton & Company, 1873.

The American Annual Cyclopaedia and Register of Important Events of the Year 1866.
    New York: D. Appleton and Company, 1867.

Andrews, C. C. Minnesota and Dacotah: In Letters Descriptive of a Tour through the
    North-West, in the Autumn of 1856. With Information Relative to Public Lands,
    and a Table of Statistics. Washington, D.C.: Robert Farnham, 1857.

Andrews, Sidney. The South since the War: As Shown by Fourteen Weeks of Travel and
    Observation in Georgia and the Carolinas. Boston, Mass.: Ticknor and Fields, 1866.

Baker, George E., ed. The Works of William H. Seward. Vol. 4. Boston, Mass.:
    Houghton, Mifflin and Company, 1884.

Bancroft, Frederic, and William A. Dunning, eds. The Reminiscences of Carl Schurz.
    Vol. 3, 1863–1869. New York: McClure Company, 1908.

Beecher, Henry Ward. Plain and Pleasant Talk about Fruits, Flowers and Farming.
    New York: Derby & Jackson, 1859.

Belz, Herman. Abraham Lincoln, Constitutionalism, and Equal Rights in the Civil
    War Era. New York: Fordham University Press, 1998.

Berlin, Ira, Barbara J. Fields, Steven F. Miller, Joseph P. Reidy, and Leslie S. Rowland.
    Free at Last: A Documentary History of Slavery, Freedom, and the Civil War. New
    York: New Press, 1992.

Beveridge, Charles E., and Carolyn F. Hoffman, eds. The Papers of Frederick Law
    Olmsted; Writings on Public Parks, Parkways, and Park Systems. Supplementary
    series, vol. 1. Baltimore and London, UK: Johns Hopkins University Press, 1997.

Beveridge, Charles E., and Charles Capen McLaughlin, eds. The Papers of Frederick
    Law Olmsted. Vol. 2, Slavery and the South: 1852–1857. Baltimore: Johns Hopkins
    University Press, 1981.

Boney, F. N., ed. *A Union Soldier in the Land of the Vanquished: The Diary of Sergeant Matthew Woodruff, June–December 1865*. Tuscaloosa: University of Alabama Press, 1969.

Boudrye, Rev. Louis, N. *Historic Records of the Fifth New York Cavalry, First Ira Harris Guard, Its Organization, Marches, Raids, Scouts, Engagements, and General Services During the Rebellion of 1861–1865, with Observations of the Author by the War, Giving Sketches of the Armies of the Potomac and of the Shenandoah. Also, Interesting Accounts of Prison Life and of the Secret Service*. Albany, N.Y.: S. R. Gray, 1865.

Bowles, Samuel. *Across the Continent: A Summer's Journey to the Rocky Mountains, the Mormons, and the Pacific States, with Speaker Colfax*. New York: Hurd and Houghton, 1865.

Brewer, William H. *Up and Down California in 1860–1864*. Edited by Francis P. Farquhar. Berkeley: University of California Press, 1974.

Bunnell, L. H. *"California As I Saw It": Discovery of the Yosemite, and the Indian War of 1851, Which Led to That Event*. New York: Fleming H. Revell Company, 1880.

Carey, H. C. *Principles of Political Economy; Part the First: Of the Laws of the Production and Distribution of Wealth*. Philadelphia, Pa.: Carey, Lea & Blanchard, 1837.

———. *Principles of Political Economy; Part the Second: Of the Causes Which Retard Increase in the Production of Wealth, and Improvement in the Physical and Moral Condition of Man*. Philadelphia, Pa.: Carey, Lea & Blanchard, 1838.

———. *Principles of Political Economy; Part the Fourth: Of the Causes Which Retard Improvement in the Political Condition of Man*. Philadelphia, Pa.: Lea & Blanchard, 1840.

Carey, Matthew. *The Olive Branch; or, Faults on Both Sides, Federal and Democratic. A Serious Appeal on the Necessity of Mutual Forgiveness and Harmony*. 1814; reprint, Winchester, Va.: J. Foster, 1817.

Catlin, George. *Manners, Customs, and Condition of the North American Indians*. 4th edition. London, UK: David Bogue, 1844.

Child, L. Maria, ed. *Speeches on Political Questions by George W. Julian*. New York: Hurd and Houghton, 1872.

Cole, Cornelius. *Memoirs of Cornelius Cole: Ex-Senator of the United States from California*. New York: McLoughlin Brothers, 1908.

Collamer, J., G. A. Grow, Sml. Galloway, et al. *Border Ruffian Code*. N.p., 1856.

Dennett, John Richard. *The South As It Is: 1865–1866*. Edited by Henry M. Christman. New York: Viking Press, 1965.

Dodge, Grenville M. *How We Built the Union Pacific Railway and Other Railway Papers and Addresses*. N.p., 1870.

Dodge, Wm. Sumner. *A Waif of the War; or, The History of the Seventy-Fifth Illinois Infantry, Embracing the Entire Campaigns of the Army of the Cumberland*. Chicago: Church and Goodman, 1866.

Driggs, George, W. *Opening of the Mississippi; or, Two Years' Campaigning in the South-West. A Record of the Campaigns, Sieges, Actions and Marches in Which the*

8th Wisconsin Volunteers Have Participated. Together with Correspondence, by a Non-Commissioned Officer. Madison, Wis.: Wm. J. Park & Co., Book and Job Printers, Harding's Block, 1864.

Eaton, John, and Ethel Osgood Mason. *Grant, Lincoln, and the Freedmen: Reminiscences of the Civil War with Special Reference to the Work for the Contrabands and Freedmen of the Mississippi Valley*. New York: Longmans, Green and Co., 1907.

Eddy, Richard. *History of the Sixtieth Regiment New York State Volunteers, from the Commencement of Its Organization in July, 1861, to Its Public Reception at Ogdensburgh as a Veteran Command, January 7th, 1864*. Philadelphia, Pa.: J. Fagan and Son, 1864.

Eden, R. C. *The Sword and Gun: A History of the 37th Wis. Volunteer Infantry, from Its First Organization to Its Final Muster Out*. Madison, Wis.: Atwood & Rublee, 1865.

Everett, Edward., ed. *The Works of Daniel Webster*. 6 vols. 1851; reprint, Boston, Mass.: Libbie, Brown, 1856.

Everts, Hermann. *History of the Ninth Regiment New Jersey Vols. Infantry. From Its First Organization to Its Final Muster Out*. Newark, N.J.: A. Stephen Holbrook, Printer, 1865.

Fleharty, S. F. *A History of the 102d Illinois Infantry Volunteers with Sketches of the Atlanta Campaign, the Georgia Raid, and the Campaign of the Carolinas*. Chicago: Brewster & Hanscom, Printers, 1865.

Franklin, John Hope, ed. *Reminiscences of an Active Life: The Autobiography of John Roy Lynch*. Chicago: University of Chicago Press, 1970.

Frothingham, Richard. *A Tribute to Thomas Starr King*. Boston, Mass.: Ticknor and Fields, 1865.

Gage, M. D. *From Vicksburg to Raleigh; or, A Complete History of the Twelfth Regiment Indiana Volunteer Infantry and the Campaigns of Grant and Sherman, with an Outline of the Great Rebellion*. Chicago: Clarke & Co., Publishers, 1865.

George, Henry. *Our Land and Land Policy: Speeches, Lectures and Miscellaneous Writings*. New York: Doubleday and McClure Company, 1901.

Giddings, Joshua Reed. *Speeches in Congress*. Cambridge, Mass: Allen and Farnham, 1853.

Greeley, Horace. *Proceedings of the First Three Republican National Conventions of 1856, 1860, and 1864*. Minneapolis, Minn.: Harrison & Smith, 1893.

Guizot, M. *General History of Civilization in Europe, from the Fall of the Roman Empire to the French Revolution*. Third American, from the second English edition. New York: D. Appleton & Company, 1842.

Hart, E. J. *History of the Fortieth Illinois Inf. (Volunteers)*. Cincinnati, Ohio: H. S. Bosworth, 1864.

Helper, Hinton R. *The Impending Crisis of the South: How to Meet It*. New York: Burdick Brothers, 1857.

Hittell, John S. *A History of the City of San Francisco and Incidentally of the State of California*. San Francisco, Calif.: A. L. Bancroft & Company, 1878.

Hurst, Samuel H. *Journal-History of the Seventy-Third Ohio Volunteer Infantry.* Chillicothe, Ohio: 1866.

Hutchings, J. M. *In the Heart of the Sierras, the Yo Semite Valley, Both Historical and Descriptive: And Scenes by the Way. Big Tree Groves. The High Sierra, with Its Magnificent Scenery, Ancient and Modern Glaciers, and Other Objects of Interest; with Tables of Distances and Altitudes, Maps, et al.* Oakland, Calif.: Pacific Press Publishing House, 1886.

Irvin, William. *Biennial Report of the Commissioners to Manage the Yosemite Valley and the Mariposa Big Tree Grove.* Sacramento, Calif.: F. P. Thompson, Superintendent of State Printing, 1877.

Jefferson, Thomas. *Notes on the State of Virginia.* Richmond, Va.: J. W. Randolph, 1853.

Jones, Henry, T. *Life with the Forty-Ninth Massachusetts Volunteers.* Pittsfield, Mass.: C. A. Alvord, 1864.

Judd, David W. *The Story of the Thirty-Third N.Y.S. Vols; or, Two Years Campaigning in Virginia and Maryland.* Rochester, N.Y.: Benton & Andrews, 1864.

Julian, George W. *Political Recollections: 1840 to 1872.* Chicago: Jansen, McClurg, and Company, 1885.

King, Charles R., ed. *The Life and Correspondence of Rufus King: Comprising His Letters, Private and Official, His Public Documents and His Speeches.* 6 vols. New York: G. P. Putnam's Sons, 1894–1900.

King, Edward. *The Great South: A Record of Journeys in Louisiana, Texas, the Indian Territory, Missouri, Arkansas, Mississippi, Alabama, Georgia, Florida, South Carolina, North Carolina, Kentucky, Tennessee, Virginia, West Virginia, and Maryland.* Hartford, Conn.: American Publishing Company, 1875.

King, Rufus. *Substance of Two Speeches, Delivered in the Senate of the United States on the Subject of the Missouri Bill by the Hon. Rufus King of New York.* New York: Kirk and Mercein, 1918.

King, Thomas Starr. *The Death of Mr. Webster: A Sermon Preached in Hollis-Street Meeting House, on Sunday Oct. 31, 1852.* Boston, Mass.: Benjamin H. Greene, 124 Washington Street, 1852.

———. *A Vacation Among the Sierras.* Edited by John A. Hussey. San Francisco: Book Club of California, 1962.

———. *The White Hills: Their Legends, Landscape, and Poetry.* Boston, Mass.: Woolworth, Ainsworth, and Company, 1869.

Kinnear, J. R. *History of the Eighty-Sixth Regiment: Illinois Volunteer Infantry, During Its Term of Service.* Chicago: Tribune Company's Book and Job Printing Office, 1866.

Lorain, John. *Nature and Reason Harmonized in the Practice of Husbandry.* Philadelphia, Pa.: H. C. Carey & I. Lea, 1825.

Mannis, Jedediah, and Galen R. Wilson, eds. *Bound to Be a Soldier: The Letters of Private James T. Miller, 11th Pennsylvania Infantry, 1861–1864.* Knoxville: University of Tennessee Press, 2001.

Marsh, George P. *Man and Nature; or, Physical Geography as Modified by Human Action.* New York: Charles Scribner, 1864.

McClellan, R. Guy. *A History of the Colonial and Republican Governments of the United States of America, from the Year 1607 to the Year 1869.* San Francisco, Calif.: R. J. Trumbull & Company, 1868.

McLaughlin, Charles Capen, and Charles E. Beveridge, eds. *The Papers of Frederick Law Olmsted.* Vol. 1, *The Formative Years, 1822 to 1852.* Baltimore: Johns Hopkins University Press, 1977.

——. *The Papers of Frederick Law Olmsted.* Vol. 4, *Defending the Union, the Civil War and the U.S. Sanitary Commission, 1861–1863.* Baltimore: Johns Hopkins University Press, 1986.

Mills, J. Harrison. *Chronicles of the Twenty-First Regiment New York State Volunteers, Embracing a Full History of the Regiment, from the Enrolling of the First Volunteer in Buffalo, April 15, 1861, to the Final Mustering Out, May 18, 1863.* 1863; reprint, Buffalo, N.Y.: 21st Reg't. Veteran Association of Buffalo, 1887.

Morison, Marion. *A History of the Ninth Regiment: Illinois Volunteer Infantry.* Monmouth, Ill.: John S. Clark, Printer, 1864.

Morrill, Justin S. *Wanderings and Scribblings; or, A Journal of a Journey South and West in May, June, and July, A.D. 1841.* Stafford, Vt.: 1841.

Morris, Edmund. *How to Get a Farm, and Where to Find One.* 1864; reprint, New York: James Miller, 1871.

Mulligan, William H., Jr., ed. *A Badger Boy in Blue: The Civil War Letters of Chauncey H. Cooke.* Detroit, Mich.: Wayne State University Press, 2007.

Myers, John C. *A Daily Journal of the 192 Reg't Penn'a Volunteers Commanded by Col. William B. Thomas in the Service of the United States for One Hundred Days.* Philadelphia, Pa.: Crissy & Markley, Printers, Goldsmiths Hall, 1864.

Nack, James. *An Ode on the Proclamation of President Jackson.* New York: Monson Bancroft, 1833.

Olmsted, Frederick Law. *A Journey in the Seaboard Slave States, with Remarks on Their Economy.* New York: Dix & Edwards, 1856.

——. *A Journey through Texas; or, A Saddle-Trip on the Southwestern Frontier; with a Statistical Appendix.* New York: Mason Brothers, 1860.

——. *Walks and Talks of an American Farmer in England.* Columbus, Ohio: Jos. H. Riley and Company, 1859.

O'Meara, James. *Broderick and Gwin.* San Francisco, Calif.: Bacon & Company, 1881.

Pierce, Lyman B. *History of the Second Iowa Cavalry; Containing a Detailed Account of Its Organization, Marches, and the Battles in Which It Has Participated; Also, a Complete Roster of Each Company.* Burlington, Iowa: Hawk-Eye Steam Book and Job Printing Establishment, 1865.

Pomeroy, Samuel, C. *The Platform and Party of the Future, and National Freedom Secured by an Amended Constitution.* Washington, D.C.: McGill & Witherow, Steam Printers, March 10, 1864.

Pratt, Richard Henry. *Battlefield and Classroom.* Edited by Robert M. Utley. Norman: University of Oklahoma Press, 2003.

Prentiss, George, L. *The Political Crisis.* New York: Somers, 1866.

Quiner, E. B. *The Military History of Wisconsin in the War for the Union.* Chicago: Clarke & Co., Publishers, 1868.

Ranney, Victoria Post, Gerald J. Rauluk, and Carolyn F. Hoffman, eds. *The Papers of Frederick Law Olmsted.* Vol. 5, *The California Frontier.* Baltimore and London, UK.: Johns Hopkins University Press, 1990.

Rhodes, Elisha Hunt. *All for the Union: The Civil War Diary and Letters of Elisha Hunt Rhodes.* Edited by Robert Hunt Rhodes. New York: Vintage Books, 1985.

Richardson, Albert D. *Beyond the Mississippi: From the Great River to the Great Ocean; Life and Adventure on the Prairies, Mountains, and Pacific Coast.* Hartford, Conn.: American Publishing Company, 1869.

Ruffin, Edmund. *Essays and Notes on Agriculture.* Richmond, Va.: J. W. Randolph, 1855.

Sanger, George P., ed. *The Statutes at Large, and Treaties of the United States of America, Passed at the First Session of the Thirty-Eighth Congress, 1863–64.* Boston, Mass.: Little, Brown & Co., 1864.

Sheldon, Winthrop D. *The "Twenty Seventh": A Regimental History.* New Haven, Conn.: Morris & Benham, 1866.

Simon, John, ed. *The Papers of Ulysses S. Grant.* Vol. 22, *June 1, 1871–January 31, 1872.* Carbondale: Southern Illinois University Press, 1998.

Simpson, Brooks D., Leroy P. Grant, and John Muldowny, eds. *Advice after Appomattox: Letters to Andrew Johnson, 1865–1866.* Knoxville: University of Tennessee Press, 1987.

Sprague, Homer B. *13th Infantry Regiment of Connecticut Volunteers during the Great Rebellion.* Hartford, Conn.: Case, Lockwood & Co., 1867.

Stowe, Harriet Beecher. *Uncle Tom's Cabin.* 1852; reprint, New York: Oxford University Press, 2002.

Tourgée, Albion W. *The Story of a Thousand: Being a History of the Service of the 105th Ohio Volunteer Infantry, in the War for the Union from August 21, 1862 to June 6, 1865.* Buffalo, N.Y.: S. McGerald & Son, 1896.

Transactions of the California State Agricultural Society during the Year 1861. Sacramento, Calif.: J. Y. P. Avery, State Printer, 1862.

Transactions of the California State Agricultural Society during the Year 1863. Sacramento, Calif.: C. M. Clayes, State Printer, 1864.

Trowbridge, J. T. *The South: A Tour of Its Battle-Fields and Ruined Cities, A Journey through the Desolated States and Talks with the People.* Hartford, Conn.: L. Stebbins, 1866.

Upham, Charles Wentworth. *Life, Explorations and Public Services of John C. Fremont.* Cambridge, Mass, 1856.

Whipple, Edwin P., ed. *Christianity and Humanity: A Series of Sermons by Thomas Starr King.* Boston, Mass.: James R. Osgood and Company, 1878.

Williams, J. C. *Life in Camp: A History of the Nine Months' Service of the Fourteenth Vermont Regiment, from October 21, 1862, When It Was Mustered Into U.S. Service, to July 21, 1863, Including the Battle of Gettysburg.* Claremont, N.H.: Claremont Manufacturing Company, 1864.

Wilson, Henry. *The Death of Slavery Is the Life of the Nation.* Washington, D.C.: H. Polkinhorn, 1864.

Wolfe, Saml. M. *Helper's Impending Crisis Dissected.* New York: J. T. Lloyd, 1860.

Wood, Wales M. *A History of the Ninety-Fifth Regiment, Illinois Infantry Volunteers, from Its Organization in the Fall of 1862, Until Its Final Discharge from the United States Service, in 1865*. Chicago: Tribune Company's Book and Job Printing Office, 1865.

Woodward, E. M. *Our Campaigns; or, The Marches, Bivouacs, Battles, Incidents of Camp Life and History of Our Regiment during Its Three Years Term of Service, Together with a Sketch of the Army of the Potomac, under Generals McClellan, Burnside, Hooker, Meade and Grant*. Philadelphia, Pa.: John E. Potter, 1865.

Articles and Parts of Books

Davis, Jefferson. "Speech in U.S. Senate, December 14, 1858." In *Jefferson Davis: The Essential Writings*, edited by William J. Copper. New York: Modern Library, 2004.

Huidekoper, H. S., and R. L. Ashhurst. "Resolution of the Soldiers of the 150th Pennsylvania Volunteers." March 11, 1863. In *Loyalist's Ammunition* (pamphlet), 7.

Jackson, Andrew. "Proclamation on Nullification." December 10, 1832. In *Life and Times of Andrew Jackson: Soldier—Statesman—President*, by A. S. Colyar. Nashville, Tenn.: Marshall & Bruce Company, 1904.

"James Knox Polk Inaugural Address." March 4, 1845. In *U.S. Presidential Inaugural Addresses*. Whitefish, Mont.: Kessinger Publishing, 2004.

King, Thomas Starr. "Discourse, Delivered in Boston, before the Ancient and Honorable Artillery Company, on the Occasion of Their Two Hundred and Thirteenth Anniversary, June 2nd, 1851." In *Patriotism and Other Papers*. With a biographical sketch by Hon. Richard Frothingham. Boston, Mass.: Tompkins and Company, 1864.

"Lecture on Agricultural Chemistry." In *The Plough, the Loom, and the Anvil*. Vol. 2. Philadelphia, Pa.: J. S. Skinner, 1849.

Lincoln, Abraham. "Message to Congress, December 1, 1862." In *This Fiery Trial: The Speeches and Writings of Abraham Lincoln*, edited by William E. Gienapp. New York: Oxford University Press, 2002.

Olmsted, Frederick Law. "Governmental Preservation of National Scenery, Brookline, Mass., 8th March, 1890." *Sierra Club Bulletin* 29 (October 1944): 61–66.

Sumner, Charles. "Justice to the Land States and Policy of Roads, Speeches in the Senate of the United States on the Iowa Railroad Bill, 27th Jan., 17th Feb., and 16th March, 1852." In *Recent Speeches and Addresses by Charles Sumner*. Boston, Mass.: Higgins, Bradley, and Dayton, 1857.

Wilmot, David. "Speech of David Wilmot." In *The Friend: A Religious and Literary Journal*.

SECONDARY WORKS

Books

Appleby, Joyce. *Capitalism and a New Social Order: The Republican Vision of the 1790s*. New York: New York University Press, 1984.

——. *Thomas Jefferson*. New York: Times Books, 2003.

Athearn, Robert G. *William Tecumseh Sherman and the Settlement of the West*. Norman: University of Oklahoma Press, 1956.

Bagley, William Chandler, Jr. *Soil Exhaustion and the Civil War*. Washington, D.C.: American Council on Public Affairs, 1942.

Baker, Jean H. *James Buchanan*. New York: Times Books, 2004.

Beard, Charles A., and Mary R. Beard. *The Rise of American Civilization*. New York: Macmillan Company, 1933.

Benedict, Michael Les. *The Impeachment and Trial of Andrew Johnson*. New York: W. W. Norton & Company, 1999.

———. *Preserving the Constitution: Essays on Politics and the Constitution in the Reconstruction Era*. New York: Fordham University Press, 2006.

Bennett, Lerone, Jr. *Forced into Glory: Abraham Lincoln's White Dream*. Chicago: Johnson Publishing Company, 2007.

Bensel, Richard Franklin. *The Political Economy of American Industrialization, 1877–1890*. New York: Cambridge University Press, 2000.

———. *Yankee Leviathan: The Origins of Central State Authority in America, 1859–1877*. New York: Cambridge University Press, 1990.

Berwanger, Eugene H. *The Frontier against Slavery: Western Anti-Negro Prejudice and the Slavery Extension Controversy*. Urbana: University of Illinois Press, 1967.

———. *The West and Reconstruction*. Chicago: University of Illinois Press, 1981.

Brady, Lisa M. *War upon the Land: Military Strategy and the Transformation of Southern Landscapes during the American Civil War*. Athens: University of Georgia Press, 2012.

Brown, David. *Southern Outcast: Hinton Rowan Helper and "The Impending Crisis of the South."* Baton Rouge: Louisiana State University Press, 2006.

Burton, Orville Vernon. *The Age of Lincoln*. New York: Hill and Wang, 2007.

Carr, Ethan. *Wilderness by Design: Landscape Architecture and the National Park Service*. Lincoln: University of Nebraska Press, 1998.

Clarke, Erskine. *Dwelling Place: A Plantation Epic*. New Haven, Conn.: Yale University Press, 2005.

Cohen, Benjamin R. *Notes from the Ground: Science, Soil, and Society in the American Countryside*. New Haven, Conn.: Yale University Press, 2009.

Confino, Alon. *The Nation as a Local Metaphor: Württemberg, Imperial Germany, and National Memory, 1871–1918*. Chapel Hill: University of North Carolina Press, 1997.

Cramton, Luis C. *Early History of Yellowstone National Park and Its Relation to National Park Policies*. Washington, D.C.: U.S. Government Printing Office, 1932.

Crofts, Daniel W. *Reluctant Confederates: Upper South Unionists in the Secession Crisis*. Chapel Hill: University of North Carolina Press, 1989.

Cronon, William. *Nature's Metropolis: Chicago and the Great West*. New York: W. W. Norton & Company, 1991.

———. ed. *Uncommon Ground: Rethinking the Human Place in Nature*. New York: W. W. Norton and Company, 1996.

Cross, Coy F., II. *Justin Smith Morrill: Father of the Land-Grant Colleges*. East Lansing: Michigan State University Press, 1999.

Davis, David Brion. *Inhuman Bondage: The Rise and Fall of Slavery in the New World*. New York: Oxford University Press, 2006.

Davis, Winfield. *The History of Political Conventions in California*. Sacramento, Calif.: The Library, 1893.

Dilsaver, Larry M., and William C. Tweed. *Challenge of the Big Trees: A Resource History of Sequoia and Kings Canyon National Parks*. Three Rivers, Calif.: Sequoia Natural History Association, Inc., 1990.

Donald, David Herbert, Jean Harvey Baker, and Michael F. Holt. *The Civil War and Reconstruction*. New York: W. W. Norton and Company, 2001.

Du Bois, W. E. B. *Black Reconstruction in America: An Essay toward a History of the Part Which Black Folk Played in the Attempt to Reconstruct Democracy in America*. 1935; reprint, New York: Oxford University Press, 2007.

Dupree, A. Hunter. *Science in the Federal Government: A History of Policies and Activities to 1940*. Cambridge, Mass.: Harvard University Press, 1957.

Dusinberre, William. *Slavemaster President: The Double Career of James Polk*. New York: Oxford University Press, 2003.

Earle, Jonathan H. *Jacksonian Antislavery and the Politics of Free Soil, 1824–1854*. Chapel Hill: University of North Carolina Press, 2004.

Egerton, Douglas R. *Gabriel's Rebellion: The Virginia Slave Conspiracies of 1800 and 1802*. Chapel Hill: University of North Carolina Press, 1993.

Egnal, Marc. *Clash of Extremes: The Economic Origins of the Civil War*. New York: Hill and Wang, 2009.

Ellis, Joseph J. *American Sphinx: The Character of Thomas Jefferson*. New York: Alfred A. Knopf, 1997.

Engs, Robert F., and Randall M. Miller, eds. *The Birth of the Grand Old Party: The Republicans' First Generation*. Philadelphia: University of Pennsylvania Press, 2002.

Escott, Paul D. *"What Shall We Do with the Negro?" Lincoln, White Racism, and Civil War America*. Charlottesville: University of Virginia Press, 2009.

Eyal, Yonatan. *The Young American Movement and the Transformation of the Democratic Party*. New York: Cambridge University Press, 2007.

Feller, Daniel. *The Public Lands in Jacksonian Politics*. Madison: University of Wisconsin Press, 1984.

Fitzgerald, Michael W. *The Union League Movement in the Deep South: Politics and Agricultural Change during Reconstruction*. Baton Rouge: Louisiana State University Press, 1989.

Foner, Eric. *Free Soil, Free Labor, Free Men: The Ideology of the Republican Party before the Civil War*. New York: Oxford University Press, 1995.

———. *Reconstruction: America's Unfinished Revolution, 1863–1877*. New York: Harper Collins Publishers, 1989.

———. *A Short History of Reconstruction*. New York: Harper & Row Publishers, 1990.

Forbes, Robert Pierce. *The Missouri Compromise and Its Aftermath*. Chapel Hill: University of North Carolina Press, 2007.

Freehling, William W. *The Road to Disunion*. Vol. 1, *Secessionists at Bay, 1776–1854*. New York: Oxford University Press, 1990.

———. *The Road to Disunion*. Vol. 2, *Secessionists Triumphant*. New York: Oxford University Press, 2007.

Gallagher, Gary W. *The Confederate War*. Cambridge, Mass.: Harvard University Press, 1997.

———. *The Union War*. Cambridge, Mass.: Harvard University Press, 2011.

Gates, Paul W. *Agriculture and the Civil War*. New York: Alfred A. Knopf, 1965.

———. *History of Public Land Law Development*. Washington, D.C.: Zenger Publishing Co. Inc., 1968.

Genovese, Eugene D. *Roll, Jordan, Roll: The World That the Slaves Made*. New York: Random House, 1974.

Gienapp, William E. *Abraham Lincoln and Civil War America*. New York: Oxford University Press, 2002.

———. *The Origins of the Republican Party: 1852-1856*. New York: Oxford University Press, 1987.

Glatthaar, Joseph, T. *Forged in Battle: The Civil War Alliance of Black Soldiers and White Officers*. New York: Penguin Group, 1991.

Grant, Susan-Mary. *North over South: Northern Nationalism and American Identity in the Antebellum Era*. Lawrence: University Press of Kansas, 2000.

Greenberg, Amy S. *Manifest Manhood and the Antebellum American Empire*. New York: Cambridge University Press, 2005.

Grimsley, Mark. *The Hard Hand of War: Union Military Policy toward Southern Civilians, 1861-1865*. New York: Cambridge University Press, 1995.

Hobsbawm, Eric J. *Nations and Nationalism since 1780: Programme, Myth, Reality*. Cambridge, UK: Cambridge University Press, 1990.

Hobsbawm, Eric J., and Terence Ranger, eds. *The Invention of Tradition*. Cambridge, UK: Cambridge University Press, 1983.

Holliday, J. S. *The World Rushed In: The California Gold Rush Experience*. New York: Simon and Schuster, 1981.

Holt, Michael F. *By One Vote: The Disputed Presidential Election of 1876*. Lawrence: University Press of Kansas, 2008.

———. *The Fate of Their Country: Politicians, Slavery Extension, and the Coming of the Civil War*. New York: Hill and Wang, 2004.

———. *The Political Crisis of the 1850s*. New York: W. W. Norton & Company, 1978.

———. *The Rise and Fall of the American Whig Party: Jacksonian Politics and the Onset of the Civil War*. New York: Oxford University Press, 1999.

Howe, Daniel Walker. *What Hath God Wrought: The Transformation of America, 1815-1848*. New York: Oxford University Press, 2007.

Hoxie, Frederick E. *A Final Promise: The Campaign to Assimilate the Indians, 1880-1920*. Lincoln: University of Nebraska Press, 1984.

Huntley, Jen A. *The Making of Yosemite: James Mason Hutchings and the Origin of America's Most Popular National Park*. Lawrence: University Press of Kansas, 2011.

Huston, James L. *Stephen A. Douglas and the Dilemmas of Democratic Equality*. Lanham, Md.: Rowman and Littlefield Publishers, Inc., 2007.

Hyman, Harold M. *American Singularity: The 1787 Northwest Ordinance, the 1862 Homestead and Morrill Acts, and the 1944 G.I. Bill.* Athens: University of Georgia Press, 1986.

———. ed. *The Radical Republicans and Reconstruction: 1861–1870.* Indianapolis, Ind.: Bobbs-Merrill Company, Inc., 1967.

Kett, Joseph F. *The Pursuit of Knowledge under Difficulties: From Self-Improvement to Adult Education in America, 1750–1990.* Stanford, Calif.: Stanford University Press, 1994.

Lankford, Nelson. *Cry Havoc! The Crooked Road to Civil War, 1861.* New York: Viking Penguin, 2007.

Lause, Mark A. *Young America: Land, Labor, and the Republican Community.* Urbana: University of Illinois Press, 2005.

Lewis, David Rich. *Neither Wolf nor Dog: American Indians, Environment, and Agrarian Change.* New York: Oxford University Press, 1994.

Majewski, John. *Modernizing a Slave Economy: The Economic Vision of the Confederate Nation.* Chapel Hill: University of North Carolina Press, 2009.

Manning, Chandra. *What This Cruel War Was Over: Soldiers, Slavery, and the Civil War.* New York: Alfred A. Knopf, 2007.

Marx, Leo. *The Machine in the Garden: Technology and the Pastoral Ideal in America.* New York: Oxford University Press, 1964.

Matthews, Glenda. *The Golden State in the Civil War: Thomas Starr King, the Republican Party, and the Birth of Modern California.* New York: Cambridge University Press, 2012.

McCoy, Drew R. *The Elusive Republic: Political Economy in Jeffersonian America.* Chapel Hill: University of North Carolina Press, 1980.

McDonnell, Janet A. *The Dispossession of the American Indian: 1887–1934.* Bloomington: Indiana University Press, 1991.

McFeeley, William S. *Yankee Stepfather: General O. O. Howard and the Freedmen.* New Haven, Conn.: Yale University Press, 1968.

McPherson, James M. *Battle Cry of Freedom: The Civil War Era.* New York: Oxford University Press, 1988.

———. *For Cause and Comrades: Why Men Fought in the Civil War.* New York: Oxford University Press, 1997.

———. *Ordeal by Fire: The Civil War and Reconstruction.* New York: Alfred A. Knopf, 1982.

———. *Tried by War: Abraham Lincoln as Commander in Chief.* New York: Penguin Press, 2008.

Melendy, H. Brett, and Benjamin F. Gilbert. *The Governors of California: Peter H. Burnett to Edmund G. Brown.* Georgetown, Calif.: Talisman Press, 1965.

Mitchell, Reid. *The Vacant Chair: The Northern Soldier Leaves Home.* New York: Oxford University Press, 1993.

Morrison, Michael A. *Slavery and the American West: The Eclipse of Manifest Destiny and the Coming of the Civil War.* Chapel Hill: University of North Carolina Press, 1997.

Nash, Roderick Frederick. *Wilderness and the American Mind*. 1967; reprint, New Haven, Conn.: Yale University Press, 2001.

O'Connor, Thomas H. *Lords of the Loom: The Cotton Whigs and the Coming of the Civil War*. New York: Charles Scribner's Sons, 1968.

Oertel, Kristin Tegteier, *Bleeding Borders: Race, Gender and Violence in Pre-Civil War Kansas*. Baton Rouge: Louisiana State University Press, 2009.

Onuf, Peter S. *Jefferson's Empire: The Language of American Nationalism*. Charlottesville: University of Virginia Press, 2001.

———. *Statehood and Union: A History of the Northwest Ordinance*. Bloomington: Indiana University Press, 1987.

Paludan, Phillip Shaw. *A Covenant with Death: The Constitution, Law, and Equality in the Civil War Era*. Urbana and Chicago: University of Illinois Press, 1975.

———. *A People's Contest: The Union and the Civil War, 1861–1865*. Lawrence: University Press of Kansas, 1988.

Parker, William Belmont. *The Life and Public Services of Justin Smith Morrill*. Boston, Mass.: Houghton Mifflin Company, 1924.

Peterson, Merrill D. *The Jefferson Image in the American Mind*. Charlottesville: University Press of Virginia, 1998.

Pierson, Michael D. *Free Hearts and Free Homes: Gender and American Antislavery Politics*. Chapel Hill: University of North Carolina Press, 2003.

Pollan, Michael. *The Omnivore's Dilemma: A Natural History of Four Meals*. New York: Penguin Press, 2006.

Powell, Burt E. *The Movement for Industrial Education and the Establishment of the University, 1840–1870*. Urbana: University of Illinois Press, 1918.

Prucha, Francis Paul. *The Great Father: The United States Government and the American Indians*. Lincoln: University of Nebraska Press, 1986.

Richards, Leonard L. *The California Gold Rush and the Coming of the Civil War*. New York: Alfred A. Knopf, 2007.

Richardson, Heather Cox. *The Death of Reconstruction: Race, Labor and Politics in the Post-Civil War North, 1865–1901*. Cambridge, Mass: Harvard University Press, 2001.

———. *The Greatest Nation of the Earth: Republican Economic Policies during the Civil War*. Cambridge, Mass: Harvard University Press, 1997.

———. *West from Appomattox: The Reconstruction of America after the Civil War*. New Haven, Conn.: Yale University Press, 2007.

Righter, Robert W. *The Battle over Hetch Hetchy: America's Most Controversial Dam and the Birth of Modern Environmentalism*. New York: Oxford University Press, 2005.

Robbins, Roy. *Our Landed Heritage*. Lincoln: University of Nebraska Press, 1976.

Roper, Laura Wood. *FLO: A Biography of Frederick Law Olmsted*. Baltimore: Johns Hopkins University Press, 1973.

Rose, Henry. *Henry George: A Biographical, Anecdotal, and Critical Sketch*. London, UK: William Reeves, 185 Fleet Street, E.C., 1884.

Ross, Earle D. *Democracy's College: The Land Grant Movement in the Formative Stage*. Ames: Iowa State College Press, 1942.

Runte, Alfred. *National Parks: The American Experience*. Lincoln: University of Nebraska Press, 1997.

———. *Yosemite: The Embattled Wilderness*. Lincoln: University of Nebraska Press, 1990.

Russell, Carl Parcher. *One Hundred Years in Yosemite: The Story of a Great Park and Its Friends*. Berkeley: University of California Press, 1957.

Sachs, Aaron. *The Humboldt Current: Nineteenth-Century Exploration and the Roots of American Environmentalism*. New York: Penguin Group, 2006.

Sanborn, Margaret. *Yosemite: Its Discovery, Its Wonders, and Its People*. New York: Random House, 1981.

Schullery, Paul. *Searching for Yellowstone: Ecology and Wonder in the Last Wilderness*. Boston, Mass.: Houghton Mifflin Company, 1997.

Sears, John F. *Sacred Places: American Tourist Attractions in the Nineteenth Century*. New York: Oxford University Press, 1989.

Shannon, Fred A. *The Farmer's Last Frontier: Agriculture, 1860–1897*. New York: Harper & Row, 1945.

Simonds, William Day. *Starr King in California*. San Francisco, Calif.: Paul Elder, 1917.

Slap, Andrew L. *The Doom of Reconstruction: The Liberal Republicans in the Civil War Era*. New York: Fordham University Press, 2006.

Smith, Henry Nash. *Virgin Land: The American West as Symbol and Myth*. Cambridge, Mass.: Harvard University Press, 1970; originally published, 1950.

Smith, Jean Edward. *Grant*. New York: Simon & Schuster, 2001.

Somerville, Duncan S. *The Aspinwall Empire*. Mystic, Conn.: Mystic Seaport Museum, Inc., 1983.

Somkin, Fred. *Unquiet Eagle: Memory and Desire in the Idea of American Freedom, 1815–1860*. Ithaca: Cornell University Press, 1967.

Stilgoe, John R. *Metropolitan Corridor: Railroads and the American Scene*. New Haven, Conn.: Yale University Press, 1983.

Stoll, Steven. *Larding the Lean Earth: Soil and Society in Nineteenth-Century America*. New York: Hill and Wang, 2002.

Summers, Mark Wahlgren. *A Dangerous Stir: Fear, Paranoia, and the Making of Reconstruction*. Chapel Hill: University of North Carolina Press, 2009.

Swisher, Carl B. *History of the Supreme Court of the United States: The Taney Period, 1836–1864*. New York: Macmillan Publishing Co., 1974.

Taylor, William R. *Cavalier and Yankee: The Old South and American National Character*. New York: George Braziller, 1961.

Thomas, John L., ed. *Abraham Lincoln and the American Political Tradition*. Amherst: University of Massachusetts Press, 1986.

Tyrrell, Ian. *True Gardens of the Gods: Californian-Australian Environmental Reform, 1860–1930*. Berkeley: University of California Press, 1999.

Varon, Elizabeth R. *Disunion! The Coming of the American Civil War, 1789–1854*. Chapel Hill: University of North Carolina Press, 2008.

Wallace, Anthony F. C. *Jefferson and the Indians: The Tragic Fate of the First Americans*. Cambridge, Mass.: Harvard University Press, 1999.

Warner, Ezra J. *Generals in Blue: Lives of the Union Commanders*. Baton Rouge: Louisiana State University Press, 1964.

Watson, Harry L. *Andrew Jackson vs. Henry Clay: Democracy and Development in Antebellum America*. New York: Bedford/St. Martin's, 1998.

——. *Liberty and Power: The Politics of Jacksonian America*. New York: Noonday Press, 1990.

Waugh, Joan. *U.S. Grant: American Hero, American Myth*. Chapel Hill: University of North Carolina Press, 2009.

Weber, Jennifer L. *Copperheads: The Rise and Fall of Lincoln's Opponents in the North*. New York: Oxford University Press, 2006.

West, Elliott. *The Last Indian War: The Nez Perce Story*. New York: Oxford University Press, 2009.

White, Richard. *"It's Your Misfortune and None of My Own": A History of the American West*. Norman: University of Oklahoma Press, 1991.

——. *Railroaded: The Transcontinentals and the Making of Modern America*. New York: W. W. Norton & Company, 2011.

Wiest, Edward. *Agricultural Organization in the United States*. Lexington: University Press of Kentucky, 1923.

Wilentz, Sean. *The Rise of American Democracy: Jefferson to Lincoln*. New York: W. W. Norton and Company, 2005.

Wilson, Douglas L. *Lincoln's Sword: The Presidency and the Power of Words*. New York: Alfred A. Knopf, 2007.

Wilson, Major L. *Space, Time, and Freedom: The Quest for Nationality and the Irrepressible Conflict, 1815–1861*. London, UK: Greenwood Press, 1974.

Winks, Robin W. *Frederick Billings: A Life*. New York: Oxford University Press, 1991.

Wood, Gordon S. *The Creation of the American Republic, 1776–1787*. Chapel Hill: University of North Carolina Press, 1998.

Worster, Donald. *A Passion for Nature: The Life of John Muir*. New York: Oxford University Press, 2008.

Articles and Parts of Books

Anderson, Ralph H. "Carleton E. Watkins, Pioneer Photographer of the Pacific Coast." *Yosemite Nature Notes* 32 (1953): 32–37.

Bushman, Richard L. "Markets and Composite Farms in Early America." *William and Mary Quarterly* 55 (July 1998): 351–74.

Gates, Paul Wallace. "Federal Land Policy in the South, 1866–1888." *Journal of Southern History* 3 (August 1940): 303–30.

Hoffnagle, Warren. "The Southern Homestead Act: Its Origins and Operation." *Historian* 32 (August 1970): 612–29.

Huth, Hans. "Yosemite: The Story of an Idea." *Sierra Club Bulletin* 33 (March 1948): 46–78.

Kuykendall, Ralph S. "History of the Yosemite Region." In *Handbook of Yosemite National Park*, edited by Ansel F. Hall. New York: G. P. Putnam's Sons, 1921.

Langsdorf, Edgar. "S. C. Pomeroy and the New England Emigrant Aid Company, 1854–1858." *Kansas Historical Quarterly* 7 (August 1938): 227–45.

McCurdy, Charles W. "Stephen J. Field and Public Land Law Development in California, 1850–1866: A Case Study of Judicial Resource Allocation in Nineteenth-Century America." *Law and Society Review* 10 (Winter 1976): 237–65.

Murray, Bronson. "Memorial of the Fourth Industrial Convention of the State of Illinois." In *The Movement for Industrial Education and the Establishment of the University, 1840–1870*, by Burt E. Powell. Urbana: University of Illinois Press, 1918.

Phillips, Sarah T. "Antebellum Agricultural Reform, Republican Ideology, and Sectional Tension." *Agricultural History* 74 (Fall 2000): 799–822.

Rodgers, Daniel. "Republicanism: The Career of a Concept." *Journal of American History* 79 (June 1992): 11–38.

Simon, John Y. "The Politics of the Morrill Act." *Agricultural History* 37 (April 1963): 103–11.

Smith, Anthony D. "The Origins of Nations." In *Nationalism*, edited by John Hutchinson and Anthony D. Smith. New York: Oxford University Press, 1994.

Stampp, Kenneth M. "The Concept of a Perpetual Union." *Journal of American History* 65 (June 1978): 5–33.

Williams, R. Hal. "George W. Julian and Land Reform in New Mexico, 1885–1889." *Agricultural History* 41 (January 1967): 71–84.

Young, Mary E. "Congress Looks West: Liberal Ideology and Public Land Policy in the Nineteenth Century." In *The Frontier in American Development: Essays in Honor of Paul Wallace Gates*, edited by Davis M. Ellis. Ithaca, N.Y.: Cornell University Press, 1969.

DISSERTATIONS AND M.A. THESES

Evans, Gail Edith H. "Storm over Niagara: A Study of the Interplay of Cultural Values, Resource Politics, and Environmental Policy in an International Setting, 1670s–1950." Ph.D. diss., University of California, Santa Barbara, 1991.

Huntley-Smith, Jen A. "Publishing the 'Sealed Book': James Mason Hutchings and the Landscapes of California Print Culture, 1853–1886." Ph.D. diss., University of Nevada, Reno, 2000.

Luebke, Peter Clayton. "'To Transmit and Perpetuate the Fruits of This Victory': Union Regimental Histories, 1865–1866, and the Meaning of the Great Rebellion." M.A. thesis, University of Virginia, 2005.

Taylor-Montoya, Amanda. "Under the Same Glorious Flag: Land, Race, and Legitimacy in Territorial New Mexico." Ph.D. diss., University of Oklahoma, 2009.

Index